PREFACE

Neither Hilary nor I can quite remember when we first thought of driving round the world. But certainly it was no later than mid 2007, knowing that we would "retire" on 30th June 2010.

10DPG, the hero of this story, is a 1956 Bristol 405 Drophead, Number 29 of forty two manufactured.

It had been undergoing a slow but painstaking restoration when we acquired it in 1999, and was finally on the road, for the first time in 24 years, in April 2001, having been put back together mechanically by Robert Hathaway. Earlier in 2010 I reported to him that we had just completed 100,000 miles in my ownership – a tribute to his workmanship. He replied that he very much regretted but the warranty had just expired!

Since 2001 10DPG has been no stranger to the inside of a container and we had already driven it on every driveable continent except Asia. Since taking delivery of the car, it has been most ably looked after by Charlie Russell.

In June 2010 10DPG was once again incarcerated – Miami bound. We flew out on 14th July and were reunited on the 16th.

In the text we have used both a day number and the date. At the end of August 2010 we flew back to Europe for three weeks, amongst other things for the celebrations of the 100th anniversary of the Bristol Aeroplane Company – until 1961 the manufacturer of all Bristol cars. As this time was not part of our Round the World Tour we suspended day numbers. Thus 31st August 2010 is day 49, but day 50 is September 22nd, three weeks later. For the rest of the trip even when the car was in a container we continued the numbering sequentially as this definitely was a part of the trip.

We are often asked; "Who did the driving?"

We both did, taking 2 hour turns.

In summary we drove from Miami, up the East coast of the USA to Canada, across Canada, and down the West coast. This forms Chapter 1. All the way round, when we told people of our plans the unanimous answer was; "Don't drive in Mexico – you will die!"

Chapter 2 covers Mexico and Central America to Panama, where we shipped the car to Buenos Aires.

Chapter 3 covers South America, Chapter 4 Australia, and Chapter 5 the journey home.

The car made four trips by container. This is a strange process, which apart from the direct delivery from the UK to Miami, involved two, or even three ships with the car being unloaded and loaded en route. While this was happening we maintained a diary entitled "Carless Days." Although not really a part of 10DPG's story we have included linking summaries of Carless Days.

In total we covered 33,196 miles, according to the odometer, which actually under reads by about half of one percent. We drove on many good roads, but some quite awful – dreadful potholes – as in Honduras, and the most vicious and frequently invisible topés, or sleeping policemen, in Mexico and Central America. We climbed to over 10,000 ft on several occasions and generally abused a 55 year old car beyond reasonable expectation. On our return to the UK the first urgency was for an MoT. We used the same station as 18 months previously and they were astounded at how well the car had stood up to it all. A great tribute to the original build quality, and subsequent servicing. As a matter of record even the tyres, new when we set out, not only passed the MoT but have covered another 17,000 miles since.

Whilst we were with 10DPG we maintained a daily diary, which we published as a "blog." This book is that diary.

ROUND THE WORLD WITH 10DPG

BY

Geoffrey & Hilary Herdman

Published by
Geoffrey & Hilary Herdman, 2013
geoffrey@10dpg.com

Design and origination by
Createability
www.createabilitystudio.co.uk

Printed by
Creeds Printers
Broadoak, Dorset, DT6 5NL
www.creedsuk.com

Cartoon of Geoffrey & Hilary in 10DPG
(within preface) with kind permission of
Fran Spencer

Illustration of Round the World Route (watercolour)
© Michael A Hill (www.michaelahill.com)

© Geoffrey & Hilary Herdman

ISBN 978-0-9576168-0-6

Round the World Route	
Chapter 1: North America & Canada	1
Chapter 2: Central America	84
Chapter 3: South America	130
Chapter 4: Australia	194
Chapter 5: Asia and Europe	238
Appendix: Facts and Figures	279
Epilogue	297

Mexico

Pacific Ocean

Townsville

Australia

Brisbane

Adelaide

← TURKEY

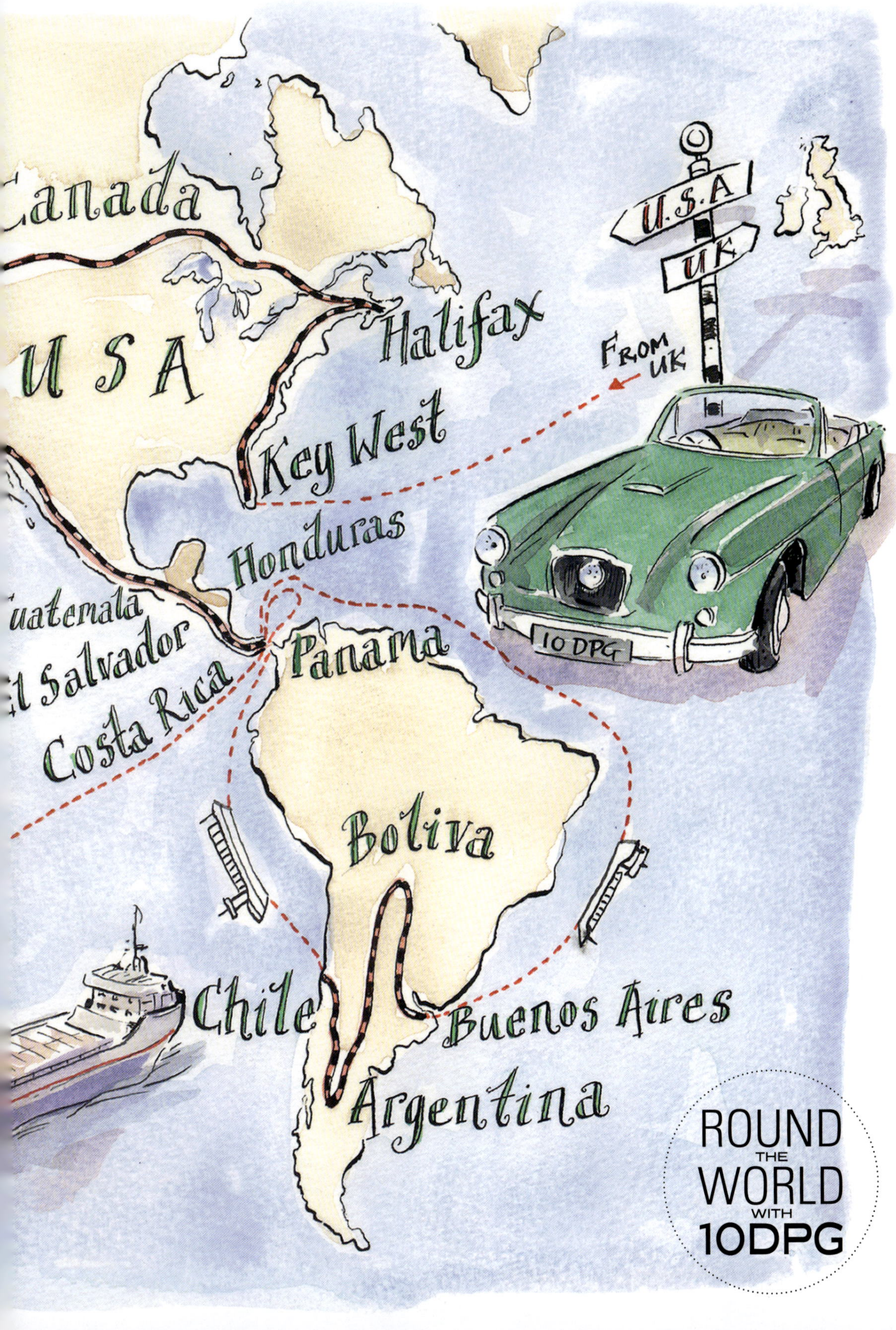

ROUND THE WORLD WITH 10DPG

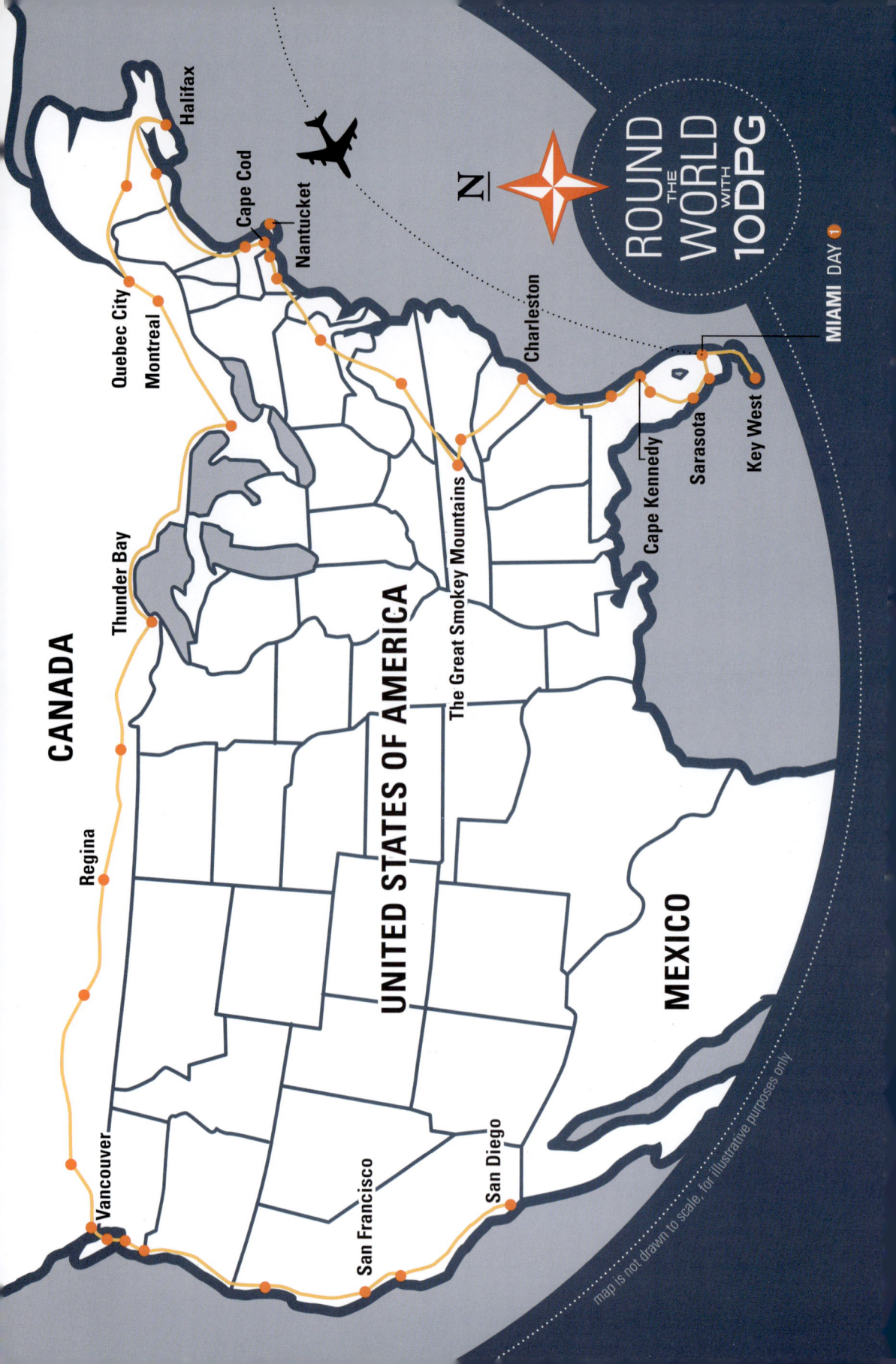

ROUND THE WORLD WITH 10DPG

MIAMI DAY 1

Halifax
Cape Cod
Nantucket
Quebec City
Montreal
Charleston
Cape Kennedy
Sarasota
Key West
Thunder Bay
Regina
The Great Smokey Mountains
Vancouver
San Francisco
San Diego

CANADA
UNITED STATES OF AMERICA
MEXICO

N

map is not drawn to scale, for illustrative purposes only

CHAPTER 1
North America & Canada

DAY: 1
14/07/10 ARRIVAL IN MIAMI Before leaving home one of us had mentioned very quietly the C word.

Fly to Miami and find campsite. The tent seems quite comfy.

DAY: 2
15/07/10 SHOPPING IN MIAMI BEACH Clearing a car in North America is going to be even slower than South. 10DPG having arrived on Saturday 10th July, 'may' be ready for collection tomorrow 16th July. We visit Miami Beach and buy essentials such as a phone and portable printer! Spectacular views from the tent balcony of a tropical storm sweeping in from the sea.

DAY: 3
16/07/10 RETRIEVING THE CAR AND A GOOD DINNER
Our container, having been x-rayed by customs at a cost of $250, is finally released, but can we go and drive the car out? Oh no, it has to be loaded on to a truck, driven 15 miles to a shipper's warehouse and unloaded from there.

It arrives at 16:55 having been promised for 13:00! With minutes to spare before everything closes for the weekend the container is opened and voila – 10DPG.

Mrs H does the difficult bit of driving down the ramp – aided by burly and very helpful Hispanic dockers, pushing with vigour.

Starting is a little difficult as I suspect humidity for the last four weeks has worked its magic, but all is well and we are finally away with a permit to keep the car in the States for a year.

We drive to Ocean Drive for a photo opportunity and are so delighted to have the car on the road that we treat ourselves to a piggy dinner in Azul at the Mandarin – possibly the best restaurant in Miami??

The waiter expresses "Utter Anguish" when he realizes one has been kept waiting for one's beer!! but the meal is superb.

TOTAL MILEAGE: 20

Geoffrey & Hilary Herdman

DAY: 4
17/07/10 TOWARDS KEY WEST
On the road proper, to Key West, 160 miles away, so we can truly start from the Southernmost tip of the USA. The first 80 miles are pretty depressing but when we cross over to Key Largo the drive becomes dramatically better with the Atlantic on our left and the Gulf of Mexico on our right. The only notable exception being Marathon, which seen from Highway US1 is a dump. We follow the route of the old railway completed in 1912 and known as Flagler's Folly, which first connected Key West by an amazing series of bridges. The railway was substantially damaged by a hurricane in 1935 and never reopened, but parts of the structure were used for the road, which opened in 1938. Not all though, and there are still long and spectacular sections of railroad bridge alongside the road.

We are enchanted by Key West and stayed in The Marquesa, as recommended by the Michelin Guide. It is a charming collection of "Conch" Houses, part Caribbean but mostly New England in style, as are most of the older houses, having been built by New Englanders who came here in the mid 19th C to join in the wrecking trade. As a result of this and cigar manufacturing, by 1890 Key West had the highest per capita income of any city in the USA. By 1930 they were bankrupt and had to be bailed out by the Federal Government.

We visit Mallory Square as does the whole of the rest of Key West to see the sunset over the Caribbean and then have dinner at A & B's on the waterfront.

TOTAL MILEAGE: 188

NORTH AMERICA

DAY: 5
18/07/10 THE SOUTHERNMOST POINT OF THE USA

We walk the length of Duval Street from Caribbean to Atlantic, a strenuous 1.2 miles and have a photo opportunity with 100 other tourists by the most southerly point of the USA marker, which is only 90 miles from Cuba. A local 60 year old athlete is proposing to swim it and I thought it was all the other way round!

We visit Hemingway's house. He lived on Key West from 1931 to 1941 and wrote "For Whom The Bell Tolls" and "The Old Man and The Sea" from here. At the time it was the largest house in Key West, having been built in the 1850's by the chief wrecker, and still has the largest garden at an acre. Hemingway's studio is a wonderful place from which to write.

We also visit Harry Truman's "Little White House" where he spent 175 days of his presidency.

Back to the hotel pool where we were enchanted by a red crested woodpecker family, which had made a perfectly circular nest high in a palm tree. Our hostess was less enchanted when we told her of the raccoon, which had emerged from under a neighbouring building.

In the evening we again cruise Duval Street, but now it is full of drag night clubs with alarmingly ambiguous greeters mostly in shocking frocks and size 11 high heels on the pavement, rivalled on the other side by gyrating males in scant g-strings.

TOTAL MILEAGE: 188

DAY: 6
19/07/10 THE EVERGLADES

We head back towards Naples on the West coast of Florida, stopping en route for an Everglades experience. This is now done by "Air boat", which is a flat bottomed boat with a draught of 2 inches driven by propellor and in our case a Cadillac 500 V8 engine. We were supplied with cotton wool for our ears which did very little to silence the incredible noise of the propeller, but we had an exhilarating trip sidesliding across the Sea of Grass, and in one case stopping so that Mrs H could paddle in the Everglades and yes, she still has both legs! although we saw several alligators on our tour.

We were reminded of the Okavanga Delta save that that was on horseback and much quieter!

Geoffrey & Hilary Herdman

We drive on to Naples and stay in a luxurious pile called the Grande Resort, hideously ugly but with a wonderful 1 k boardwalk to the most spectacular white beach, full of birds.

Although it is quite warm, there is one very good thing to be said for coming at this time of the year: the prices are between a third and a quarter of those in January. We don't actually need to look too hard for campsites so far.

The day time temperature is around 34ºC or in American 94ºF. We find it much cooler with the hood up and have discovered that if you rotate the quarter lights through 135º there is a gratifying cooling draught. On the road the water temperature varies between 95º and 98º and as soon as we stop at lights I put the fan on. Thus far the cooling seems to be coping. Once when we stopped, after a little while the water temperature was reading 105º, so I gingerly loosened the radiator cap but there was no pressurization, so maybe the gauge is overreading?

TOTAL DISTANCE: 430 miles. At 320 we filled up with 14 gallons (US) and have added half a litre of water.

DAY: 7
20/07/10 SARASOTA To Sarasota and the Ringling Art Museum, of which needless to say we had never heard! despite it being one of the great American art collections with four massive Rubens cartoons taking pride of place. Ringling made his fortune as a circus entrepreneur and real estate developer but lost a large part in 1929, and despite the amazing collection died in 1936 with $311 in the bank (according to Wikipedia!!). He also built as his home the Ca' d' Zan an extravagant Venetian style palace on the waterfront. The collection includes a circus museum including the Ringlings' private rail car built in 1907 by the Pullman company.

We stayed at Longboat Country Club, on the water's edge with beautiful white sandy beaches and NO oil. (This was after the BP Macondo disaster on 20th April 2010)

CUMULATIVE MILEAGE: 556

DAY: 8
21/07/10 ORLANDO We have booked-in to the Courtyard at Lake Lucerne in Orlando – as recommended by the green Michelin Guide.

The direct route is to cut inland but the route via St Petersburg over the skyway bridge looked more attractive and turned out to be quite spectacular. The old bridge had its Southern carriageway bisected by a drifting ship in 1980, causing several deaths. The only survivor was a truck driver whose vehicle fell onto the ship and landed the right way up.

Ron, the receptionist at the Courtyard, recommended that we visit Florida Southern College at Lakeland, most of whose campus was designed by Frank Lloyd Wright. We duly pay our respects. It is the largest collection of Lloyd Wright buildings anywhere, designed in the early 1940s. Equally amazing is the fact that the Dean, Dr Ludd Spivey, with no money was able to persuade him to

NORTH AMERICA

come and build twelve buildings and 1.5 miles of terraced cloisters largely using student labour, with hand made concrete forms.

We have lunch in the student café overlooking Lloyd Wright's fountain and lake, at student prices! This is more like it!!

On our return to the car the inside temperature is 52ºC but on the run we settle down to a more comfortable 37º.

The Michelin has triumphed again and the Courtyard is an absolute gem of 1880's houses with a leafy tiled courtyard; one is completely unaware of being surrounded by high rises and the East West Expressway, or being in the centre of town.

H did have an encounter with a large live frog in the loo bowl. No amount of kissing or flushing would remove him so a cup was placed over with some plastic on top and he was despatched to the garden, where he went leaping off – doubtless a very relieved frog. We were assured that frog encounters are the norm in Florida.

CUMULATIVE MILEAGE: 723 and en route we have bought 10.3 US gallons, but were unable to fill up!!

DAY 9

Geoffrey & Hilary Herdman

DAY: 9
22/07/10 COD VENICE Despite all our better judgements we thought we should visit one of the Disney experiences, and on the advice of our dinner waiter no less, chose Epcot, a 20 mile drive. A $14 car park fee plus $75 per head entrance left the words "rip off" quivering on the tip of the tongue. To find there were 1-2 hour queues for most of the better rides did not improve matters. However in the end we managed to do most things, apart from soaring, and had a surprisingly enjoyable day. We even had an excellent dinner in the Doges Palace, before a spectacular firework display – just such as they do on all the other 364 days of the year!!

CUMULATIVE MILEAGE: 755

DAY: 10
23/07/10 THE MORSE MUSEUM Again on the recommendation of Ron we visited the Morse museum in Winter Park, a sleepy but VERY affluent suburb of Orlando. Morse was a distant relative of the inventor of the code but an eminently successful industrialist, who retired to Winter Park and became a great philanthropist in Orlando. His grand-daughter married Hugh McKean, who was a student of Louis Tiffany, and together they set up the Museum, of which Hugh was the first Curator. We met, by chance, the present Curator, who had worked with Hugh for 2 years before his death, and has been the Curator for the past 16 years. The McKeans were childless, and the Museum has inherited a generous endowment, which includes much of the main street in Winter Park. Accordingly, they are shortly opening an extension which will double the size of the Museum, and enable them to redisplay their wonderful collection of Tiffany, Art Nouveau and Arts and Crafts, including Liberty, and William Morris. (Charles Morse had a collection of Arts and Crafts, some of which is on display.) Because Hugh had studied with Tiffany at his country house, Laurelton Hall, subsequently largely destroyed by fire, he and his wife were able to hunt down and piece together many works (including the Chapel, first designed for the Chicago 1892 World Fair) from memory of their display at Laurelton.

Altogether we had had a much more interesting time than the previous day and yet there was NO mention of the "Morse" in our trusted Michelin Guide!

CUMULATIVE MILEAGE: 775

DAY: 11
24/07/10 CAPE KENNEDY To the Kennedy Space Centre. Entry $41 per head and no car parking fee! We had thought that a couple of hours would cover it, but 7 hours later we still had many things to do and see with the highlight at the end being a simulated shuttle launch. H's most vivid memory is of the viewing gantry overlooking the two launch pads 3 miles away with their huge tanks for water, liquid oxygen and liquid hydrogen. The assembled shuttle

is driven a 3 mile distance from the assembly point to the launch pad at up to 1 mph and takes 8 hours to complete the journey. The cranes finally lifting it into place are accurate to within 1/64th of an inch in any horizontal direction and 1/50,000 inch vertically, and at launch the shuttle burns 15 tons of liquid hydrogen and oxygen per second.

Each shuttle has 300,000 man hours of meticulous checking between launches.

We left with a very strong impression that the NASA effort was a dying duck so far as Congress is concerned and they have only two more shuttle launches agreed. It was a wonderfully romantic experience, but having landed twelve men on the moon the last one did say rather wistfully that he didn't think that 24 years later he would still be able to say he was the last man on the moon. We did rather come away with the feeling that maybe Congress had a point.

Being alongside a nature reserve the wildlife was abundant – including ominously circling vultures, and having left the centre we set out to see some of the wildlife via unfortunately a military area. "Hi folks you're not in England now – no cars allowed here" so we u-turned and wended our way towards St Augustine.

It has to be said that the hotel there was not our first choice and we found ourselves somewhere North of St Augustine in a golfers' paradise, with a completely empty mini bar and a "complimentary" bottle of water costing $4. The a/c blew alternately very hot and very cold during the night but the elevator had glass walls and the view was not bad!!

TOTAL MILEAGE: 955 and petrol taken on – again where we weren't able to fill up 12.5 gallons US.

DAY: 12
25/07/10   ST AUGUSTINE

Back down to St Augustine, as we were staying 10 miles to the North. It is pronounced in American with the emphasis on the first syllable as St AUg'stine. It was founded in 1513 by Ponce de Leon, who claimed Florida for Spain, and was settled in 1565, making it the oldest continually occupied European settlement in North America.

The Spanish built a wooden fort for the protection of the treasure fleets. Drake burnt it down in 1586. After subsequent pirate raids the Spanish commenced construction of the present day fort built from coquina in 1672, completing it in 1695. Coquina is a local material, mostly limestone and shells with the flexibility to resist repeated cannon ball attacks, rather than fracturing as does harder stone. The fort was never thereafter taken, despite two long sieges, and St Augustine only changed hands according to the political fortunes of Europe.

St Augustine itself was largely destroyed by fire in 1912, but several houses have survived including the oldest dating from the early 18th C. The house is now a museum and the excellent tour highlighted the changing fortunes and styles of its successive Spanish, British and American owners, including a spell as a tap-room for the barracks opposite. The old town has been largely recreated. Although it is now full of shops and cafés, it still has a wonderful charm to it.

Geoffrey & Hilary Herdman

There is both a Greek and Minorcan community. The Greeks still have their church, which also serves as a museum recording how they arrived, originally as indented labour for the ill fated 18th C community of New Smyrna. The few survivors resettled in St Augustine.

Later that afternoon we set out for Savannah. A very hot drive with in-car temperature nudging 40ºC but engine water temperature holding steady.

TOTAL MILEAGE: 1,165. Filled up en route 13.5 US gallons at 1,103 miles.

DAY: 13
26/07/10   SAVANNAH   Savannah was founded in 1733 by James Oglethorpe, who founded the State of Georgia. He had intended Georgia to be a place where "the British working poor and 'societal misfits' could carve out a living". It also conveniently provided a barrier between South Carolina, in English hands, and Florida, in Spanish hands, which was to be a cause of anguish on both sides.

Savannah was laid out as a "Citta ideale" by Oglethorpe. The old city is a perfect rectangle of 2.2 square miles, set out on a grid system with twenty four squares – now reduced to twenty two. Each of the squares is planted with live oaks, as are the streets linking them; most but not all are adorned with Spanish moss, which is neither Spanish nor a moss but a very attractive epyphite, or air plant, adding to the romance of the view.

During the Civil War when so many Southern towns were destroyed the townspeople of Savannah handed General Sherman the keys and thus it has been preserved almost intact from the 18th C.

We were staying at the Eliza Thompson house (1740) on Jones St, which claims to be the prettiest in town.

In the morning we took an open bus tour, and after lunch on Factors Row, overlooking the Savannah river, we visited the Owens-Thomas house, complete with original slave quarters. The house was designed by William Law, an English architect aged 21. It was the first house to have plumbing, which necessitated a 2,000 gallon water tank in the roof, and the strength to support it. The house was thus built from tabby, a very strong local building material reinforced with steel. Not bad for a 21 year old! As with most other houses of the period most of the building materials and finishes were imported from England, including the plaster. It is a lovely house.

Finally dinner at Elizabeth on 37th, which was actually outside the old town but very good.

NORTH AMERICA

DAY: 14
27/07/10 CHARLESTON

To Charleston, via Hilton Head for a swim. Bizarrely despite it being one of the great beaches, we had difficulty finding it as TomTom took us into the centre of Hilton Head. Once located though we had miles and miles of pure white sand with sun loungers and umbrellas, which turned out to be free as the attendant had fallen for 10DPG.

We both loved Charleston and were very glad we had done Savannah first. It was rather like the difference between Prague and Budapest. The former is very beautiful but slightly like living in a museum. In the latter, as well as beautiful buildings, people are getting on with their lives and there is a sense of get up and go.

Charleston has just as beautiful houses as Savannah but bubbles with it.

We arrived hot and tired in the early evening, but the staff were exemplary at the Harbor View Inn. They wanted to valet park 10DPG, but I took the porter as passenger. He was so overwhelmed he sent a bottle of champagne up to our room!

Just outside the hotel was a fountain where children were paddling. The water was a maximum of 6" deep and yet they had to have a notice saying "No lifeguard on duty"!!

Dinner was at Fleet Landing. As we had to wait they gave us a disc, which when our table was ready would flash and vibrate. Good idea – except I put it in my pocket and was totally unaware that anything was happening, and they had to come and find us!!

CUMULATIVE MILEAGE TO CHARLESTON: 1,335

DAY: 15
28/07/10 SIGHT SEEING IN CHARLESTON

We wander along E Bay Street lined with the most beautiful houses.

Until the Civil War, South Carolina was the most prosperous state in the USA, mainly thanks to rice, which had been imported with African slaves. By the late 18th C it was the most important crop and slaves were bought for their ability to work the rice fields. Although they had introduced it they were not allowed to eat it themselves, but had to live on corn instead.

Charleston is bounded by the Ashley and Cooper rivers and many of the great plantations were on their banks. However the land is soft and could only be worked by manual labour so with the end of slavery the rice industry in South Carolina died and it wasn't until tourism in the mid 20th C that the economy picked up again.

The legacies from its heydays are some absolutely gorgeous 18th and 19th C houses overlooking the bay.

Geoffrey & Hilary Herdman

In the afternoon we took the ferry across to Patriots Point where on decommissioning in 1975, the USS Yorktown, a WW2 aircraft carrier has been a floating museum. Alongside is a submarine, built at the end of WW2 and not seeing active service. On the outside the hull is covered in barnacles and badly rusting, on the inside I would think it is much as it was when operational. It has a displacement of 1,800 tons, which by WW2 standards makes it a very large sub, and a crew of 90. How did they manage, crammed into what seems an impossibly small space?

Dinner at Poogans Porch, reputedly haunted!

DAY: 16
29/07/10 PLANTATIONS

We visit two of the great plantations; Middleton Place and Drayton Hall. Each one was only a very small percentage of their owner's total number of plantations, but they were the favourites. Each plantation was of about 5 or 600 acres out of an original total of perhaps 30,000.

The main house at Middleton was burnt by the Unionists at the end of the Civil War and only one "flanker" building remains. To compound matters in 1886 there was a severe earthquake, which destroyed much of what the Unionists missed. S Carolina is on the second biggest geological fault in the States.

What is left of Middleton is now air conditioned and furnished with most of its original furniture donated by members of the family. The gardens are beautifully laid out, much as they were in 1740, when they were the foremost landscaped gardens in the States attracting visitors even then; beautiful water gardens and an abundance of birds.

We were instructed and entertained by an actor/carpenter, working with original tools making casks for the transport of rice. The hoops being made of saplings, rather than iron.

Drayton Hall survived the Unionists, possibly because the owner had a hospital there and put up warning signs that it was a smallpox centre.

The Drayton who built it was 23 and certainly built to a grand design. Eventually

NORTH AMERICA

he would become one of the most successful of all the plantation owners.

The house never had electricity or plumbing, despite being used by the family for vacations until the 1950s and is now without any furniture, which allows one to see the design of the rooms; fine plaster ceilings and carved fireplaces.

Dinner at Hanks, probably the best of our three meals in Charleston.

CUMULATIVE MILEAGE: 1,375

DAY: 17
30/07/10   TO ASHEVILLE To try and escape the heat we elect for Asheville and the Great Smokies, at the bottom of the Appalachian Range. A distance of 265 miles.

We set off in searing heat 35 or 36°C at about 10:15. Rather impressive! we were only 15 minutes behind intended departure time!!

Asheville is 2,100 ft above sea level. We arrive at about 16:30 and check into a charming B&B. We had had this fond idea that B&Bs would be cheap but at $215 per night plus taxes it turns out to be much the same as the hotels. Pinecrest is however very folksy, run by Janna Martin and her daughter Stacey and we are cosseted and well looked after.

We walk downtown to check out eateries and back again. One of us has a quick drink of rather vicious Sangria. As downtown is 1 mile each way that probably wasn't the most sensible drink!

An hour later we retrace our steps but arrive at the restaurant a bit late and have an underwhelming reception. At least for the first time for a long time we are able to eat outside, in comfort and well, if somewhat anonymously as there was no outdoor lighting.

Filled up at 1,416 miles with 14.85 US gallons. TOTAL MILEAGE: 1,635

DAY: 18
31/07/10   THE GREAT SMOKIES One of the purposes of staying in Asheville was to visit the Great Smoky Mountains, some 50 miles away. The whole National Park was bought by the State in the 1930s with a grant of $5,000,000 from the Rockefellers. Outside the park is a sprawl of motels, casinos, and shopping centres. Inside, it is absolutely beautiful, but on our entry it started raining and continued all day.

We drove to the summit, where the Appalachian Trail crosses the road and sat in the car applying hide food to the leather whilst waiting for the rain to ease. The AT, as it is known, runs for 2,200 miles to Maine and here marks the divide between North Carolina and Tennessee. Eventually we ventured out under an umbrella and walked for at least 100 yards along the trail, including one foot each across the State boundary.

We returned to Asheville via the Blue Ridge Parkway starting from the very bottom, but we were in thick cloud and the Looking Glass Rock was completely obscured.

Geoffrey & Hilary Herdman

Dinner at The Bier Garten, which advertised a huge range of beers, most of which seemed to be off, so settled for a glass of draught Pisgah, local and very good.
TOTAL MILEAGE: 1,840 Filled up at 1,754 miles 15.8 gallons US.

DAY: 19
01/08/10 THE BILTMORE ESTATE As there was no sign of a nearby Episcopalian Church, Mrs H took her courage in both hands and went to the Greek Orthodox instead, which was immediately next door to the B&B, and proclaimed (in English) that visitors were welcome.

It is a charming little building, put up 2 or 3 years ago by the relatively small Greek community. Liturgy was billed to start at 10:30, but seemed to be well under way at 10:25, with a handful present. However, as the service proceeded more and more families appeared (many at about 11:30, when the sermon had just finished) and ultimately there were well over 100, any of whom could have been a Paxiot. The service moved seamlessly between Greek and English, was sometimes repeated in both (they are very keen to maintain the Greek language), and was almost entirely in Gregorian chant, very well sung.

Geoffrey meanwhile was conscientiously blogging away, as rather like Edwin the boy scout, we seem to be a few days behind our good intentions...

We then visited the Biltmore Estate, where as you will see from the photo, another mirror pond awaited our photographer. The house, completed in 1895, was inspired by the Chateaux of the Loire (but of course is built to USA dimensions), and was absolutely fascinating. The owner, George Vanderbilt, commissioned John Singer Sargeant to paint portraits of the architect and of the landscape gardener, which hang at opposite ends of a long gallery. Although vast, the house has a very easy and hospitable style; in the basement there is an indoor bowling alley, and a swimming pool, with original underwater lighting and a depth of 10′ so the young

NORTH AMERICA

men could dive. They also had a gym, complete with rowing machine and Indian clubs. The gardens are lovely (Olmsted, the designer, also landscaped Central Park) and include verdant wooded landscapes planted on what was originally scrubland.

We finished at the winery, set up about 25 years ago, on the basis that a French Chateau should have a vineyard. Of the first efforts it was said that the label was the only good thing; but they persevered and now have a very successful enterprise. In its own right it is the most visited winery in the USA.

An excellent dinner at what subsequently proved to be a Gluten free restaurant, called Posana's, so it was probably good for us too!

CUMULATIVE MILEAGE: 1,848

DAY: 20
02/08/10 BLUE RIDGE PARKWAY The Blue Ridge Parkway runs South West from Waynesboro in Virginia to Cherokee in the Great Smoky Mountains. It was started in 1935 as part of the New Deal to provide work, and completed in 1987 with the construction of the Linn Cove Viaduct. It extends for 469 miles along the ridge of the Appalachian Range. We thought we would drive its whole length, albeit in sections. No commercial vehicles are allowed, so it is, or should be, gorgeous driving.

Geoffrey & Hilary Herdman

On Day 18 we drove the section from Cherokee to Asheville and today we are heading for Blowing Rock. It is measured in mileposts starting from the North and Blowing Rock is at milepost 290.

The drive today was horrible. Warm air from the East meets cooler air from the West or vice versa and we drove for most of the day in very heavy cloud. For much of the time visibility was so bad we could only see the double yellow lines in the middle of the road.

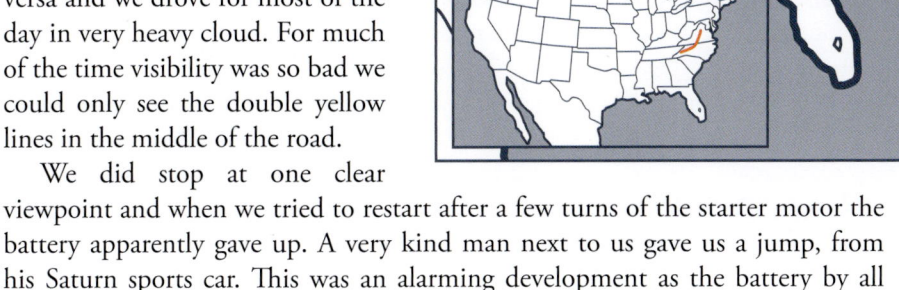

We did stop at one clear viewpoint and when we tried to restart after a few turns of the starter motor the battery apparently gave up. A very kind man next to us gave us a jump, from his Saturn sports car. This was an alarming development as the battery by all appearances is fully charged.

At our next stop, Linnville Falls, the starter completely refused to turn, so although tight I undid the battery terminals, twisted them around and redid them and all was then well, although the starter motor has been sounding a little strange of recent.

We stayed the night in Blowing Rock, which had been recommended to us by a man in Savannah, and were heartily thankful to be off the Parkway. The hotel, The Inn at Ragged Gardens, was strange and had changed hands many times but we had an adequate meal in their restaurant, the Best Cellar, which did not live up to its name.

TOTAL MILEAGE: 1,963

DAY: 21
03/08/10   THE FIRST PROBLEM! Having checked the car and put in a litre of oil, the first used on the trip at 1,963 miles, we set out from Blowing Rock about 11:00. The weather was completely different from yesterday and the Parkway was a joy to drive. However after about 5 miles the road was closed off. We pulled off onto a gorgeous country road and the postman advised us how to circumvent the blockage. Whilst talking to him we had switched off the engine.

When we tried to start there was a dull moaning, wheezing gasp. It has to be said it had been making slightly odd sounds for about a week. As we were on a hill I tried a rolling start but the starter was permanently engaged and so kept turning with the engine. I tried turning the shaft at the other end and that seemed to be free. I tried a rolling start again but still the starter turned with the engine.

NORTH AMERICA

"Clayton the post" stayed with us and recommended Millers Car Clinic in Boone 8 miles away, and then, and then... in the immortal words of Leiber and Stoller "along came Jones". Actually he was Jim but he might have been Jones. He drove me into town, where I helped him bare handed clear a load of asbestos from the back of his truck into the local tip and then we went to see Millers. They put us straight in touch with Jon the starter King. Jim then fixed up a flat bed truck and poor 10DPG was ignominiously towed into town.

Whilst Jim and I were doing our rounds Mrs H diligently applied hide food to the leather – what a star!!

We stayed at the Holiday Inn Express in Boone and took a taxi to Jim's restaurant where for $40 we had an excellent meal and the rules of baseball explained to us.

Our taxi driver, Samantha aged 23 going on 40 came with attitude and a taser in case of trouble.

DAY: 22
04/08/10 "JON THE STARTER" 10DPG overnighted in the safety of Hampton's Bodyshop and Wreckers! but the next morning Mexican Joe picked me up from the hotel, and by 09:00 we were at Jon's. Charlie had told me he can remove a starter in 4 minutes. By 09:03 Jon had it out. I had taken off the power lead but Jon had the requisite ratchet socket to be able to remove the bolts.

At 11:00 I phoned Jon fearing the worst because any spare parts were probably going to have to come from the UK with a 2-3 day delay, but Jon was just putting the starter back in the car. A lock nut, which holds the bendix had come undone and the whole assembly had come loose. Whoa Geoffrey we're getting technical here! but it was something like that. The fastenings for the nut were worn but Jon figured it should last me a while and when back in the UK I will acquire a spare.

We phoned the redoubtable Samantha to drive us back out to Jon's and we learnt in the space of 10 minutes that: she had run away from home at 15 because her mother was a drug addict, she is very clever, she had had a child at 17 (now aged 6), she was a member of the army reserve and is a very good shot, and that one day she is going to be world famous as a musical artist and we can follow her prowess at myspace.com/rougemererocks and logging in to Samantha O'Brien from Boone NC!!

Jon had the car all fixed by the time we arrived and the starter sounded as good as new. He thought all the parts looked in reasonable shape and charged $50, cheap at many times the price!! We had also had to pay $125 for the tow truck so the whole exercise including taxi had cost under $200 and we were underway in 24 hours. As the Holiday Express is $116, as opposed to the usual B&B at $216 our two nights in Boone had paid for the repair!!

Just South of Boone on the Parkway we had driven over the Linn Cove viaduct in the fog and also Grandfather Mountain with the mile high bridge, so we decided to retrace our steps. Sadly, as we climbed, the clouds surrounded us and we were

Geoffrey & Hilary Herdman

denied the mile high bridge but did have a chance to drive over and walk under the viaduct. Impressive. It had not been built until 1987 because they wanted to create a viaduct without the use of heavy equipment, which would destroy the ecology for years to come. We also visited Flat Top, the beautiful house of Moses Cone, who made his fortune in the late 19th C from Denim, and whose family had donated it, and 4,200 acres of the Parkway to the nation in 1950.

We also went to see our saviour Jim to show him the car in working order. He was absolutely delighted to see us and we parted with many handshakes.

Finally, as the same section of the Parkway was going to be closed the following day from 08:00 to 15:00, we drove the 10 miles so as not to miss any of the road.

On our return to Boone we filled up at 2,043 miles 13.08 imp gallons.

Gas comes as 87, 89, and 93 octane. Costs vary but average in Virginia, which only has 5% sales tax, is $2.60, $2.70 and $2.80 respectively per US gallon which in English equates to 50p per litre for the highest rating.

DAY: 23
05/08/10 AND THEN A PUNCTURE

It never rains but it pours – in all senses of the word!! As I was loading 10DPG a kindly passer-by pointed out that the nearside rear tyre was practically flat. Fortunately we carry an electric pump, but after an hour we had lost a couple of pounds so we visited the Boone Tyre Centre. They were alarmed when they found it had an inner tube and promptly removed it and put in a tubeless valve. The tube had perished where it was being pinched by the rim, but for "belt and braces" I asked them to repair it which they kindly did. By about 12:00 we were underway heading for Roanoke, some 170 miles up the Parkway. It was very good to be underway again!!

That afternoon the skies ahead were looking more and more ominous. To the North they looked clear, to the East black, black and very black. We drove on. The top was down. It started raining. It started thundering. Then the thunder became instantaneous with the lightning. In driving rain we stopped and put the hood up. It made no difference to the dampness inside the car, but irrationally we felt more secure from the constant lightning overhead. We had to shut the windows to keep out the torrential rain. The windscreen misted up and visibility through the rain was pretty marginal. At one stage we stopped for tea, but the electricity had been off for 2 hours and tea was off. The ranger cheered us by telling us that there were two storms and the one where we were heading was just as bad as the one we had come through. She was right!!!

We had made no reservations in Roanoke so looked up B&B on TomTom. The first was enchantingly named Rose Hill, but when we found it it looked very drab and on pressing the bell a dog barked mournfully from within, but there was no sign of life. We did a runner just in case someone should appear. We then tried the Ramada. It too looked pretty desperate and a King bed cost $60 breakfast included. We took one look at the room and did a second runner, settling finally for the Holiday Inn Express again. Ramada in the States is NOT the same as Ramada in the UK.

We had been recommended to eat at "Awful Arthurs" downtown. It was vast and we thought completely misnamed until the live music started when we hastily moved outside.

After our accommodation experiences in Roanoke we decide to book ahead in Charlottesville for tomorrow night on the internet. The recommended B&B is full and we end up reserving two nights at the Mark Addy some 25 miles out of town in a small village called Nellysford.

CUMULATIVE MILEAGE: 2,223

DAY: 24
06/08/10   CHANCE ENCOUNTER

Weatherwise this was the best day we had had thus far. Clear sunny skies, temperature in the 70s as opposed to 90s, and just a joy to be motoring at 45 mph, the speed limit in the Parkway. No commercial vehicles are allowed and if we catch up with a car we stop for a minute and then drive alone. There is no advertising, no electricity or phone cables, very few buildings and such as there are were all from before construction of the road. We have spectacular views to both left and right as we twist and turn and climb and descend. We are between 3,500 ft and at the lowest point 800 where the James river cuts through the range.

We stop and walk over to the remains of a lock and canal. The lock is mostly there, but the canal has just a few yards and then is completely overgrown. We also go on a "tree trail" but on questioning the warden he tells us that the signs are old and many of the trees they point out are no longer in existence. We also ford a very dangerous river (See photo!!)

A little further we stop for lunch. I try cat fish, which is very good!

We are very sad when the Parkway ends, but the continuation through the Shenandoah National Park is called the Skyline Drive and we decide to do that in two days time.

We did not see any bears (probably staying in the dry in the Smokies), but saw muskrats, wild turkey, lots of deer, including a doe with twin Bambi fawns, and the most enormous and beautiful butterflies, not to mention a large black snake

Geoffrey & Hilary Herdman

wriggling its way across the road in front of us. Although it is August, there are still lots of flowers and everything brilliantly green and verdant; lovely!

We find the B&B in the middle of nowhere, a typical wooden house from 1836 set in 12 acres and with a parrot. We dine on excellent pasta at Vito's in Nellysford and return home. As the night is young we sit out on the verandah gently rocking on the rocking chairs. Senile? Us?

About 22:00 a car draws up and the passenger comes up the stairs and utters the immortal words "The Herdmans I presume?"

The USA has a surface area of 3,787,422 square miles, and a population approaching 300,000,000 of whom we know two. One of them, who we supposed was in Europe and in any event lives in Maryland, miles away, just happened to pass 10DPG in Nellysford that afternoon as he was being driven in to Charlottesville. His host said: "Oh look an old Merc" to which the reply was: "No a Bristol 405 Drophead and the name of the driver is Geoffrey, but where would they be staying?" They thought it just possible we might be staying at the Mark Addy and there was Michael Christie.

It's a small old world.

TOTAL MILEAGE: 2,385. Filled up at 2,354, 12.49 gallons. The last couple of fills have been with 89 octane. This time we use 93. 10DPG certainly seems to go better with same.

DAY: 25
07/08/10
MONTICELLO AND A GOOD DINNER

Michael, it transpired, was staying about a quarter of a mile away from our B&B in Keith's country cottage. I still can't work out the laws of chance that dictated we should meet up. Keith kindly invited us to supper, so Michael came over at breakfast with navigational instructions. We agreed that we would provide the wine and fortunately we were right in the heart of Virginia wine country.

After breakfast we set out for Charlottesville and Monticello (Jefferson's House which I had visited in 1970 and we had both visited on the BOC Tour in 2001). En route we stopped off at the Veritas winery. This was in superb premises and had been started as a retirement project some 10 years ago by an English couple called the Hodsons. He had been a neurosurgeon in Jacksonville for 25 years. Now they produce 10,000 cases of wine a year, and increasing, as well as having catering facilities for up to 250. After a very knowledgeable sommelier had taken us through a winetasting we bought two different reds and a white and drove on to Monticello. A car park attendant remarked that he had never seen a car like 10DPG to which I replied that it had been there only 9 years ago!!

We were given a ticket with a timed start of 15:20 so drove back into Charlottesville for some lunch. The main street was formerly named Three Notch Street and formed part of the main road from Washington to the Shenandoah Valley in the 18th C.

Monticello itself had a vast new visitor centre completed only 18 months ago, and crowds of visitors, but it was Saturday in August. At the end of a visit one is left in awe at the sheer breadth of Jefferson's abilities and knowledge.

That evening we had a splendid barbecue chez Keith and the four of us managed to consume not only our three bottles of wine but another as well!!

We both think that this part of Virginia is absolutely gorgeous.

CUMULATIVE MILEAGE: 2,482

DAY: 26
08/08/10 THE SKYLINE DRIVE

The plan was to drive the Skyline Drive and head for Philadelphia. Michael wondered why we would bother with the latter, but it does have 3 Stars in the "Good Book."

Entry to the Skyline costs $15, whereas the Blue Ridge is free. The Skyline is only 105 miles long against 469 for the Blue Ridge and there is a speed limit of 35 mph so minimum time to do the drive should be 3 hours.

Needing some exercise we stopped at Bearfence Mountain. This is NOT a mountain but is a pretty steep scramble over the rocks for a couple of geriatrics. We were nervously making our way when along came a family of four. Father with youngest child aged 11 months on his back and Ruth and Frankie aged 5 and 3 respectively. Once at the top he turned to the children and said "Give me your eyes. Now look around and be careful where you walk." It turned out he was a serving Marine with at least one tour of duty in Afghanistan. We still felt a modest sense of achievement and the view was well worth the scramble.

By the time we had done our hike and had some lunch it was 16:30, rather than 14:00, when we exited the Drive so there was no question of Philadelphia. Instead we settled for Chambersburg – not one of the glories of North America.

Again we asked TomTom for a B&B and again we ended up at a depressing looking building, but fortunately no-one came when we pressed the bell so we made for the Marriott Fairfield instead. It was identical to the Holiday Inn Express even down to the plastic knives and forks and paper plates, but $10 cheaper!

We filled up in Chambersburg and also found we were out of One Shot, but garages only sell engine oil. Fortunately there is an Advanced Auto Parts in town, which we will visit tomorrow.

CUMULATIVE MILEAGE: 2,698. Petrol bought 15.23 gallons US.

Geoffrey & Hilary Herdman

DAY: 27
09/08/10 **INTERCOURSE VILLAGE!** We are aiming for New Haven, home of Yale, 301 miles up the road. It is only a 4½ hour journey according to TomTom.

However the navigator suggests a detour via the Dutch Amish country, and indeed drives for part of what is a slow but fascinating walk in the car. We are impressed by the Amish one horse buggies, which bowl along at a brisk trot, despite the heat, seemingly impervious to enormous trucks looming behind them. As it is Monday, there are spectacular lines of laundry hanging out to dry, neatly arranged in descending order of size. Surprisingly large fields of hay are being turned by two horse ride-on spinners.

We visited Ephrata, the carefully restored site of an 18th C vision in community living, established by a refugee from war and religious persecution, from Heidelberg.

The life was rigorous, to put it mildly. It started as a Protestant monastery, to which a convent was added, and ultimately a third building for 'householders' who were families. They produced beautifully printed books, and composed hundreds of hymns, which at that stage could only be printed in part, with the notes being handwritten. The monastic community lasted until the early 19th C, but the householders continued to maintain the property and live there until the 1930s. Ultimately it was acquired by the state.

The result of this diversion was arrival at the George Washington Bridge in New York at 19:00, which turned out to be the height of the rush hour; despite

NORTH AMERICA

lovely views of the sunny Manhattan skyline, both car and driver grew increasingly hot and bothered. In the thick of it we were cheered up by a convertible mini driver who asked if the car was a Bristol, a first thus far in N America. Amazingly 10DPG ground slowly over the bridge, and through the preceding 3/4 hour traffic jam without boiling, and we arrived at the wonderfully comfortable Study Hotel in New Haven in one piece, where Geoffrey had several well deserved beers.

TOTAL MILEAGE: 3,045. Filled up at 3,003 miles 14.23 US gallons.1 litre of one shot added at 2,692 miles.

DAY: 28
10/08/10 SIGHTSEEING IN NEW HAVEN

The Study at Yale is a quite excellent hotel, rebuilt only 18 months previously and with very good service. After yesterday's exertions not to mention bottle of Long Island wine at dinner, we are a little tired and it is the ideal day for sightseeing.

In the morning we visit the Centre for British Art at Yale, which should really be called the Paul Mellon collection of British paintings, complete with purpose built and beautiful gallery.

In the afternoon we take the 90 minute tour of Yale. In the early 20th C to stop students from going to Oxbridge the idea was to create a replica, even down to pouring acid over the stonework to age it, but instead having the effect of weakening it. For us, the two most memorable things were the Women's Table, and the Beinecke Library.

The Table is a tribute to Women at Yale, designed by Maya Lin, who also designed the Vietnam Veterans' Memorial in Washington. It is an oval flat topped marble table with water flowing absolutely evenly over the whole surface.

The Library houses rare manuscripts and books. The Beineckes invented S&H stamps, the equivalent of Green Shield stamps and the building was meant to look like a page of stamps. Each square was of semi translucent marble which gave the most beautiful light inside, and also helps conserve the exhibits on display, including a volume of Audubon; lovely.

A no driving day!

The Beinecke Library

DAY: 29
11/08/10   MYSTIC SEAPORT   H returned to the Centre for British Art and we both gave the Yale University Art Gallery the once over before setting off for Mystic – just 53 miles up the road.

We checked into the Taber Inn founded and run by Maggie, now 84, who when she had retired as a school teacher 19 years previously decided she needed something to do. Maggie was born in Cavan but emigrated aged 2 and still has a farm back home.

The Seaport is a living museum to the art of shipbuilding and they are 2 years into rerestoring the Charles W Morgan, the last sailing whaler in existence. Inside it looked in pretty good shape and the captain had very comfy quarters including a double bed on gimbals for him and his wife. The only problem was that they had to sail round the Horn to the Pacific, and voyages could take anything up to 3 years. It is said you could smell a whaling ship from 25 miles away as all the rendering was done on board in a furnace, known as a tryworks and fuelled by bits of whale. A ship would typically hold two thousand barrels of 31 gallons each of whale oil and needed to slaughter sixty whales for a full load.

The Charles W Morgan should be ready to sail in 2013.

We also took a trip on the Sabino, a passenger boat built in 1908, with a double expansion steam engine. The voyage was for 90 minutes and we had to have the road bridge lifted, and the rail bridge swung for us to pass out and pass back again. As noted with the Earnislaw out of Queenstown a steam reciprocating engine is the most beautifully peaceful way of going to sea.

Our captain had a wonderful life and lived on a 42 ft boat called Calypso. He wintered in Florida and each spring he motored up to Mystic taking about six weeks, where he lived aboard. His 6 year old Scottie had never slept ashore.

Dinner was at A&B by the road bridge outdoors; a lovely setting but with absolutely no lighting so when the lobster came we had to request that they crack and separate it for us.

TOTAL MILEAGE: 3,098

DAY: 30
12/08/10 NEWPORT – SUMMER COTTAGES

To Hyannis via Newport. Newport is THE most extraordinary town. Breakers was a Summer home for the Vanderbilts and built by the same architect, Richard Morris Hunt, and at the same time as Biltmore 870 miles to the south. It is just one of many such "Summer cottages" built in the 1890s in Newport although probably the largest.

We didn't have time for a full visit so drove on stopping en route at a seaside resort, which could well have been anywhere downmarket on the S coast of England, for lunch. The snack bar was unprepossessing in the extreme but served up the most delicious lobster roll and chips. Maybe we were just hungry!!

We were staying in Hyannis at the Simmons Roadside Inn. It had been found for us by friends as a safe place to leave 10DPG whilst visiting Nantucket. Bill, the owner, had a collection of sixty five sports cars of which the vast majority were British and all painted bright red with the exception of one Lotus in its original colours. I cleaned 10DPG in honour of the occasion but next morning found paw marks all over the car from one of his huge family of cats.

TOTAL MILEAGE: 3,220

DAY: 31
13/08/10 THE WAY TO FLY

For the Herdmans an early (09:00) taxi to Hyannis International airport. You can go to three places, Martha's Vineyard, Nantucket and Boston and only by 8 seater Cessna 402. But boy this is the way to fly. At check in we gave our names and were given boarding cards. No ID, no tickets required. We were taking a bottle of champagne so had packed it in a suitcase. No x-ray and no question of security or searching.

My computer went in a small luggage compartment in the rear of the engine nacelle!

The flight to Nantucket is just over 10 minutes and flying at 1,500 ft you have a spectacular view, albeit that I was in the back seat and lying almost horizontally. Headroom was not good.

Our friends and Bristol owners, Colin and Dorothy Harper from Ontario, met us and took us to their Summer house, which they have owned for 30 years. En route we had a guided tour of Nantucket, whose fortune came from the whaling industry.

It is an enchanting island, but we are not alone in thinking so, and mansions for the mega rich are being constructed, although they must all have shingle

Geoffrey & Hilary Herdman

cladding. To join the Nantucket Golf Course 20 years ago cost an entry fee of $250,000 and annual subs were I think of the order of $15,000. From the air it looked pretty desolate to us, but is apparently the sine qua non for golfers.

Colin's father bought his 405 new from Bristols, and had long correspondence with the factory on the subject of overheating. I have always understood that at the Paris Motor Show, where the 405 was launched, there were problems with overheating which Bristol hotly (get it??) denied, but Colin's father was able to get the factory to fit a Kenlowe free of charge. Sadly the correspondence has gone missing.

DAY: 32
14/08/10 SIGHT SEEING IN NANTUCKET

To the whaling museum where we learnt of the only recorded case of a whale attacking and sinking a whaling ship in 1820 and the horrific two months before the remains of the crew were rescued. Then to the harbour where nestling amongst the multi million $ yachts were two 12 metre class America's Cup boats including Columbia, winner of the trophy in 1958 and now doing day charters!

After an excellent lunch chez Harper time for the return flight and again the bliss of informal procedures at check-in. The pilots of these twin engine planes are apparently paid $10 an hour as their main ambition is to accumulate flying hours.

Back to Simmons Inn and an excellent dinner at Alberto's in Hyannis.

NORTH AMERICA

DAY: 33
15/08/10 CAPE COD The plan was to drive up Cape Cod to Provincetown and probably to drive back the same day. It is no great distance but being a Sunday we were advised not to attempt the return as both bridges to the mainland, (Cape Cod is an 'island', because of the canal) could take an hour or more to cross.

This week is also Carnival week in P'town so accommodation was going to be interesting. In the event we stopped at a tourist info, who despaired but eventually found us an excellent B without B at Truro just to the South.

After sixty seven days at sea the Pilgrim fathers first landed at Provincetown in November 1620, some 200 miles North of their intended landfall. They stayed for five weeks before one of the crew suggested, from past experience, that Plymouth would make a better site for a permanent home.

Provincetown is now in some ways rather like Key West only much cooler

DAY 34

Geoffrey & Hilary Herdman

– with a vibrant gay community. Being carnival week there were all manner of shows on offer with all manner of people advertising them.

Driving up the peninsula we stopped off for a beach walk and found a line of camper vans all about 10 yards back from the sea and each with its own high powered fishing boat. The method of beaching these was to rev the 200hp outboard to maximum, whilst still at sea and run the boat up the beach, whilst hydraulically lifting the motor. I enquired as to the damage to the propeller and one owner did say he had gone through a couple. He also showed us his catch of yellow striped bass. The shore was strewn with fish skeletons, which the seagulls had cleaned very effectively.

On entering town 10DPG suddenly started running very roughly so when we parked I inspected under the bonnet and found petrol all round the middle carburettor; clearly grit in the needle valve and a few taps on the top of the float chamber seemed to cure the problem. Our last fill up had been with some dubious petrol called "Pepsi". It obviously came with lumps! I also rather alarmingly noticed that the leads to the brake lights had come detached from the master cylinder. This can only have happened when the starter was being replaced some two weeks previously!!

We managed to avoid any of the entertainments, but dined excellently in a Tiffany style restaurant called Napi's.

For the return to Truro the engine was once again its usual sweet self. Tapping the top of the carb seemed to have done the trick.

TOTAL MILEAGE: 3,320 – more or less spot on intended average of 100 miles per day.

DAY: 34
16/08/10 THE MAYFLOWER

Marc & Ruth Atkinson had told us we must go and visit 403 owners, the Carlsons, who live at Milton just South of Boston. They in turn went along with this suggestion, although Keith was taking the "red eye" from Pebble Beach and arriving at about 10:00 in the morning.

However our first visit was to a seal colony. Low tide was at 10:04, when they come up to the sandbanks. Although we were a little late there were literally hundreds basking and swimming, making soft cooing sounds. We stayed for an hour or so enchanted, watching the diminishing colony gradually setting out for the sea as the tide rose. Unlike the sea lions in Argentina there was no overpowering stench.

We took the opportunity to pay our respects to the Mayflower in Plymouth, moored about 100 yards from where it is alleged the Pilgrims first stepped ashore, before making our way to Milton.

Keith and Kathy gave us a most gracious welcome. They live in a mansion and Keith, as well as the 403, has four assorted Jaguars including a replica XKSS which he races successfully. He also has a "man" who fixes all his cars. As we had now covered nearly 3,500 miles this was of great interest!!

TOTAL MILEAGE: 3,420. Filled up at 3,335 miles 16.64 US gallons.

NORTH AMERICA

DAY: 35
17/08/10 THE FIRST SERVICE In convoy with Keith's immaculate 403 we visited the excellent Warren, who was able to drop everything to give 10DPG the first N American service. Warren asked how much my engine moved on depression of clutch. We examined and saw that there was a slight movement, whereas in Keith's there was something like an inch. Clearly new mounts are called for!

Having dropped the car at 09:30 we collected it at about 15:00, and yet Warren charged me for only 2 hours labour at $85 per hour, but he said he loved working on the car. He pointed out that I was using the "one shot" too often as there was a great accumulation of oil all over the inside of the front wheels, but otherwise it seemed in good shape.

For the return journey Keith drove 10DPG and I drove his XKR. I think the word is "awesome!"

Keith and Kathy very kindly accommodated us for another night and we dined on scrod at Siros in Quincy. Scrod's derivation is apparently "small cod remaining on dock!"

Geoffrey & Hilary Herdman

DAY: 36
18/08/10 **MARBLEHEAD** We visited Marblehead in 2001 with the BOC and loved both it, and the Harbor Light Inn, so determined to return one day. It is no great distance from Milton and we were there before our room was ready, but they very sweetly dropped everything and we moved in by midday.

With the possible exception of the Mandarin in NY it is quite our favourite hotel in North America. Nine years have only gone to improve it with the addition of a small swimming pool and even a bar.

After a splendid lunch at The Landing we walked round "The Neck", wondering at the splendid houses – in particular "Carcassonne", complete with formal knot garden. At one stately mansion a party was clearly in progress and as we watched a Range Rover drew up with the registration WEALTH!!

CUMULATIVE MILEAGE: 3,460.
We are back under our intended average of 100 miles per day.

DAY: 37
19/08/10 **USS CONSTITUTION** In 2001 we drove to Salem and took the train to downtown Boston. In 2010 we had a much more elegant alternative and took the catamaran, also from Salem. It is a journey of 55 minutes with spectacular views of the Boston skyline. At $8.50 for wrinklies we thought jolly good value too.

We had to pay homage to USS Constitution, which features in two of the Patrick O'Brian series. Launched in 1797 as one of six frigates to protect American commerce from Barbary pirates – despite paying $1M a year for them to desist – she is now the oldest serving warship afloat. (Victory is of course in dry dock).

During the war of 1812-14 she unfortunately was able to defeat British ships sent against her. Her first encounter was with HMS Guerriere and lasted only 33 minutes before the latter hauled down her flag. She became known as "Old Ironsides" as cannon balls appeared to bounce off her hull. Her construction was a laminate of white oak, live oak, and white oak. We have already encountered live oak in Savannah. It is immensely strong and sinks in water. Constitution is towed out into the harbour every year on Independence Day and fires a twenty one gun salute, but is under a major restoration and will sail again in 2012, although not very far because of the risk of a terrorist attack!!

To get to Constitution we had taken an old style open tourist trolley. Rather than a recorded commentary the driver kept up a running dialogue with repartee, as well as driving the bus. On the route, at any one time there are eighteen buses so that is probably 18 x 2 or more drivers with the most wonderful knowledge. One driver I spoke to had been doing it since the beginning of the year and had spent 120 hours in the library before venturing out. He was practically losing his voice and it was still only 14:00.

We completed the tourist circle with only one more stop for lunch and some minor retail therapy!

NORTH AMERICA

On the return boat trip we passed close to Logan airport and were amazed at the frequency of landings and take offs.

CUMULATIVE MILEAGE: 3,470

DAY: 38
20/08/10   SAILING   H wanted to go to Harvard, but having been to Yale only recently, and the Blog being sadly in arrears, I elected to stay behind to diarize, and play with the car.

The right trafficator was sticking on. The clockwork mechanism was working, but the lights would not stop flashing when the clockwork had unwound itself. As soon as the left flasher stopped the right started again continuously. For the present I removed the bulbs and stuck my arm out. This doesn't of course make much difference, as I am on the right hand side of the car, and all other drivers are on the left so probably can't see my gesture, but it salves the conscience.

Having wrestled for an hour I took sage advice from Spencer, which was on no account to examine the entrails of the clockwork mechanism or I would end up with a handful of cogs and springs. I determined to fix up a jury rig.

However, just as I was considering how best to do this a 1960s Oldsmobile 98 convertible floated topless into the car park. To cut a long story short I was invited to join a small but select luncheon club, called the Romeos.

We established that:

Property still had some way to fall in the US, probably another 10%. It is currently about 80% on average of where it should be.

Geoffrey & Hilary Herdman

Obama had been left a terrible legacy by George Dubbya. When Clinton left the presidency there was money in the coffers. GWB had not only spent it all but left the biggest deficit in history, rather like Caligula after Tiberius, only he was assassinated!

Obama was a better president than Hillary would have been,
and:
No-one could explain what the healthcare bill was all about!

After lunch the Plymouth owner, John Foster, who could trace his descent directly back to 1639 immigrants, invited me to go sailing in his Rhodes 19. There wasn't much wind but we had a blissful afternoon, followed by drinks at the Eastern Yacht Club.

On collecting H from the boat I tried to put on a serious face and say what a terrible time I had had whilst blogging and spannering but it lasted at least 15 seconds!

H had felt very guilty having had a lovely day in Boston including a visit to Harvard. Like Yale, Harvard is carrying out an enormous redevelopment of its art museums, but the Sackler remains open with a wonderful exhibition selected from all four museums. Accordingly she was delighted that I had also had a day's holiday.

CUMULATIVE MILEAGE: 3,490

DAY: 39
21/08/10 TANGLEWOOD An early visit to an auto store to buy a 3 way switch and various bits and pieces. What to do with them was of course another story and as we had some way to go would have to wait until tomorrow.

What with one thing and another it was practically midday by the time we left Harbor Light. Having paid our respects to Peter our host we set out for the 180 mile drive. En route we revisited Leominster, pronounced Lemminster, and stopped for lunch in a rambling old barn filled with the most appalling tat and calling itself an antique emporium, but the chocolate brownies were to die for.

As in 2001 we followed the Mohawk trail, because as in 2001 we were staying in Lenox, albeit not in the Village Inn. Everything was full, but we were able to book the last room in a grossly overpriced B&B at $335 for the night. Driving along the Mohawk we made a small diversion to Shelburne Falls. In 1929, when the tram service stopped, some enterprising ladies turned the tram bridge over the river into a Flower Bridge. Eighty years later it is quite beautiful. A pathway down the middle, and flower beds on either side, effectively two 400 ft herbaceous borders with mature trees.

No sooner had we arrived at the Kemble B&B than we realised that Tanglewood was only a couple of miles away and the Boston Symphony Orchestra was playing Mendelssohn and Beethoven there that evening. Tanglewood has what is called the "Shed" which is a roof covering, but open at the sides. The shed was apparently full, but our landlady gave us tickets for the lawn, plus umbrellas, and better, a car pass. After a speedy Italian supper at Alta we set off and found the car park badge

NORTH AMERICA

DAY 39

a Godsend as we were in VERY exclusive parking, which meant avoiding queues. We also managed at enormous expense – well $99 each – to buy two tickets for a "box" and sat in wonderful rocking chairs. It was a quite excellent concert, with a vast and enthusiastic audience.

TOTAL MILEAGE: 3,715. Filled up at 3,635 miles 15.25 gallons US

DAY: 40
22/08/10   TROUBLES WITH TRAFFICATORS

We awoke to rain. H elected for church, I elected to play with 10DPG.

After about an hour I had a jury rig for the trafficators with a lever switch. Left for left and right for right, I surprised myself! So far so good but in the absence of anything more secure the switch was attached precariously and very unsatisfactorily to the underside of the dashboard with velcro.

On examination the back of the clockwork unit is covered only with what appears to be thick greaseproof paper. On removing this the electrical part of the mechanism was exposed and is happily completely divorced from the clockwork. A cam actuates either arm of a brass V and one of the arms was bent. Bending it back had the system working again, until of course metal fatigue sets in, and we now have proper working trafficators.

Whilst in the middle of operations H came over with the vicar who said "Ah! 2 litre Bristol, copy of a BMW engine." You get a better class of clergyman in Massachusetts, and the sermon was pretty good too apparently.

In the afternoon the rain appeared to have eased so we walked a mile and a half to Edith Wharton's house, The Mount, and had a guided tour just for the two of us. For the return the heavens had opened and there was some discussion as to who had the greatest portion of the umbrella!

En route we passed a Shakespeare Company, who were doing A Winter's Tale that evening, but in view of the inclement weather our stomachs overruled our minds.

Geoffrey & Hilary Herdman

DAY: 41
23/08/10 THE CLARK AT WILLIAMSTOWN

We were not sorry to leave the Kemble Inn. The owners were very sweet but had only bought the place eight weeks previously, clearly never having owned a B&B before – and it showed. Yet it was by far the most expensive accommodation we had stayed in.

We were aiming for Ashland on the fringe of the White Mountains in New Hampshire, but en route had to visit the Clark. In 2001 we just had time to dash in and see the Virgin and Child with four Angels by Piero della Francesca, before the gallery closed. This time we were able to spend a comfortable 4 hours there. The highlight was an exhibition of Picasso/Degas, demonstrating clearly the former's debt to the latter, with many examples of pictures by both, side by side, on exactly the same theme.

They are about to lend their substantial Renoir collection for an exhibition, so we were treated to the unusual sight of a gallery remaining open while one side was stripped of works, and then rehung by a friendly and informative curatorial team, including some Monet canvases which were hanging on another wall in the same room when we first went through it that morning.

I eventually dragged H away at about 15:30 with three and a half hours driving to go. This was the coldest day we had had thus far. The water temperature far from struggling to keep under 100° was now struggling to keep above 80°. An inspection of the thermostat or lack thereof is clearly called for.

Ashland is a sleepy backwater in New Hampshire. Our B&B, Glynn House, was run by Glen, and his English wife Pamela, very efficiently. Glen was the ex Far Eastern manager for DHL, having previously done 8 years in the military including two tours of Vietnam.

For dinner we were directed to "The Common Man", 5 minutes walk away, where we met Steve, a regional sales manager for Hershey ice cream (nothing to do with Hershey chocolate). He again tried to explain the rules of baseball, which features on every TV in every restaurant we have been to, punctuated with even greater frequency than in the UK by advertisements.

TOTAL MILEAGE: 3,903

DAY: 42
24/08/10 MT WASHINGTON AND THE COG RAILWAY

One could happily spend a long time in Northern New Hampshire. Options include; white water rafting, kayaking, hiking, sailing, trains old and new, and of course Mt Washington in the Presidential range. In the event we decided on the White Mountain scenic drive and Mt Washington.

The first "cog" railway in the world (1859) was built at Mt Washington. The first engine, Peppersass, had a vertical boiler, but worked for 41 years. Until 2 years ago all motive power was by steam, but about 2 years ago six biodiesel locomotives were introduced, although the first and last trips of the day are still by steam.

NORTH AMERICA

Tickets are $62 each or $57 for wrinklies for the return. The distance is only 3 miles, but the train reaches a maximum of 7 mph and the journey takes 45 minutes each way. In the old days railway workers had a kind of rail sledge for the descent and the record for the 3 miles is 2 minutes and 45 seconds. Errol Flynn once described the Cresta as "the ultimate laxative". He should have tried this.

The summit is 6,288 feet. It had been snowing the previous day, and in 1935 recorded the fastest wind speed ever in the States at 235 mph. Today they told us it was 42°F with an 11 mph wind factor so we took barbours.

In fact there appeared to be no wind at all and we were rather too hot. Some cloud, but visibility was generally good. Under perfect conditions you should be able to see the sea 100 miles away. The Appalachian Trail crosses at the summit. As already mentioned it is 2,200 miles long and for a fit hiker takes about 110 days. The oldest person to do it was 81 and the youngest 6!

The round trip with waiting for the return train takes about 3 hours. We just missed the 13:00 going up, so by the time we returned it was about 17:00. Mrs H was intent on a walk, but first we drove the rest of the White Mountain loop before finding an old logging railway track running beside a river. Despite dire warnings of Black Bears there were no encounters with wildlife.

Back in Ashland Glen warned us the forecast for the morrow was less clement.

TOTAL MILEAGE: 4,053. Filled up at 3,976; 16.1 US gallons.

DAY: 43
25/08/10 MAYUMI EXPLAINS RESTAURANTS

Looks like the front suspension is broken but this is one of the steam engines for the Cog. Once it starts climbing it does of course become level.

Glen sadly was right and we woke to a downpour. We also drove in a downpour. Time was when 10DPG used to leak on the passenger side. Now the passenger remains remarkably dry, but the driver had VERY wet feet. Steps will have to be taken.

En route we stopped for coffee and as always 10DPG scored again and we chatted to Carol and her husband, who were just about to relocate back to Monterey. They had been married for 51 years – certainly didn't look possible – and had now sold up in New Hampshire and were heading South.

Glen had advised us that on entering Kennebunkport there is the Clam Shack just on the bridge and we had a rather bizarre lunch of lobster roll and lemonade in the rain.

Our B&B "Captain Jefferds" was run by a very efficient ex-physiotherapist, called Sarah, and her husband.

That evening Sarah pointed us towards The Hurricane. We arrived a little early but had a charming waitress called Mayumi, who although living most of her life in the States, had just come back from a 2 year UNESCO project in Liberia, where she had been born. Clearly a touch above your average waitress, but 'That's Kennebunkport!'.

We told her we were confused by American restaurant protocol. She explained that in order of appearance you have:

NORTH AMERICA

A hostess, who can only show you to your table
A buss boy, who can only fill your glass with water
A server, who can only take your food order
A sommelier, who can only take your drinks order
A captain, who can only deliver your food.
We didn't progress as far as the one who clears the plates!

I suppose it is probably much the same in a smarter restaurant in the UK, with the major difference that at least the hostess can get you a drink.

As the Herdmen usually arrive at a caff with their tongues hanging out we do prefer the European system!!

TOTAL MILEAGE: 4,140

DAY: 44
26/08/10 DEER ISLE MAINE
Mrs H on top of Mt Washington.

Peter at the Harbor Light Inn in Marble Head had given us a book called "The Select Registry of Inns". Captain Jefferds of course features, as does Pilgrims on Deer Isle. Sadly they could only accommodate us for one night as they had a wedding and were choc-a-bloc on the Friday.

The weather had completely changed from yesterday. Despite 10DPG being rather damp we had a glorious topless drive along the 1, which wimbles all the way from Key West to the Canadian border. Deer Isle is utterly gorgeous and reminded us both of the West coast of Scotland or Ireland, with coves and bays and fishing boats and just a handful of clapboard houses.

We didn't arrive until about 18:00. On check-in H discovered a trail to Barred Island. We walked along a forest track for about a mile and a half before coming to a spit joining the island to the mainland, walkable only shortly before and after low tide. We made the island, but by the time of return it was getting pretty dark and for the last quarter of an hour we were stumbling through the forest looking for markers on trees. On reaching the car park we met some other people who had found, and returned by, the road!

CUMULATIVE MILEAGE: 4,331

DAY: 45
27/08/10 CROSSING INTO CANADA
Just a little trepidation today. To bring 10DPG into the States had been a major hassle with paperwork and we needed to have Environmental Protection Agency clearance and a

Geoffrey & Hilary Herdman

certificate. We just sort of assumed that once in the States there would be no problem driving into Canada.

We were recommended to The Algonquin hotel in St Andrews in New Brunswick, but first decided to see more of Deer Isle. For some time the previous day we had been on reserve so a fill up was called for. In New Hampshire the predominant petrol (gas) is Irvine and the octane ratings are 87, 89, and 91, rather than 93 which we had been used to, but 10DPG seemed not to mind.

A glorious walk through an old farmstead surrounded by sea and with a couple of apple trees where the kitchen garden had once been, followed by circumnavigation of the Isle. The only town of any significance is Singleton on the edge of the sea with probably no more than five hundred inhabitants, a very pretty artists' retreat and complete with the Singleton Opera House, where they were performing Measure for Measure.

Onwards and upwards, North through New Hampshire, with a spectacular view from the top of the Caterpillar Hill over the bay with its dozens of islands, all that remains visible of a vast submerged mountain range, and the scene of the scuttling of an American navy fleet to avoid surrender to the British in the War of Independence. Lieutenant Paul Revere (he of the ride) was discharged the militia but later exonerated. The Admiral was dismissed the service.

We followed the 1, and cut the corner via the 191, through wonderfully named Meddybemps. A lovely afternoon's drive in beautiful weather, over attractive roads with very little traffic, to Calais on the St Croix river, which is the boundary between the USA and Canada. The US official just waved us through. On the North bank we stopped at a very efficient border post where we showed our passports; 10DPG's registration was punched into a computer, a couple of questions about where we were going and we were through. There were no cars in front of us and the whole process took 5 minutes. Let us devoutly hope that future border crossings will be as easy – but somehow I doubt it.

The Algonquin is a huge old Canadian Pacific railway hotel. The railway no longer comes to St Andrews and the hotel division of CP has been taken over by Fairmont, new owners of the Savoy in London, so it was very comfortable and the lobster was excellent.

TOTAL MILEAGE: 4,510. Almost filled up at 4,331, 16 gallons US

DAY: 46
28/08/10   ST ANDREWS, NB   Cleaning and polishing day!
Weather perfect so 10DPG parked in the shade for the process.

Later a walk downtown in St Andrews. As in Marblehead many of the houses have plaques with their dates and original owners. The town is on the banks of the St Croix with Navy Island a little way off, and on the opposite bank, Maine. Seen on a perfect August day we are bowled over by St Andrews, and fancy a reviver by the water's edge. H spots some tables pied dans l'eau. I point out that the bar seems to be under construction but Evan, the owner, pops out and asks us what we would

NORTH AMERICA

DAY
46

like, and pours us tumblers full of Sauvignon Blanc. Another visitor arrives, who is Austrian and selling Biomass central heating, which depends on wood chips.

We are dining at the hotel as we have discovered there is a wedding, and better, fireworks that evening, so after dinner we sit on the veranda and have pole position for a spectacular display.

DAY: 47
29/08/10 THE FERRY TO DIGBY

Our original plan was to reverse the ferry crossing of 2001 from Yarmouth, at the foot of Nova Scotia to Bar Harbor in Maine. But we discovered that on 31st December 2009 the service had been shut down. Our two options were to drive to Halifax via Moncton, or take the ferry from St John to Digby. In the event we opted for the latter, a 3 hour crossing.

A gorgeous drive to St John. In 2001 we had been warned not to even think about driving through NB due to monotony of trees, but today was lovely. The loaders put us in pole position for leaving the ship, despite being well back in the queue!

Once under way H found a travel guide who recommended going whale watching from Freeport at 17:00 that evening.

To get to Freeport meant firstly a drive of 30 miles along the Digby Neck to East Ferry, not featuring on map, but opposite Tiverton. The ferry runs on the half hour from East Ferry and on the hour back from Tiverton a distance of perhaps half a mile. The fare was $5 which covered us both ways. Another 11 miles further on we came to Freeport, where H went whale watching and I repaired to the bar

Geoffrey & Hilary Herdman

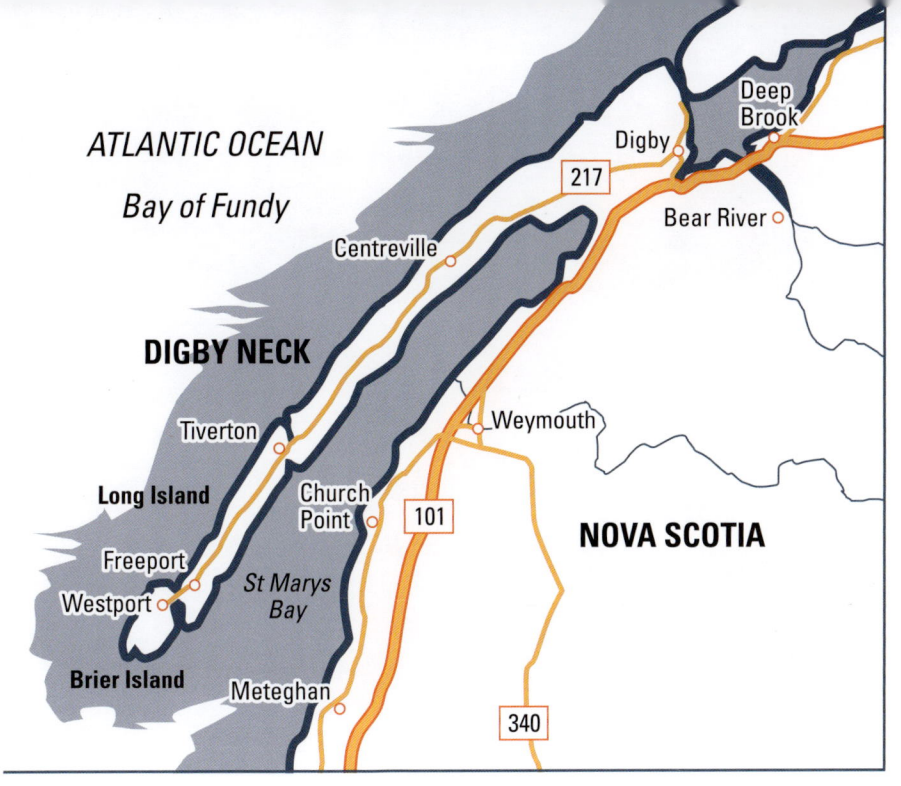

for a couple of Coronas (Mexican beers) before setting to on the chrome.

The good ship Georgy Porgy, a lobster fishing boat in the winter, and a whalewatcher in summer, did not let us down, and we got close to a humpback mother and calf, who spouted and dived for an hour or so in a beautiful calm evening sea. A lovely trip, which lasted as long as the chrome polishing, rather conveniently for H.

We set off from Freeport just too late to make the ferry, and no sign of a hostelry, so considerable loss of morale, when by good luck the local Mountie, who had been admiring the car and the polishing efforts earlier, turned up on an urgent mission, and summoned the ferry, which kindly took us as well, thus avoiding a tedious 45 minute wait.

TOTAL MILEAGE: 4,656

DAY: 48
30/08/10   10DPG BEING WELCOMED Being already on reserve we stopped in Digby for petrol and as I was filling a voice said "Hello Geoffrey" twice before I realised he was talking to me. It turned out to be our friendly RCMP from the previous evening who had spotted us.

There are two roads to Halifax, the 101, which is the main road bypassing most towns and the 1, which preceded it and potters through all the villages like Paradise. Our travel guide on the ferry had recommended scenic places to visit en route. The weather was one of the hottest days we had had since North Carolina with temperatures in the 80s and we had a glorious drive.

First stop was Annapolis Royal, named after Queen Anne, but the most fought

NORTH AMERICA

DAY 48

over place in Canada during the 17 / 18th C and changing hands more than most. On to Look Off, which as its name suggests was on an escarpment overlooking the Bay of Minas and even vineyards, although the wine has a little way to go we are informed. Finally Freeport, which has a 35 ft tide and rather attractive sun worshippers(!) for a paddle.

We arrived on the outskirts of Halifax at around 17:00 to a mega traffic jam, from which we took emergency avoiding action and the faithful Simon (TomTom) took us unerringly to our friends John & Susan.

Dinner was prepared by them and was by far and away the best lobster we had had with a sensational lemon butter, washed down with superb home made lemonade. We cleaned poor Patrick out of his reserves.

TOTAL MILEAGE: 4,834. Filled up at 4,656 miles, 58.5 litres.

DAY: 49
31/08/10 **THE END OF THE REHEARSAL** Our friends the Venns in Halifax, with 10DPG under new cover. Patrick is holding a bottle of his excellent lemonade (pictured opposite).

As 10DPG was due to be here for three weeks we went in search of an upholsterer, who might be able to repair some wear to the driver's seat. He said he could pull the leather back into place and restitch, but it would be preferable if we could procure a complete front seat cover from the UK, and he would sew it into place very quickly on our return. An e-mail was despatched to the excellent David Nightingale.

Bob the upholsterer suggested we go and visit Peter Osborne who worked on UK cars. Peter had built for himself the most immaculate garage from granite and

Geoffrey & Hilary Herdman

had a delectable range of cars both British and American all in superb condition.

Meanwhile H & Susan went to the Pier 21 Museum, the Canadian equivalent of Ellis Island, which records the arrival of pre and post war immigrants, including refugees from various conflicts and the largest mass immigration to Canada of the 48,000 Second World War brides and their 200,000 children.

In the afternoon we dropped the seat off to Bob, and for the first time tried out the car cover. It wasn't until we had it in place that we read it was NOT meant as an outdoor cover, but if it was to be thus used to tie it down, which we duly did. Hurricane Earl is due at the end of the week!

Tonight we are due to catch a 23:45 Air Canada flight to the UK for three manic days before setting off on the Tour of Switzerland and the BAC100 events.

It has been a most wonderful seven weeks and we can't really believe this is only the rehearsal. 'Touch wood' (very hard) the starter has been our only significant problem, but 10DPG has been a joy to drive and the greatest crowd puller. They all think we are mad but hey!

Note: We returned to Europe on 1st September 2010, however this did not form part of our Round the World trip. We therefore continue the next part of our journey with Day 50, having returned to Canada on the 21st September.

NORTH AMERICA

DAY: 50
22/09/10   UNDER COVER

We flew back to Canada on the 21st, a day later than expected, as we had:

a) to muck out our London flat in readiness for tenants – it's amazing how much junk you can dispose of from a small flat! Fifteen black sacks in our case and another twenty boxes of stuff to go into storage and four clothes boxes!

b) to spend a day going through the accounts of the excellent BAC100 weekend. 215 for dinner on the Friday night and 150+ cars at the Concours on Saturday.

En route to the BAC100 dinner I stopped off at David Nightingale's to collect the new seat cover and panicked as I thought the pattern wasn't correct. He assured me it was standard 405, but having only owned the car for 12 years and driven over 100 k miles I was convinced that my seat was NON standard.

We were met at Halifax airport by our very kind friends, complete with the seat in the "trunk" of their car and of course the new seat back was a perfect match – stupid boy!!

So we took the entrails to Bob who assured us he would have everything ready for the morrow.

Whilst we were away 10DPG had been under cover. As we left Hurricane Earl was threatening, but fortunately the strongest part bypassed Halifax. The main danger being falling branches. John had added a tarpaulin, and the result was a dry as a bone car.

DAY: 51
23/09/10   ON THE ROAD AGAIN

A glorious day if slightly chilly, but definitely top down stuff. We had both brought an extra suitcase with us so the packing was a work of precision. At a later date we will photograph all of it to emphasize how much luggage one can travel with in a 405 Drophead!

We were en route at about midday with the aim of driving to Fredericton, capital of New Brunswick. The Trans Canada Highway, Route 2, was mostly empty dual carriageway and driving was a joy. I am told that from Moncton to Fredericton is the least interesting bit, but I slept soundly, curled up rather uncomfortably in the passenger seat.

When we stopped for petrol, and a belated lunch we were advised to approach Fredericton by the riverside drive, which turned out to be spectacular.

Geoffrey & Hilary Herdman

On arrival at the Crowne Plaza Hotel we found we had been upgraded and had the most magnificent room thus far, complete with open plan bath and jacuzzi.

Fredericton is a most attractive town. Christchurch Cathedral – illustrated opposite – is magnificent and the footbridge across the St John river is the longest footbridge in the world, although needless to say an old railway bridge.

Filled up with 60 litres at 4,960 miles. TOTAL DISTANCE: 5,116 miles

DAY: 52
24/09/10 HOTEL TADOUSSAC

We set out from Fredericton in cold and very wet conditions and things only got worse as the day progressed.

The plan was to visit Tadoussac, where a friend has a family Summer house. Tadoussac is at the confluence of the Saguenay and St Lawrence rivers and is world famous for whale watching, as vast quantities of krill come down the Saguenay.

We had first to cross the St Lawrence. Fortunately we checked on the internet and found that the Riviere du Loup St Simeone crossing, the logical one, was closed for a year. We tried to book the alternative, Les Trois Pistoles – Les Escoumins by phone but the answer machine said it was full and could take no more messages and the internet was not even an option.

The trans Canada in New Brunswick was magnificent dual carriageway, but as soon as we entered Quebec the road deteriorated and when we went off piste towards Les Trois Pistoles the road was one mass of road works.

At the ferry they asked for our reservation, having none we were waitlisted, fortunately successfully.

The Saint Lawrence is 26 k wide at that point and the crossing took one and a half hours. There were distant whale sightings (to the eye of faith) through the downpour, but it was so cold that it was not conducive to staying out on deck.

And so to the hotel, which gave us a wonderful dinner.

Filled up at 5,246 52 litres. TOTAL MILEAGE: 5,406 miles

DAY: 53
25/09/10 TO QUEBEC

It had rained all night and was very cold. Tadoussac has laid out a very pretty and informative boardwalk around the headland for whale watching. In the rain we tramped round, but visibility was poor and the whales obviously thought they were better off deep at sea than in this cold climate!

We tried to set out at about midday in the rain, but poor 10DPG, cold and miserable, refused to start and then produced a dull click from the solenoid when turning the key. This was the first time we had had a nonstart. H had suggested the previous evening using the cover and of course she was right!! Fortunately a friendly porter saw our dilemma and helped H, or rather the other way round, push the car to where I could roll down a hill. Even better he had done a runner before we could thank him appropriately. The hill start worked and having parked

NORTH AMERICA

on another hill I tightened up the battery terminals, which seems to have done the trick re the clicking solenoid.

There is a large ferry which runs every 20 minutes 24/7 across the Saguenay and is completely free. Thereafter we took the 138 to Quebec, deviating only at Malbaie to take a very pretty coastal drive, where we stopped at a boutique paper manufacturer. The 138 of course is also the old Roman road from Rouen to Tours!!

We had wanted to stay in the Chateau Frontenac – see photo, but all six hundred and fifty rooms were taken, so we settled for the Hotel Manoir Victoria also in the old town, which involved interesting car parking with tight turns and a lift!

On the recommendation of both the green Michelin Guide and the hotel we dined at Le Saint-Amour. They couldn't feed us until 21:45 and even then were absolutely storming and we came away with a bill for $300, our most expensive dinner thus far! But even walking through it by night we were enchanted by Quebec City.

Filled up 5,547 miles 57 litres. TOTAL MILEAGE: 5,583

DAY: 54
26/09/10 SIGHTSEEING IN QUEBEC Mrs H went to the Anglican Cathedral; beautiful interior of oak donated from Windsor Great Park by George III. The service was bilingual, in honour of a Christening for a francophone family, but otherwise familiar.

We scaled the Heights of Abraham, under heavy restoration, but still in use as a military barracks, and looked down in wonder at the Port. The Crown Princess, 116,000 tonnes of cruise liner, with 3,500 passengers and 1,500 crew dominated the harbour. The Aida Luna at a mere 69,000 tonnes looked small by comparison.

After a quite excellent lunch in "1640" – escargots and Caesar salad – both neat garlic, surprise surprise!, we took the rather dramatic funicular to the Old Town, heavily restored but none the worse for it. The Place Royale – see photo – boasting a splendid head of Louis XIV. At least there wasn't a bust of the abominable De Gaulle, who single handedly by his cynically calculated cry of "Vive le Quebec libre" in 1967 has caused such problems within the province to this day.

We had imagined that Quebec City especially would be completely French speaking but due perhaps to tourism everyone seemed to be bilingual and hardly knew if they were speaking French or English. So our fractured attempts were met with either language at will.

A rather mediocre dinner at what attempted to be a recreation of Relais de Venise in Marylebone Lane!

DAY: 55
27/09/10 NORTH HATLEY A fairly leisurely start, which involved extricating 10DPG from the upstairs garage via a lift, but all was well.

A motorway drive to Sherbrooke, before heading off to N Hatley and Peter and Helene's enchanting house.

NORTH AMERICA

North Hatley is located at the Northern end of Lake Massawippi, which has a fine pier with what looks like a bandstand at its end. A few days later this would all be submerged by heavy rains.

In the evening we drove into Sherbrooke for dinner at the quite exceptional "Le Bouchon" with panoramic views of the river. Just upstream there are some falls which were floodlit in colours of changing hue. All very attractive.

The food and decor were excellent and the wine list was like a computer screen. When you opened it the two pages were back lit. A brilliant idea.

TOTAL MILEAGE: 5,739

DAY: 56
28/09/10   TO MONTREAL

One only ever drives a Bristol engined car in Montreal! From 1968 to 1972 it was an AC Greyhound with 100D2 engine and now of course a 100B.

We woke in the peaceful wooded calm of North Hatley, to find the rain had almost stopped.

In the morning Peter took us round Bishops University. I had been on a course there in 1968, but regrettably had no memories. The chapel is particularly fine with all the pews facing each other and magnificent carved angels in the choir stalls.

The university was founded partly by Dr. Doolittle; sadly no sign of a pushmepullyou, but some fine 19th Century buildings, as well as a modern campus.

We lunched at the local tavern in N Hatley, where just a few days later the ground floor would be completely submerged, and rather later than we had perhaps intended set out for Montreal.

The weather looked forbidding but in the event we made it in the dry, albeit with the top up. The approach to the Champlain bridge was very slow, as we had been warned, partly due to renovations, but we then swung right for the Jaques Cartier and the East end. We were staying in the Auberge de la Fontaine on the Parc de la Fontaine. The hotel was – adequate, the Parc quite attractive.

As soon as we arrived the rain started but we were not going to risk Montreal traffic, so took a taxi to Peter and Helene's son Dave, and his partner Lara. When I left Montreal in 1972 I sold my B&O to Peter, who in turn passed it on to Dave. The dual turntable long ago gave up the ghost but the rest sounded wonderful, installed in their very pretty apartment, reached by the typical Montreal exterior staircase from the street to first floor.

We took a trip down memory lane to the Alpenhaus on St Marc St. On entering we were greeted by an Indian who had bought it in 1992. It opened in 1967, and really nothing had changed apart from the prices! We dined on chopped veal Zurich style with rosti, and chocolate fondue. We were practically the only people in the place and the decor certainly had neither changed nor been cleaned in 40 years. Goodness knows what Dave and Lara made of it!! There is a moral here, somewhere....

TOTAL MILEAGE: 5,834

DAY: 57
29/09/10 RIGOLETTO We had arranged to meet David Horlington for lunch. He suggested O Thyme on De Maisonneuve (founder of the city of Montreal), as it is a BYO caff, and he had some excellent wine which he wanted to share with us.

We wandered through the East end in the morning and around the Place des Arts, which seemed to be a total mess of reconstruction. Rather unsurprisingly downtown had changed out of all recognition in the last 40 years.

Lunch was excellent and we managed a half bottle of champagne, a bottle of white, and an excellent St Julien, before David suggested we repair chez lui for coffee. He has a Jaguar XFR, which was seriously impressive, even on the short run home.

The apartment turned out, unsurprisingly, to be sensational, with ceiling to floor glass, and spectacular views from his bed, not to mention his exercise bike, over Montreal. Privacy was afforded by electrically operated curtains, which Louise was in the process of changing.

Rigoletto was on that evening at Salle Wilfred Pelletier. Only the second time I had seen it, and although a dubious story, it was beautifully performed with a deserved standing ovation. Gilda was quite gorgeous, with a stunning voice. As we exited a trumpeting busker was playing "La donna e mobile" in ever higher keys.

David had suggested for dinner T Brasserie, just outside, and the latest Montreal sensation, but at 22:55 they were desolated, the kitchen was shut, despite us having made a reservation. Worse they couldn't think of anywhere else where we could eat. For better or worse the Hyatt bar next door was open, and we dined at about 23:30 on very welcome hamburgers.

What is the second largest city in Canada coming to if you can't get a proper meal after 22:30? Not like my days there.

DAY: 58
30/09/10 DINNER WITH THE McGOUGHS Many years ago, when I lived in Montreal, opposite the Westmount police station, the AC would be parked externally and we would climb in through the back window of the apartment. The police did once come round and stop me more or less "in flagrante delecto," but as I explained it saved going round to the front again.

Forty years on the apartment block is much the same. The back parking area has been patched a bit, but the window now has an aircon box, thus precluding clandestine entry.

NORTH AMERICA

We had left Auberge de la Fontaine in the rain, and visited Stanton St., site of said apartment, in the rain. We then headed for Decarie, the route out to the Metropolitan Bvd in the rain, and on approaching it were warned that it was stationary. Fortunately there are side roads and we took these all the way to Metropolitan, which was pretty solid with traffic leaving, but not half as bad as entering Montreal. There had been an accident causing a 20 mile tail back.

The autoroute was dreadful, thick traffic, driving rain and low visibility, so we decided to take another trip down memory lane and drive through Hudson, where we had a Summer cottage in 1972.

We stayed on pleasant country roads, via Vankleek Hill (lunch) until forced to rejoin the motorway shortly before Ottawa.

We had decided to visit the newly opened War Museum. The traffic on entering the city was horrendous and we were in serious danger of running out of petrol, or gas as it is quaintly called. TomTom misled us once but when we did at last find a gas station we were driving on fumes.

The War Museum lived up to its reputation, but unfortunately we had only about 45 minutes to spare, rather than the 3 - 4 hours it deserved. The vehicles on display included a German 'Kreig Elefant' motor-bike used in the North Africa campaign, which we realised must have been the type used by Count Metternich, when he took our friend Oliver captive after he had crash landed in the desert.

And so on to our hotel in Kanata, half way between Ottawa and Dunrobin, where the BOC North American secretary, Peter McGough lives, with his elegant wife Verne.

They had advised that they would feed us and asked if we had any dietary requirements. I replied that I didn't eat Welsh rarebit, so Verne prepared by way of hors d'oeuvre, quite the most sensational 'cheese on toast'.

Peter has a working 412, two and a half 405s, an Arnolt, and two – yes two BS1Mk 4 engines. One day he will have some amazing cars!

We had a very good evening with them.

TOTAL MILEAGE: 5,933. Filled up at 5,897 67.5 litres.

DAY: 59
01/10/10   TO BARRIE Some serious motoring again, 300 odd miles from Kanata to Barrie and mercifully at last the weather was clear.

The logical route and as recommended by TomTom would have been to take the motorway all the way, going down to Lake Ontario, but judging by yesterday's traffic we would not have been alone.

Colin and Dorothy had recommended that we take the cross country route via Renfrew, Griffith, Denbigh, and Bancroft, which we proceeded to drive and had a more or less traffic free run. The scenery was lovely, with fall colours. Even when the sun is not shining, the colours give the illusion that it is. We saw a stopped car with its bonnet up, and then realised it was an artist, who had halted at the top of a winding downhill stretch, where the grey of the road and the strong yellow of the

Geoffrey & Hilary Herdman

roadmarkings were echoed by the surrounding trees; a vivid picture seen from the car, and I hope he survived to complete it!

We stopped at a large barn of a place called Mapleton House for lunch and gorged on pancakes and maple syrup. The proprietor told us she had two thousand taps into maple trees which finally produced 2,000 litres of syrup. The sap has to be reduced by a factor of 40:1, ergo her two thousand taps yielded 80,000 litres of sap. Seventy five percent of the reduction was done by osmosis and the rest by steam injection – however that is achieved! Anyway the result was delicious.

In Barrie, as Laura was recently out of hospital we stayed in the Harbour View B&B, overlooking Lake Simcoe. Having established communication with the B&B we thought we would check out downtown Barrie, and walked round the edge of the lake as far as a mini Lake Geneva type water fountain.

On our return I was rather alarmed, but hardly surprised after the recent rain, to find water still trickling out of the nether regions of poor 10DPG.

It came as a welcome surprise that rather than kitchens shutting down at 10:30 a la Montreal we were able to eat when we liked. Indeed one of the restaurants was open until 02:00. In the end we elected for Shirley's as recommended by our landlady and had a very good meal.

TOTAL MILEAGE: 6,212 Filled up at 6,204 63 litres

DAY: 60
02/10/10 A FAMILY AFFAIR A day spent with Laura Crook in Barrie. Her brother Andrew was over, partly looking after her, as she had just had a back operation. H had not seen him for approx 50 years. Neither Laura nor Paddy (84), who housekeeps for Laura, can drive at the moment, so Andrew was something of a Godsend.

A well deserved wash and clean for 10DPG in the afternoon with water still trickling out of the back and then a family dinner. Rob and his brilliant and attractive wife Anya were in attendance although Anya was on call at the hospital and had to dash out to diagnose an MMR scan. She commutes between Barrie and Ottawa hospitals. In the latter she is head radiologist in charge of quite a team. Also dining was Sheila, another UCH medic, who had started the trend to Barrie, and again H thought they had last met 50 years ago. Rob produced wonderful barbecued steak, followed by Paddy's justly famous chocolate mousse: delicious!

Anya has driven to Ottawa some eighty times and always takes the cross country route as recommended by the Harpers, and followed by us. It came as a revelation to her that Mapleton House was open.

NORTH AMERICA

DAY: 61
03/10/10 TO PENETANGUISHENE

From Barrie to Penetanguishene is only some 34 miles, but we took the scenic route (98 miles).

First, by keeping to the shores of Lake Simcoe, passing the most amazing estates, and then following, as best possible, the canal system from Lake Huron to Ottawa.

The bad weather of Quebec was now well behind us and so it was top down stuff all the way.

By about 14:00 we were feeling just a little peckish and stopped at Severn Falls to find the Corvette Club of Ontario had beaten us to it and there must have been at least fifty of them. We were warned that lunch would take at least half an hour, so decided to press on.

One of the Corvette owners asked what we were doing and when we told him he said we were totally mad and that we would be killed by drug gangs in Mexico. In that case I said you will be able to read all about it in the Globe and Mail. I never read that rubbish he replied. He may be right but I just think he might have had a problem or two.

A little later we came to Big Chute and were attracted by an alarm bell ringing, and then some gates coming down across the road. Fortunately just after we had passed. We parked up to see a boat lift in operation. Boats float into the lift and are strapped up. The lift then rises out of the water, over the road and down the other side to a lower level. To keep it even it has two sets of rails, one for the front and one for the back wheels, which follow different inclines. It can apparently take boats up to 100 ft long, and was constructed as it was thought that a lock would allow lampreys from the upper water into the fisheries of the lower water.

And so we arrived at the Harpers' lovely house on the edge of the water in Georgian Bay.

I mentioned to Colin that water seemed to be dripping out of the back of 10DPG. When we checked his car we found drain holes on both sides at the back. 10DPG had one, where the fuel overflow pipe comes through, but nothing on the offside. A few minutes later with the aid of a drill, about 2 litres, maybe more, of water came pouring out. It looked absolutely clean so perhaps not too much rust had been created. We had a delicious dinner of Mennonite duck, and were joined by John McGill, who is President of the Lincoln association, and was off next day to the Hershey concours, where we had first met Dorothy and Colin in 2001.

TOTAL MILEAGE: 6,310

Geoffrey & Hilary Herdman

DAY: 62
04/10/10 **THE SECOND SERVICE** 10DPG garaged in eclectic company; Maserati Mistrale, Lamborghini Espada, and 405 saloon owned since new by Colin's father and now by him.

We had only covered some 2,800 miles since the last service in Boston, but this would be the last chance before the West coast. Colin has an amazingly well equipped garage complete with electrically operated hoist. Together – well he did most of it – we carry out a service. He even greased the lubrication points in the universal joints. I had worried that the thermostat might be permanently open as we seem to run very cool in the cooler weather, but on examination it was completely closed, so I guess is just set for a low temperature. The water gauge shows 80° - 85° on a cold day, but on rereading the handbook it suggests that when testing a hot engine the water should be above 70°, so as we should be heading for warmer climes it is probably sensible to have a cooler rather than a warmer thermostat.

Colin even had some K&N cleaner and we were amazed at the colour of the water after the filters had been washed. Despite being 10,000 miles old we examined the spark plugs but they all seemed in pretty good condition so left them for the next time.

Both Colin and Dorothy are heavily involved with Wye Marsh, a wetland habitat, and in the afternoon we walked the couple of miles of boardwalk around the peaceful reserve. Sadly we didn't have time to visit the old mission in Midland.

That evening we dined in a converted library also at Midland.

TOTAL MILEAGE: 6,335

NORTH AMERICA

DAY: 63
05/10/10   TO SAULT STE MARIE, GLORIOUS WEATHER

With sadness we say goodbye to Colin and Dorothy and set off for the West. It was always our intention that once having left Penetanguishene we would "go for it" to Vancouver. The total distance is 2,800 miles.

The weather is chilly but we motor barboured up and top down. The colours are magnificent.

Sault Sainte Marie is a link between Canada and the States. It is also the link between Lakes Superior and Huron, but there is a small strip of land between the two, which is the link to the States. The St Mary's river runs between the two lakes and has a fall of 12 ft, hence the name Sault or Rapids. We check-in to our hotel and are upgraded to a suite and then in the gloaming walk along the old canalway. There are now newer and bigger canals with road and rail bridges high enough above to allow Lakes ships to pass below. Unsurprisingly there are also two hydro power stations, whose output is limited by the amount of water they are allowed to pass through.

Reception tells us about Murios, an Italian restaurant downtown, but when we arrive it looks more like a sandwich bar and is fortunately closed. En route we had passed Arturos and returned there to be greeted by Arturo himself, and had an excellent, if garlicky, meal. We told Arturo he needed to have a word with the receptionist at the Delta, and on our return cross questioned the rather large receptionist as to why she had not recommended Arturos. "Oh" she said "I didn't realise you wanted fine dining!"

TOTAL MILEAGE: 6,702.
Filled up at 6,404 32 litres

Fall colours in Ontario

Geoffrey & Hilary Herdman

DAY: 64
06/10/10 — **HALF WAY ACROSS; THUNDER BAY** Typical road in Ontario. NB dense traffic!

Yet another sunny day – topless all the way.

The road from Sault to Thunder Bay follows the North shore of Lake Superior and is most attractive, with wonderful colours. We had been warned that everyone runs out of petrol on the Lake Superior road so took the necessary precautions!

Going by the most direct route Halifax to TB is 1,890 miles and TB to Vancouver 1,866 miles. In fact we have covered 2,296 miles, an extra 430 miles.

We stayed at the Valhalla Inn – perhaps appropriate for Thunder Bay? and at dinner were served by a very mouthy waitress, who advised us to stay at the Fort Garry in Winnipeg, and kept mastiffs with muzzles, one of which weighed 130 lbs and the other 230 lbs!

She also advised us not to drive by night for fear of hitting an animal. There are loose moose on the road. Their legs buckle and you are liable to have half a ton of moose coming through the windscreen. We assured her it was not our intention to drive after dark!

TOTAL MILEAGE: 7,130 days run 428
Filled up at 6,702 33.5 litres and again 6,897 32.5 litres

DAY: 65
07/10/10 — **TO WINNIPEG THROUGH THE PRAIRIES**

On leaving Thunder Bay there were major roadworks and a girl doing aerobics with her stop sign. Three lots of traffic came through our way before we could get going and a very angry truck driver behind us had words with the girl. A 15 minute hold up.

Of the 438 miles all but the last one hundred were in Ontario along single carriage way or highway as we call it over here. There is very little traffic and we are hardly held up. Passing places are marked well in advance so one has a chance to close up to a truck for the final overtake. Trouble is the trucks tend to go almost as fast as 10DPG so even in a 2 mile overtaking lane it can take a while, and close behind trucks there is a lot of turbulence which causes one to be alarmed for the safety of one's hat!

NORTH AMERICA

DAY 65

A varied drive through lovely countryside, a little wilder than before. H saw a bald eagle perched on a crag above the roadside.

We were sad to leave Ontario, land of shining waters, where we have had so much kindness and hospitality.

As soon as we reach Manitoba the road changes to twin highway, and about 50 miles from Winnipeg the trees stop and we are into flat Prairie.

We had booked into the Fort Garry, which is a magnificent hotel. All of a sudden we felt as if we had joined the grown ups. Porters come out to meet us and collect the luggage – not something we had had since St Andrews NB. Wonderfully maintained grand Edwardian decor in the lobby and bar.

Dining ends early in Winnipeg and we were delighted to find Sydneys, built in some converted stables.

TOTAL MILEAGE: 7,568, day's run 438 miles.
Filled up at 7,134 miles 45 litres and again at 7,327 miles 38 litres

DAY: 66
08/10/10 TO REGINA SASKATCHEWAN A totally glorious day weatherwise. Temperature up to low 80s in early October and shirtsleeves driving for most of the way. We asked one pump attendant how long the weather would last. "Until it rains" was the laconic reply!

TomTom aka Simon threw a wobbly first thing and exiting Winnipeg took us onto a dirt road for about 15 miles to the South. One day it may be a ring road but I think we should have just turned left out of the hotel and kept going.

Breakfast was included at the Fort Garry and we had a showman of a chef doing the day's specials of omelettes with asparagus, mushrooms and parmesan cheese. So we decided to pig out and bypass lunch. The cheese was perhaps a mistake, but we gave him $2 for presentation!

Apart from a sign for a closed tourist information centre there was no

Geoffrey & Hilary Herdman

indication that we had entered Saskatchewan, nor any indication that we had changed time zone. The need to retard watches came as a complete surprise on checking-in to our hotel.

The road is relentlessly straight and most of the scenery VERY boring. They may not have twin highways in Ontario but the landscape there for the most part is gorgeous.

We had been recommended to take a scenic divert via the Qu'Appelle valley, which I suppose means "No name". This involved a diversion up the 201 and all of a sudden, behold, hills and lakes and smallish farms all rather attractive and a welcome change; there were even some bends.

One sight on the Trans Canada which was impressive was a goods train, which must have been ninety trucks long, all double loaded with containers and keeping up with us despite only being drawn by one engine. That means one hundred and eighty trucks/lorries were not on the road. Not only was it being drawn by one engine but there is a gradual incline all the way from Winnipeg 780 ft to Regina at 1,893 ft.

We stayed in the Radisson, which was large and comfortable on Victoria Street, which is actually the Trans Canada through town. Dinner was at a strange windowless restaurant called Golfs Steak House.

TOTAL MILEAGE: 7,960
Filled up at 7,624, 48 litres

DAY: 67
09/10/10 REGINA TO BROOKS

Another glorious day. We can't believe our good luck.

The original plan was to drive to Calgary but that is an extra 100 miles and then a very short drive to Lake Louise, so instead we break the journey at Brooks.

Driving out of Regina is rather attractive. The hotel is on Victoria Street, and we turn off onto Albert St to exit town, through a very elegant park and presumably the legislative building for Saskatchewan (see illustration). This looks imposing and much like the one for Manitoba.

The road is unrelenting, more or less dead straight dual carriageway and we cruise at 3,000 rpm all day. The speed limit in Saskatchewan is 110 ks, which is almost exactly 3,000 rpm. We have gone from 90 in Ontario to 100 and even 110 in parts in Manitoba and now here. Occasionally we pass something – once an hour. We are passed more often – maybe four or five times an hour.

Although the road is straight, the countryside does roll and the drive is much less boring than we had feared, and no risk of the driver dozing off. The road runs through some wonderfully named places – Moose Jaw, and Swift Current, not to mention Medicine Hat, although there was more romance in the name than the actuality.

The drive is worth it, apart from anything else, just to experience the vastness of this country and appreciate the efforts of the pioneers.

There are freight trains everywhere; one with four engines is 2 miles long. H wonders how ever long it would take to stop.

There is absolutely no indication when we cross into Alberta, where the speed limit remains the same 110, and the only town we pass is Medicine Hat, which is supposed to be the historic centre of the "gas" industry.

We reach Brooks, also an oil town and drive through on brand new roads to a resort on Lake Newell. Mrs H is v. nervous about her choice of night's lodging, as G is not so keen on B&B's as she is, and it does seem to be an alarming distance from a very charmless town into a featureless interior. We eventually find the B&B. "A Lakeshore Bed and Breakfast". It is cheap and comfortable and about like living on the moon – no atmosphere. For dinner we head back into town and eventually settle for O'Sheas, where we have a rather good dinner. The waitress, who in real life is a mortgage processor for Scotia Bank, tells us a three bedroom house on Lake Newell costs $1M. We are amazed!

Breakfast tomorrow is at 08:30 so we retire early.

TOTAL MILEAGE: 8,346
Filled up in Regina 7,961 58 litres and again in Medicine Hat 8,247 miles, 56 litres.

DAY: 68
10/10/10 INTO THE ROCKIES. LAKE LOUISE

More or less as soon as we rejoined the Trans Canada one of us thought we could possibly see the Rockies in the distance but I think it was just cloud! H assures me it was NOT clouds.

Calgary itself seemed to be a complete dump. The Trans Canada passes straight through it with traffic light after traffic light. As seen from the road we were underwhelmed. We did however stop at Tim Hortons for excellent coffees. Every Tim Hortons we have passed seems to be doing a storming trade and H wants to buy shares in the company.

After Calgary we definitely were able to see the Rockies and it was very good to have topography after the flatness of the Prairies.

Our big concern had always been whether we would be able to get through the Rockies before snow set in. As a fall back we had established that we could train the car from Calgary to Vancouver for $450. We had imagined we could travel on the same train, but that wouldn't have been the case.

Normally it doesn't snow until the end of October and even then the Trans Canada is kept clear with apparently no salt.

Today there was no sign of snow as we approached, but it did begin to rain quite hard.

We visited Banff briefly and were stuck in traffic before taking the old road up to Lake Louise and the Chateau at 1,740 metres. We had booked a room

Geoffrey & Hilary Herdman

Chateau Lake Louise

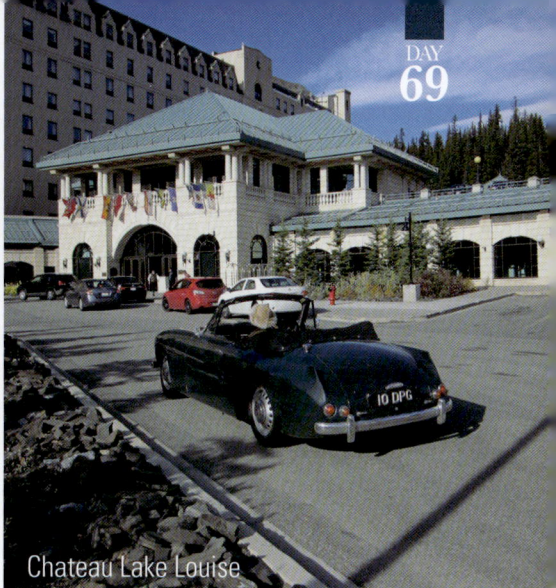

facing the lake. The hotel is vast, 650 rooms, and there seemed to be at least three weddings taking place simultaneously.

Lake Louise is fed by three glaciers, one of which can just be seen in the photo, and is a most beautiful turquoise blue.

Local knowledge in Tim Hortons had advised the walk up to the Tea House on Lake Agnes, and once the rain had stopped we set out rather late, albeit still with very strong winds. As we climbed we heard tales from the rather shaken descenders, of three trees blocking the path, which hadn't been there when they were ascending. We did hear one tree fall but the wind (which had been whipping up white horses on the lake) soon died down, as forecast. We were also told that the Tea House had shut for the season at 17:00 so we would have no refreshments! In the event, as it was getting dark anyway, we climbed as far as Mirror Lake at 2,010 metres, a climb of about 270 metres, and called it a day.

TOTAL MILEAGE: 8,584
Filled up at 8,469 45 litres

DAY: 69
11/10/10 THROUGH THE ROCKIES – PHEW We had been promised cold weather for today but we also had sun so took the top down and wrapped up.

Our first stop was the "Spirals" at Kicking Horse Pass. When Canadian Pacific first built the railroad through the Rockies in 1884, due to financial constraints they had to come over Kicking Horse Pass, which meant a gradient of 4.5%, twice as steep as permitted. Escape routes for out of control trains were created so that in the words of one driver "You could have your accident without holding up oncoming traffic!". The uphill ascent was equally troublesome and required many extra engines for the 7.5 k ascent. In 1909 after 25 years of near and total disasters the "Big Hill" was replaced with two spiral tunnels to reduce the gradient. The Big Hill is now part of the Trans Canada, along which we drove.

NORTH AMERICA

We stopped to watch as a freight train, at least 1.5 miles long, rumbled past us, entered the tunnel and then exited lower down. As the front emerged the rear hadn't even entered the tunnel. A fantastic sight and there are two Spirals.

The notice boards telling us about it all were covered in ice. We had thought we were cold. Now we knew we were and the top quickly went up.

Immediately after the Spirals we made a divert to watch the Takakkaw Falls, one of the highest waterfalls on the Continent. We also stopped to walk down a boardwalk through wetlands that at other times of year are full of birds, attracted by the giant skunk cabbage. The birds had flown, but the cabbage still made its presence felt.

We reached our B&B in Kamloops at about 18:30 but as it was Thanksgiving our landlady had left the place open. She had also left a phone by the front door so I could call her and ask for instructions. Apart from the proximity of the Trans Canada Highway and Rail the location was rather good, on the banks of the Thompson River. Even the traffic was pretty well deadened by good insulation. Cynthia had left us instructions for where to eat and with some difficulty we found Storms.

TOTAL MILEAGE: 8,885
Filled up at 8,654 33.6 litres

DAY: 70
12/10/10 ARRIVAL IN VANCOUVER

Our co-guest at breakfast, Sheri, turned out to be Conde Nast's No. 1 recommended Tour Guide for the North West Pacific, so we picked her brains unmercifully, and then cleaned a well deserving car.

Having been to Paradise in Nova Scotia, here we are at Hell's Gate in BC, so called for the torrent of water in the Fraser River rushing through a narrow gorge. The stricture was made worse in 1911 by CN blasting a railway track and causing a landslide! In 1945 the Fisheries dept. created salmon runs, as the water was often too fierce for them to swim against. There is an aerial cable car from the road down the 600 ft to the river, but it had closed the day before (Thanksgiving Day) so we walked down and back up.

As I keep telling Mrs H it's good for the ticker to work a bit sometimes. She gets rather bored with this comment as she enjoys walking for its own sake!!

There are two routes from Kamloops to Vancouver, old and new. We elected for the old via Cache Creek, as Michelin judges it the prettier. It was also the route the miners from the 1860s took, when some 20,000 fortune seekers walked it the reverse way to us, along the Cariboo Trail.

After Kamloops the scenery becomes very barren for a time, with no trees and very little vegetation or habitation, although unlike the prairies there are steep scarps and valleys. The Fraser Gorge is dramatic, and the road swings and curves in a way that Mrs H finds a pleasure to drive.

Approaching Vancouver we were astonished and quite unused to the amount of traffic pouring out.

Geoffrey & Hilary Herdman

And finally we made it to the Vancouver Club. We had booked a suite, which is magnificent with private sitting room and here we are in the heart of downtown Vancouver paying little more for a suite than we had for B&B in Kamloops.

Needless to say dinner in the Club was excellent.

TOTAL MILEAGE: 9,155
Petrol $40 33.8 litres but not full at 8,888 miles.

DAY: 71
13/10/10   SIGHTSEEING IN VANCOUVER   Breakfast in the glorious atrium of the Vancouver Club, surrounded by plants.

AND then to the BLOG – sadly in arrears.

However in the afternoon in perfect weather we took a trolley bus to Stanley Park. The park was opened in 1888 and covers the tip of downtown Vancouver. It covers an area of just over 1,000 acres, half the size of Richmond Park, and is surrounded by Vancouver harbour. We walk the whole way round, 8.5 ks. This involves underpassing the Lionsgate Bridge, opened in 1938, and financed by the Guinness family at a cost of $6M but not before they had been granted 4,700 acres of the North shore, which it now connects to downtown.

The views of the harbour on a day such as this are spectacular, with sea planes for the islands taking off and a very busy port going about its business.

We took a couple of hours dawdling slowly round and realised we were very hungry, so had crépes from a Chinese crépe stand, which were rather good.

On our return to the Club we had quite a reception committee, which impressed us until we found it was for Sarah Palin, who was promoting her book

NORTH AMERICA

and giving a talk. She charges $75K for the latter and they had 188 guests paying $500 a pop to hear her.

In the evening John Gunn, whom I had known since Montreal days, came and picked us up and took us to an excellent fish restaurant on the N Shore overlooking the sea. This did of course entail passing over the Lionsgate bridge.

DAY: 72
14/10/10 **SKYTRAIN** Our very efficient Polish waiter, (married to a Chinese wife) told us about the Skytrain and how we should sit in the front and see where we were going.

After some important shopping we tried it out and found we could indeed sit at the front and through the rain see the track ahead. The picture below of downtown Vancouver is what we would have seen if we had gone the day before. Skytrain is I suppose like the Docklands light railway, but much longer with 42 miles of track and three lines. The trains have no drivers, and the effect is rather like a very gentle rollercoaster. We crossed the Fraser river before heading back downtown, H to go to the museum of anthropology at UBC and me to return to the blog. The trip to the museum involved an hour's trolley bus ride, which meant only about 20 minutes were available for the museum. Some might argue this was perfectly adequate. (They very kindly did not charge for such a limited visit!) Vast modern campus, with an adjoining 'University' golf club, where we were told the members are very surprised to find that their First Nation landlords are in two minds about renewing the lease which has just expired.

Geoffrey & Hilary Herdman

In the evening we had arranged with John that as we each felt we should buy a dinner he would come to the Club and sample its fare. The Georgian room gave us an excellent meal in elegant surroundings. Our pretty German waitress had been on duty the previous day so had heard the Palin speech. She told us that when time was up Sarah more or less stopped in the middle of question time and retreated to dinner.

DAY: 73
15/10/10 SALT SPRING ISLAND

To get to Salt Spring we had to take a ferry from Tsawwassen, 45 minutes South of Vancouver. There are actually two ferries; one leaving at 10:10 and visiting all the Gulf Islands before arriving in Salt Spring and taking 3 hours. The second one leaves at 11:00 and goes directly to Swartz Bay on mainland Vancouver Island. This only takes 90 minutes, but one then has to take another ferry across to Salt Spring. The Herdmans don't do early if they can help it so elected for the 11:00, which apart from not stopping at each island goes much the same route as the slower ferry with the same views.

On checking out we established that membership of the Vancouver Club is in decline. It had been 2,000 but is now around the 1,800 mark. The thought did occur that membership might be a good idea as it is surrounded by high rises and there must surely come a time when it will no longer be viable so the members will cash in? A pity if that does happen as it is beautifully appointed. Although the building is old, the whole of the interior is very modern and well designed. The staff are exceptionally charming and welcoming.

A very easy drive out to the ferry in glorious weather – how much longer can it last? followed by probably one of the great sea crossings of the world through the Gulf Islands of Mayne, Galiano, and Pender. On arrival at Swartz, instead of just moving over to the next ferry, we have to drive out of the terminal for a couple of miles, do a U-turn and return to the adjacent berth. The crossing to Salt Spring is only about 20 minutes, and again breathtakingly lovely in this perfect weather. We saw grey seals swimming and diving near the boat.

Salt Spring is the largest of the Southern Gulf Islands with an area of some 70 square miles and now a population of 10,500. It has the feel of being very laid back and arty, but also very expensive!

We drive to Ganges, the capital, and check-in to Hastings House, built in 1940 by Warren Hastings – yes a descendant, who had permanently emigrated in 1937 with his new wife Barbara, and thereby hangs another tale! He had Hastings House built as a replica of his 11th C house in Kent. It is quite beautifully done. We had a VERY expensive suite overlooking the Bay, but it was well worth it for the view alone. Additionally we had a working fire in our sitting room. The photo (overleaf) is the view of Ganges Harbour from our sitting room window.

The dining room is apparently renowned for its food but we found the prices more mouthwatering than the meal itself!

In the afternoon we foolishly took poor 10DPG up Mt Maxwell. The first part was tarmac, but the road became steeper and rougher and it was not a kind thing to do. 10DPG of course made it and the views from the top over the islands and mainland were spectacular.

TOTAL MILEAGE: 9,206

DAY: 74
16/10/10   VICTORIA BC   10DPG on the ferry from Vesuvius Bay, Salt Spring Island, to Crofton, Vancouver Island. Remarkably the ferry was free. Having paid to get on to the island there is no charge to get off.

It has to be said that Crofton does not inspire. It has a huge wood pulp plant at the water's edge with chimneys spewing steam or smoke, but we were soon on our way South, rather surprisingly on the Trans Canada highway.

Our friend John had told us that he found Victoria, which is not only capital of Vancouver island, but also the Provincial capital of BC, to be creepy. First impressions of the Union Club rather reinforced this view. From the outside the building has an imposing facade with a splendid stairway. On arriving at reception we were handed a failed delivery ticket from UPS. Despite knowing that we were coming they had rejected a delivery for us but blithely handed over the note. UPS were needless to say closed by now for the weekend.

We had a suite with sea view, which was even better than the Vancouver Club, but the rest of the place creaked. They have about 900 members of whom only 450 are "resident" and 450 "non resident", and appear to rely on their 450 affiliated clubs for guests. We were by far the youngest people there!!

We thought we would go walk about that evening and found ourselves sequentially, near, closely followed by: in, the one theatre, for the Pacific North West ballet from Seattle. This turned out to be excellent. And when it was over, unlike Montreal, we were able to have an excellent dinner in Pescatores.

23 litres added in Ganges (gas is much cheaper in the US!!)
TOTAL MILES: 9,256

Geoffrey & Hilary Herdman

DAY: 75
17/10/10 BUTCHART GARDENS

Mrs H tried to go to the cathedral, but ended up in a local parish church, although the "bish" was in residence and gave a spirited sermon, and the communion wine was served in individual thimbles for fear of contamination!

In the afternoon we visited one of the great joys of Vancouver Island – Butchart Gardens. R P Butchart set up the first cement works on Vancouver Island in 1902. His wife Jennie immediately started gardening on a grand scale. When a lime pit became exhausted she created a sunken garden, see photo, lowering herself on a bosun's chair to plant ivy into the rock face. The gardens now extend to 55 acres, attract one million visitors a year, and at the height of the season employ five hundred staff, and are still family owned. The weather was perfect and it is quite one of the most magnificent gardens I have ever visited.

In the evening our friends Keith and Kathy, on whom we had shamelessly imposed ourselves in Boston, were in town so we returned to Pescatores with them and had a thoroughly agreeable evening. Our waiter Joseph, from N Ireland, told us it was the best restaurant in Victoria, and we have no reason to disbelieve him.

TOTAL MILEAGE: 9,290

NORTH AMERICA

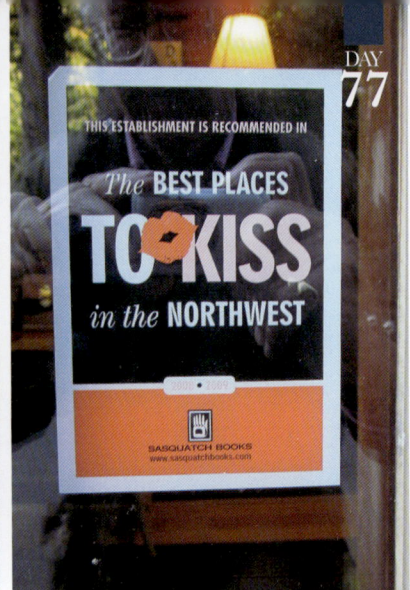

DAY: 76

18/10/10 ONE'S BIRTHDAY! And no it's not Harrods! The provincial legislature or government building of BC, lit by night, and partly obscured by a tree.

In 1891 24 year old Francis Rattenbury, newly arrived from England, entered a competition for the design of the building – and won. Despite running $400,000 over budget it was eventually opened to universal praise in 1898.

The architect thereafter had a chequered career, before being murdered by the lover of his second wife in Bournemouth in 1936. Terence Rattigan immortalised the proceedings in his play Cause Celebre. The murderer got life, commuted to 7 years, and the wife, having been convicted as an accomplice, committed suicide a few days later.

Much more importantly H's b'day. We drove out to UPS and recovered the parcel minutes before it was about to be returned to Amazon. Emma had, with great care, sent two books, but a combination of Amazon, UPS and pig headed surliness at the Union club, had very nearly confounded.

What with the excitements of receiving a month's supply of mail from flat 24 and coping with the laundry – we do lead exciting lives – we left ourselves with only 90 minutes for the BC Museum, which was quite extraordinary. Needless to say the two enduring memories left are a replica of the Endeavour in which George Vancouver surveyed the N W coast in the early 19th C and a quote that Victoria is "Where old folk go to meet their parents!" (Some of us also remember, in an exceptionally well designed museum, the fascinating 'First Nation' floors, including pieces that were nearly 2,000 years old, and some very sad statistics about the ravages of smallpox and other European diseases. And let us not forget the woolly mammoth!)

Our two travel gurus John Gunn and Brian Wadsworth had told us about Sooke Harbour House, both with modified raptures. Keith and Kathy joined us for dinner, with Kathy kindly driving. Despite a rather pretentious wine list, that extends I think to 88 pages, we ate wonderfully. They have the three requisites of real

Geoffrey & Hilary Herdman

estate – location – location – and location, overlooking the Straits of Juan de Fuca, with the mountains of the Olympic Peninsula Washington in the background.

On our return to the club we pottered out for some fresh air and to take the adjoining photo (far left). Eleven o'clock at night and Victoria was dead.

All in all a thoroughly satisfactory day!

DAY: 77
19/10/10 ADIEU CANADA; HELLO AGAIN USA

We say farewell to Canada with mixed feelings. Montreal was a big disappointment, Quebec was a revelation. The weather has overall been astonishingly kind. We have driven from Barrie Ontario to Vancouver with the top down more or less all the way in October. We have had great kindness from friends and feel a pathetic sort of achievement that we have made it from East to West.

In Ontario I was asked on four separate occasions how I managed to drive on UK plates, the only place where it has happened, and meal portions are sensible sizes. To all intents and purposes the Canadian $ is at parity with the US $, although in reality it should be at a premium.

We take the Coho, owned since new in 1959 by Black Ball Lines, across the Juan de Fuca Straits from Victoria to Port Angeles – a voyage of 22 miles and 90 minutes. We clear US immigration in Victoria and find our passports were only stamped to 14th October in Miami so we have to refill green immigration cards.

I had been worried that there might be queries about 10DPG on re-entering the States and had every piece of paperwork I could think of to hand, but with a cheery enjoinder to remember to drive on the right hand side we were waved on and in.

Our goal was the Lake Quinault Lodge in the Quinault Rain Forest, as recommended by Sheri, whom we had met at Kamloops. As seen from the photo it is apparently one of the best places to Kiss in the North West!!!

En route we stopped at Rialto Beach, which looked as if an atom bomb had hit it. The whole beach was piled high with dead and bleached storm tossed tree trunks, a part of the forest coming down to the water's edge which had been blown down. It went on like that for miles.

Lunch was in a strange caff outside Forks, which was in dire need of ventilation or extraction and was festooned with vampires and ghouls. Forks is apparently the setting for an American soap about vampires and popular with a certain age.

And so finally to Lake Quinault Lodge. Built in 1926 on the water's edge. From turning of first sod to having the first guest took ten weeks. It is also the cheapest accommodation we have had thus far at $120 for the night. We decide to stay for two nights and find the second night is half price. The location is superb and the drawing room has a huge fireplace. This is mostly a gas fire but they put especially wet logs onto it which burn very slowly. The hotel is a total gem.

TOTAL MILEAGE: 9,440

Filled up in Port Angeles 16 gallons US 9,291 miles.

DAY: 78
20/10/10   THE QUINAULT RAIN FOREST

Relief rain dumps 100+ inches on the West side of the Olympic Mountain range and perhaps 20" on the East. This high rainfall and constant mist causes the rain forest. There are three separate visitor centres of which Quinault is reputed to be the least crowded. The whole area was designated a protected area by FDR in 1937 after a visit to the very Lodge where we are staying.

In the morning we walk along 4.5 miles of beautifully laid out trails and wonder at Douglas Pines 400 years old, ram rod straight and growing to 300 ft. Also lichen encrusted cedars, waterfalls and rushing streams. Along the trail there are helpful notices explaining what we are seeing.

In the afternoon we decide to circumnavigate the Lake – 31 miles, of which ten are unmetalled and rather pot holey. These are difficult to see because of sun and shade through the trees. We are trying to find Bunches Meadows where a homesteader by the name of Bunch eked out a living at the beginning of the 20th C using a tame Elk to tow his plough.

Despite the high annual rainfall we have glorious sunny weather.

10DPG has a deserving wash down and I even found a vacuum.

TOTAL MILEAGE: 9,470

Geoffrey & Hilary Herdman

DAY: 79
21/10/10   JIM AND JEANNETTE McQUAY
On the road by 09:20 as we have 270 fairly slow miles to do to Seal Rock along the 101. GPS says it will take us six and a quarter hours, but that is without one or two little diversions.

At Astoria we cross the Columbus river, which is the largest river flowing into the Pacific from the USA. It also marks the boundary between Washington and Oregon. The bridge itself must be 3 miles long and is a Forth rail bridge type construction in Washington, which immediately changes structure as we cross the state line in mid bridge.

The coastline of Oregon is dramatic and rugged. There are long breakers rolling in all the way down and almost a sea mist created by the blowing spume.

At Tillamook the 101 cuts inland so we take the scenic drive round the three Capes; Meares, Kiwanda, and Lookout. Unfortunately large sections of the road are in very poor condition.

We arrive at Jim and Jeannette's beach house by about 17:20. It is perched high over the ocean with dramatic views.

The original idea had been to take them out to dinner, but apparently the local tavern is going to be packed as the local college football team is in action. Instead Jeannette cooks us sublime spaghetti and meat balls. The meat balls are partly Moose, shot by Jim.

Jim has an Arnolt with a Chevrolet V8 engine which is under restoration. He bought the car in 1963 and for a long time it was his only means of transport, with no roof whatsoever. It was last on the road in 1982 and they have just started the restoration process. Jeannette has total recall for all the part numbers and history of the car. I don't even know the tyre size on 10DPG but she has it all off pat.

We are their second BOC visitors. Kenneth Andren was by last year with his Arnolt which he had had flown to Seattle. To fly it he had to drain every drop of liquid including the battery acid. Maybe it was not such a bad idea shipping 10DPG.

We are royally looked after and Jeannette's key lime pie was sensational. At

NORTH AMERICA

one stage Jim turned on the shipping forecast, which is dire, with gale force winds, high seas and heavy rain for the weekend.

Filled up at 9,611 15.4 US gallons
TOTAL MILEAGE: 9,750

DAY: 80
22/10/10 STARTING PROBLEMS! Having taken Bizzy, Jim and Jeannette's gorgeous German short hair for a beach walk we thought Jim might like to try 10DPG, but when we try to start there is a dull click from the solenoid. This has happened before but this time no amount of wire waggling makes any difference. Jim produces a voltmeter and we find that despite the click nothing is coming out of the solenoid. And then it does start. Jim takes Jeannette for a drive and as they live up a steep slope leaves 10DPG pointing downwards!

We have a full tank and so decide to press on and try and leave the car pointing downhill each time we stop. In the event I don't think we needed to switch off all day. We are only driving 140 miles.

The coast is rugged and dramatic with the sea sweeping in, in a white spuming froth, all the way down. At one point we drive down to the beach and find a group of Inmates clearing up the parking area.

Geoffrey & Hilary Herdman

Around 16:15 we enter Port Orford, pop 1,090 and declining. As we enter I notice a Kar Kare Auto Parts store. Having checked in to our rather bijou chalet, complete with smoking courtier stove, I drive back to the store. The prop looks rather like a university professor and is quite unfazed by a Bristol needing a starter solenoid. He produces his catalogue, which has a 405 listed!!! determines the generic type, and sells me a new one for $12.50. The invoice comes with the heading; "This is the day the Lord has made "REJOICE"", and I think it may have been right.

I ask where I can get the solenoid installed and despite it being 16:45 the answer is right over the road. 10DPG refuses to start so "over the road" is able to determine that it is indeed the solenoid, which has caused intermittent problems for years, and 20 minutes and $35 later I have the new solenoid installed. The starter works better than ever, so even though the old solenoid worked mostly, it must have been in pretty poor shape internally.

We find that Port Orford has a brand new restaurant, with dramatic sea view, called the Red Fish. As it still hasn't rained we walk down and have one of the three great meals of the trip, and are given a lift back by two fellow guests.

TOTAL MILEAGE: 9,890

DAY: 81
23/10/10   THE FIRST 10,000 MILES

We drive down to Port Orford and view Battle Rock where in 1851 nine white, would-be settlers were besieged by the local people. Having escaped, they returned with stronger forces and the local people were rounded up and shipped to reservations further up the coast, having for generations lived in the area.

The 101 continues along all 362 miles of the rugged and windswept coast of Oregon, apart from a brief cut inland through some splendid sand dunes.

It's funny; both of us somehow expected that once we crossed the State border into California, we would suddenly be amongst flesh pots and millionaires' palaces. Instead we have redwood forests and then more rugged coast. San Francisco is about 380 miles south of the border and for at least 330 miles we see very few signs of civilization.

Forty miles into California we clock up our first 10,000 miles. If anything the odometer underreads by about 0.5%, so it is by no means an optimistic total.

On the advice of the National Parks Information we divert to Requa. We stop at the Requa Inn, and ask if it is possible to have a coffee. Despite them being a B&B, and not doing lunch we are welcomed in, so long as we promise to come back and stay sometime. They also give us excellent shortbread cookies in the shape of acorns. Our charming waitress explains that in the old days "her" people used acorns for flour. The secret was to leech the ground acorns thoroughly with cold water to get rid of the bitterness.

Requa is on the Klamath river, which is a tribal reserve for the Yurok people. The Inn has been here since 1914 and Hilary surmises that the Inn, in the same family since it was started, is owned and run by Yurok people. We drove to the

NORTH AMERICA

mouth of the estuary in the hope of seeing grey whales – no luck – but the views were spectacular of the ocean and the mist shrouded river valley.

Later we walked through the Redwoods and saw herds of Elk.

That night we stay in Eureka at the rather expensive Carter Inn. One night with dinner costs the same as two nights at Lake Quinault. Just across the way is the magnificent Carson House (1885) – pictured.

In Oregon you are not allowed to self serve petrol. There is also no sales tax, but gas costs $3.20 per gallon, a whole lot more than the E coast.

TOTAL MILEAGE: 10,069. 14.5 US gallons at 9,931

DAY 82

Geoffrey & Hilary Herdman

DAY: 82
24/10/10 AVENUE OF THE GIANTS

It has been raining hard all night and removing the car cover is wet making!

The main road down the West Coast of America, the 101, runs 1,200 miles from Port Angeles, where we crossed from Canada, to Los Angeles. At Leggett 200 miles into California the old road, the 1, branches off the 101 and swings back to the coast. It is the road recommended by the Michelin Guide.

Before we have even reached Leggett we divert onto the Avenue of the Giants, a 20 mile tunnel of Redwoods. The trees surpass the hype; immense and grand. We find when walking beneath them that, unlike most groves of conifers, there is light and life. Their branches are surprisingly slight in proportion to the vast trunks.

We pass isolated habitations of ramshackle buildings. These are creepy by day and you certainly don't want to break down here on a wet and foggy night.

We come to the small village of Myers Flat, complete with Post Office and "drive through tree"; $7 thank you. But we have to do it. It is a squeeze! (see photo opposite)

Shortly afterwards we turn onto the 1. H is driving and there is a warning that the next 22 miles are VERY twisty. If they were honest they would have said the next 122 miles! Not only that but they are hilly too, and driving is made no easier by; a) continuous rain and b) coming round a particularly tight bend and finding a tree across the road. It has either broken in falling or someone has rough hacked it. Fortunately we manage to squeeze through.

We stay in Little River at the Little River Inn. As we arrive the rain eases off and I am able to chammy the car before putting the cover over.

TOTAL MILEAGE: 10,218

DAY: 83
25/10/10 THE RAC IN CALIFORNIA

Breakfast for some reason is served in one's bedroom. When the boy arrives I ask him if it has rained in the night, to which he replies; "I don't know. I'm new here"!

We have sunshine, and once again are able to have the hood down.

Our first stop is at Fort Ross, the site of the RAC in California. The RAC in this case was the Russian American Company. In 1812 a group of Russians landed and set up a stout wooden fort with forty one cannon. California belonged successively to Spain, until Mexico won its independence in 1821, when it became part of Mexico, and then to the USA in 1850. In 1812 it was still Spanish and both the local militia, and the local Indians, many of whom would work for the Russians, realised they were not strong enough to take on such a formidable fort. (The photo is of the chapel in the fort.)

NORTH AMERICA

The purpose of the colony was twofold:

To collect sea otters' skins, which commanded a huge price in China, and to provide food for the Russian settlements in Alaska. The former enterprise was more successful than the latter as the land is bleak and overrun with gophers. By 1841 however the sea otters had been wiped out and the Russians gave up and sold the site lock stock and barrel to John Sutter, a very successful Swiss emigré, and by now huge Californian landowner.

We were alarmingly low on gas. TomTom said there was a gas station 5 miles up the road, but TomTom misspoke himself. Eventually all was well and in Gualala we were able to fill up, doing it ourselves being out of Oregon, but at an eye watering $3.50 a gallon!

We had another lovely coastal drive, along a winding and precipitous highway, prompting a change in drivers, owing to Mrs H's tendency to admire the scenery. A large colony of grey seals was basking on the rocks at the Russian River estuary.

And so, driving over the Golden Gate Bridge, we came to San Francisco and the Olympic Club, by reciprocity with the "proper" RAC. Neither of us had visited the City before, and the sunlit evening view from the North side of the bridge was wonderful.

TOTAL MILEAGE: 10,420
Filled up at 10,270 17 US gallons

DAY: 84
26/10/10   SIGHTSEEING IN SAN FRANCISCO We have been given a very comfortable room in the Olympic Club, which is just off Union Square.

Apart from the entrance hall, grandiose marble, and the bedrooms, the Club appears to cater solely for the body corporeal. Breakfast facilities make a UK railway café look good – plastic plates and cutlery – and the dining facilities are only open twice a week despite 14,000 members. The whole of the rest is taken up with gyms, squash courts etc. and each morning we are woken by the muted thump, thump of people running on treadmills over our heads.

Today we gave 10DPG a rest, and were total tourists, taking a coach trip round the City from Fisherman's Wharf, which we thoroughly enjoyed. The weather was glorious, so the views from the Twin Peaks and the Bridge were spectacular. Had a late and piggy lunch at Scoma's on the Wharf.

We returned on the cable car; much queuing but well worth the thrill of hanging on the side of the car for a series of switchbacks. One was so steep that the driver was forced to reverse to a level cross street, after an unexpected halt, and then attack again con brio.

We discovered that Placido Domingo was singing Cyrano in a farewell tour at the Opera tomorrow. No luck on the internet, but after a rather scary walk to the box office, we were rewarded with two return tickets.

Geoffrey & Hilary Herdman

DAY: 85
27/10/10 CAROL AND RAY

We had met Carol and Ray quite by chance over coffee in a café on a rain soaked morning in New Hampshire. They had just sold their house, and were planning to go to Monterey, renting a house while they looked for somewhere to buy. Carol had very kindly emailed us to get in touch when we made it to California: we did!

As it turned out, they had rented a house in Oakland, her childhood home, just over the bridge. They asked two total strangers to lunch with them there, only three weeks after they had moved in, and before they had finished unpacking. We had a delicious lunch and very enjoyable visit. We really have met with the most extraordinary kindness and hospitality on this trip, and just hope we may have the chance to reciprocate.

Their Volvo still has its New Hampshire registration plate, with the State motto 'Live free or die,' which has been promised to their garageman as a trophy for his walls.

We went to the opera in the evening; unsurprisingly it was packed. Domingo made his debut there in La Boheme in the 60s, and has maintained a link with the company over the subsequent decades. The opera, which Domingo has recently championed, comes in the 'rarely performed' category, but was well staged, and the last scene in particular, very moving.

This very grand opera house put up a surtitle in the interval to give the score in the San Francisco Giants v. Texas Rangers opening game in the World Cup Baseball series (11 - 7), greeted by cheers and whistles.

We had an excellent dinner at La Jardiniere, where the atmosphere was celebratory, and the decor rather like Le Caprice.

NORTH AMERICA

DAY: 86
28/10/10   THE 3RD SERVICE

Shawn Thomas, who I think has seven Bristols plus an untold quantity of memorabilia, and is the Arnolt Registrar, had recommended a garage called Phil Reilly, who would do a full service on the car.

Back over the Golden Gate bridge and we were greeted by Shawn himself at Phil Reilly's, then handed over to Ivan Zeremba. As he showed us the four Bugattis in various stages of undress – not to mention the workshop dedicated to over sixty Cosworth DFV rebuilds a year, Ivan made it very clear that he wasn't interested in Bristols per se, but liked the story of our trip, and so was prepared to help.

Shawn took us off in a 1951 Packard shooting brake with a 700hp 8 litre motor, to show us the car collection he was currently looking after. One Ferrari he pointed out had just come in at a cost of $400K and after two weeks work setting up the fuel injection properly had already been sold for a price that made one wistful to be in the Classic car business.

He then took us to a micro brewery for lunch with the enticing aroma of mashing malt wafting through the restaurant.

As we had time to kill we walked round the wildlife sanctuary at the back of Phil Reilly's before collecting the car. Ivan took me out for a test run. He told me that when he lubricated the advance retard mechanism he had also altered the timing. Round the block it seemed o.k., but as we drove back to the Club it clearly wasn't.

I rang Shawn in despair who told me to take it to him in the morning.

By the time we set out for dinner it was past 21:00 and we ended up in Gitane, where we had excellent tagine (anagram of Gitane!)

Geoffrey & Hilary Herdman

DAY: 87
29/10/10   MORE VISITING A quick call to Charlie established:

a) that my 110 engine was finally ready with wonderful torque and power curves – so now I have an emergency fall back – and

b) that the timing on the 100B should be 38º at 3,500 rpm.

Shawn quickly established that it had been set for 44º and as soon as he reset it to 38º the problem was resolved.

The previous day Ivan had not been able to give me an invoice and didn't take credit cards, so I dropped in to pay him $828, which for the amount of work done I thought reasonable.

Whilst I was doing this H took a trolley bus to the Botanical Gardens, and the De Young Museum, which was showing Part 2 of an exceptional loan exhibition from the Musée d'Orsay, whose 19th and early 20th C galleries are temporarily closed for refurbishment. A lovely exhibition, in a beautiful museum building, full of space and light.

The programme has a letter from President Sarkosy, saying the loans are being made available 'to several countries that have longstanding associations with France, especially at cultural level'; not sure if any are going to the UK!

In the afternoon we visited Nadine, who works for i-escape, and has been living in San Francisco for the last 4 years. She has a lovely apartment in Mission, with humming birds in the trees outside her windows, and beautiful views of the city. We picked her brains shamelessly, and she gave us enthusiastic and knowledgable advice. Later, her dear little 3 year old daughter Esmé came home from school with Colman, very excited about Hallowe'en and her new party outfit.

Good dinner at Cafe de la Presse that evening.

TOTAL MILEAGE: 10,504

DAY: 88
30/10/10   MONTEREY The plan was to go to Yosemite National Park; however, accommodation was hard to find, and the only place that could help said it was snowing, and we might need chains which we felt would not suit 10DPG. So we decided to go on to Monterey, and perhaps back track from there, as the snow was not expected to last long at this time of year.

We had been told at Lake Quinault that the same company had a hotel in Monterey, and eventually tracked down the Asilomar in Pacific Grove. It is a collection of old shingled buildings in wooded dunes by the shore, with a slight feeling of old fashioned institution about it; we wondered if they served alcohol! It turns out to be the property of the State Parks, having been bought from the YWCA, who founded it as a leadership centre in 1916. The older buildings are now national monuments, and the complex has been sympathetically extended over the years.

Having been reassured on the alcohol point, we like it very much. There is a board walk through the dunes to the white powder sand beach, and some spectacular displays of surf-boarding; exhilarating just to watch them, and it must be fantastic to be able to do it.

Poor G is getting some nasty 'lurgy, so we decided to stay here pro tem.
TOTAL MILEAGE: 10,624
Filled up in SF at 10,504 12.5 gallons US

DAY: 89
31/10/10 CHILLING OUT IN MONTEREY

Poor Geoffrey still feeling rotten, so he stayed on the balcony with aspirin and John Le Carré, leaving Mrs H and 10DPG to venture into downtown Monterey, first to the tiny wooden Episcopal church of St Mary by the Sea, and then to the Aquarium. Car and driver both on best behaviour and got back safely. Had dinner in the redwood and rubblestone dining room of Asilomar, part of the Arts and Crafts buildings designed by the architect and engineer Julia Morgan, of whom we had not previously heard, and more later; this was to prove serendipitous.

DAY: 90
01/11/10 MORE CHILLING

Patient still not much better, but sure that time, aspirin and John Le Carré would do the trick. Mrs H and 10DPG made another exciting foray to the Aquarium (two day ticket) where there is a remarkable exhibition of sea horses and sea dragons; these beautiful and fascinating creatures have very sensible child rearing arrangements, as the male houses the female's eggs in his kangaroo like pouch, from where they are hatched. Saw wild sea otter in the bay.

The photo is of San Francisco City Hall – eat your heart out Boris! There happened to be an Asian arts festival on at the time hence sculpture.

DAY: 91
02/11/10 MONTEREY

Geoffrey still not well, so we had a quiet morning. Went for a walk in the afternoon, on mid term election day, and looked into the local village hall, expecting to see high tech voting arrangements, perhaps even a pregnant chad machine, but was told that while there is some electronic voting the majority remain paper ballots, and the whole set up was reminiscent of voting with blunt pencils in the village school at home.

Geoffrey & Hilary Herdman

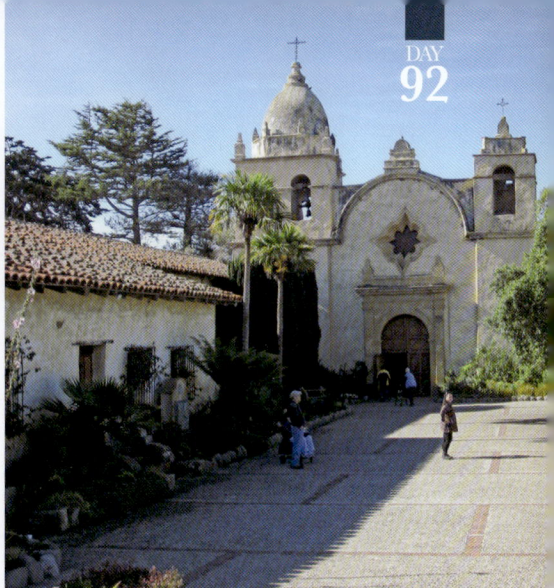

Although the weather remains glorious, there must have been storms at sea, as the surf was tremendous, and the beach in theory closed, although it was very easy to step over the rope as many others had done.

Walked to the Fishwife for excellent dinner.

The photo is of a section of cable used for SF Golden Gate Bridge. The cables are just over 3 ft in diameter and each contains 27,572 wires for a total wire length of over 80,000 miles.

The bridge opened under budget at $37M in 1937 and is the most popular place in the world for committing suicide. 1,200 by 2005 and growing at one a fortnight. There is a telephone hotline to Samaritans!

DAY: 92
03/11/10 STILL CHILLING

G woke up feeling worse than ever, and Le Carré finished, so drove to Doctors on Demand, who quickly diagnosed wryneck, and supplied anti-inflammatory drugs and a course of exercises, which had remarkable effect; huge relief in every sense, so we had an excellent celebratory lunch in hot sunshine on the deck in Cannery Row, followed by a massage! and then drove round 17 Mile Drive at Pebble Beach. We walked along the dramatic coastline from Spanish Bay, with the surf still crashing down. Saw some golfers struggling, (and in some cases succeeding) to tee off from a tiny square of grass perched on top of a rock, about 100 yards across the open sea to a fairway on the other side.

Dinner at Fishwife again.

We are a day ahead of ourselves but the photo (pictured top right) is of the Mission at Carmel.

TOTAL MILEAGE: 10,690

NORTH AMERICA

> DAY: 93
> 04/11/10

HEARST CASTLE Is it an abbey? Is it a cathedral? No, this is Hearst Castle built between 1920 and 1947 by William Randolph Hearst. He did not inherit the site until his mother died in 1919, by when he was 56. It came with 250,000 acres and spectacular views over the coast at San Simeon.

It is reckoned to have cost over $10M and is built entirely of reinforced concrete. The architect was the same Julia Morgan who designed Asilomar. She was a busy lady, with over 700 projects in her lifetime. Despite the vastness of this one she managed it at weekends. As well as being the first female qualified architect in California she also had a degree in civil engineering. When the earthquake of 1989 struck, the bells in the towers rang for the first time in 40 years but the building was found to be absolutely sound.

The floor area covers over 70,000 sq ft. Water is entirely gravity fed, despite the Castle being 500 metres above sea level. Each of the towers has a 2,500 gallon reservoir underneath the bells and just above two beautiful bedrooms.

Life was not made easy by "WR" constantly changing his mind, so reinforced concrete had to be pulled apart and re-erected. Julia Morgan said of her client; "He had the disease of Changeability!"

We took the introductory tour and were so bowled over we resolved to return next day for a tour of the bedrooms.

En route we stopped at a magnificent restaurant hanging on the edge of a cliff called Nepenthe at Big Sur. In the car park were an Elva Courier and XK120. Sadly we only wanted coffee. What a location for lunch.

And finally to Cambria, 6 miles to the South where we stayed at Moonstone Landing, with panoramic views of the sea.

TOTAL MILEAGE:10,795

The outdoor pool, having been enlarged twice. Originally it was heated, but no more.

Geoffrey & Hilary Herdman

DAY: 94
05/11/10   HEARST AGAIN & VENICE BEACH Thick fog when we woke, so no view from our expensive sea view room. Surprise surprise we just about made it in time for the 10:20 tour at Hearst 6 miles away. You park as soon as you enter the property and then take a 20 minute bus ride climbing up 500 metres. As soon as we started the climb we were in brilliant sunshine but can see the fog bank on the coast.

Today we are taking Tour 2, which all the guides describe as their favourite, and visit some of the bedrooms and the two libraries. On WR's death he bequeathed Hearst Castle to his children. They, realizing they could never afford it, gave it to the State of California without an endowment. California accepted in 1957 on the basis that if they couldn't make it pay within 2 years they would hand it back. They are still there 53 years later!

We had planned to stay four nights at the Los Angeles Athletics Club, but they couldn't accommodate us for the Saturday night. Rather than playing musical hotels we chose the Venice Beach House, as recommended by Bernard Dawson.

The plan was to stick to the coast on the 1 as much as possible, but we were back on the 101 for a large chunk, including very heavy traffic round Santa Barbara. It was consequently dark some time before we reached Venice.

The hotel is enchanting, ivy clad and built in 1911, just after the creation of Venice and with its own private garden.

TOTAL MILEAGE: 11,045
Fill up at Cambria 10,808 miles 17 gallons US
Gas v expensive $3.70 per gallon as opposed to $2.90 on the E coast.

DAY: 95
06/11/10   THE GETTY CENTER It has to be said that Mrs H and I are not in agreement over the Getty Center. To me it is a classic case of having too much money and not enough to do with it. The result is of a massive sprawl of rather ugly buildings, costing $1.3billion. The galleries themselves, which are spread rather unnecessarily over four of the buildings have all the atmosphere of railway stations, and are incredibly badly laid out with no directions.

The gardens, not large, require forty seven gardeners. Let's get real here, it's an art gallery. Anyway that's what happens when you set up a posthumous Foundation run by committee.

Despite entry being free we have to pay $15 to park the car and then take an air suspended train half a mile to the centre.

Probably the only good thing is the access, which is by route 405!

PS. There is another school of thought, which is that this is a beautiful space, with wonderful light.

So far as the gardeners are concerned (I think there are forty six for the central gardens) their lives must be rather like the ones in Alice, painting the roses. In this case, they must:

NORTH AMERICA

1. remove by hand each alternate leaf from the avenue of plane trees, in order to maintain the dappled light demanded by the artist. (They are less busy in the winter months, but the light is less dappled!)

2. prune by hand (to avoid electrocution) the rather wonderful azalea maze in the lake at the foot of the gardens, and

3. comply with local regulations which prohibit killing or artificially feeding the local fauna, by staying up all night with a flashlight to deter nocturnal marauders.

All the above may of course just prove G's point.

However, apart from the parking fee, everything is free, and the place was packed, including a group of schoolchildren busily sketching. It was lovely to see so much activity in a museum.

DAY: 96
07/11/10 CALIFORNIA BOC Bob Schmitt (on the left) and Greg Woog by Greg's 411S2.

Bob has invited us to a French/Italian car get together in Woodley Park. We also meet Bill Watkins and his wife Beth. Bill has had four Arnolts and has raced them all over the years. He used to build Big Dippers, so clearly has nerves of steel! He tells us he built his first at the age of 8, which resulted in his first broken arm!!

There is a collection of Citroëns including two SMs. Must be most of the Citroëns in the USA gathered together in one place!!

Afterwards we go back to Bob and Shannon's house to try some of Bob's excellent home brew. Shannon also makes beer – now that's rivalry for you. And then out for an early dinner. As clocks went back this morning it is dark by 17:30 and we have an interesting drive back in the dark.

Los Angeles seems to be a complete maze of highways. Nobody indicates right or left and clearly nobody takes any notice if I do. They probably have no idea what the flashing light is for. On a five lane highway, where exiting can be either from the fast or slow lane this makes for somewhat fraught driving!!

Bob has a Frazer Nash, which he bought in Hawaii in pieces many years ago but has recently had restored in Invercargill NZ. The car now lives there and every year he flies down to drive it for a month or so.

Geoffrey & Hilary Herdman

DAY: 97
08/11/10 NORTON SIMON MUSEUM What an absolute gem, and what a contrast with the Getty. Norton Simon was a hugely successful industrialist, who "discovered" art at the age of 40 in 1947 and thereafter collected over 11,000 pieces. Finding that it wasn't possible to buy "old masters" individually he bought one of the most famous dealers, lock, stock, barrel, including the building.

For many years he had nowhere to exhibit his collection, but in 1977 bought the bankrupt Pasadena Art gallery and renamed it the Norton Simon Museum. Although physically crippled from 1984 onwards he still maintained control over it until his death in 1994.

The result is, as we both agreed, one of the great art galleries, set in beautiful sculpture filled gardens. We spent far longer than we intended there, with the result that by the time we made it to the Huntington library it was closed for the day and not open until Wednesday. The Norton Simon had a loan of the Washington Gallery's Raphael of the Cowper Madonna and Child, painted only two years after their own Raphael, which made an extraordinary contrast. Similarly, the Getty had a lovely Rembrandt portrait, on loan from a private collection, of the girl who was a frequent model for him, including Europa in the Getty's painting hanging nearby.

In the evening we walked along the beach – not terribly salubrious! to the Enterprise Fish Co in Santa Monica for an excellent dinner.

TOTAL MILEAGE: 11,181
Filled up at 11,121 15 gallons US

DAY: 98
09/11/10 BLOGGING IN VENICE Our ivy clad hotel 100 yards from the beach with its own private garden.

Today was given to Mrs H doing "real work" and me bringing the Blog up to date – all very exhausting, so in the afternoon we walked round the Marina del Rey – or a small part of it as it is the largest marina in the world.

Part of the walk took us alongside one of the canals dug at the beginning of the 20th C to drain the marshes and give Venice its name.

A day of rest for 10DPG.

NORTH AMERICA

DAY: 99
10/11/10 COMPLETING THE HORSESHOE Having set out from the bottom right hand corner of the USA, Miami and Key West, on 17th July, today we reached the bottom left hand corner at San Diego, 11,334 miles later. As the route took us trans Canada we have in effect completed the horseshoe.

But first to the Huntington Library, Gallery and Gardens; home of Gainsborough's The Blue Boy. Slight danger of overdosing on culture here! but absolutely worth the visit. The Library has a wonderful exhibition, from the millions of works it holds, including an illustrated edition of Canterbury Tales, produced just after Chaucer's death, a first folio Shakespeare, and Audubon's birds. It is a continuing collection, and as well as letters by Coleridge, they had letters and work by Kingsley Amis, Auden and most recently, Hilary Mantel's manuscript of Wolf Hall.

The beautifully landscaped gardens are on an astonishing scale; I would love to go back one day.

It meant leaving Pasadena at about 15:00 and then freeway, mostly the 5, all the way to San Diego, 130 miles to the South. TomTom often refers to HOV lanes and today we found out what they are; car pool lanes in which you can only drive if you have two or more people in the car. For at least 30 miles coming out of LA we more or less had the HOV lane to ourselves while a five lane highway sat gridlocked.

The traffic was dreadful. San Diego is the second largest city in California and sixth largest in the States and the 130 miles took us 3 hours, the last 45 minutes of which were in the dark surrounded on all sides by drivers not giving an inch. But we're here and going for a beer!

The arrival was slightly fraught as we were booked into the Hillcrest B&B, TomTom took us instead to the Hillcrest doss house and we were heartily relieved to find this was not to be our accommodation. The correct one was enchanting.

TOTAL MILEAGE: 11,334

DAY: 100
11/11/10 BALBOA PARK SAN DIEGO Wonderful start to the day. Midnight Haze, in which one has a modest investment, led from start to finish in the 2 o'clock at Ludlow. H took this as an omen that all would be well with Mexico!

Our lovely landlady, Ann recommended that we visit the Prado for lunch in Balboa Park. The park itself is much the same size as Stanley Park in Vancouver, i.e. rather larger than either Central Park, or Hyde Park and Kensington Gardens combined.

In the 1920s the city fathers commissioned the city architect to travel to Europe for inspiration to design a central feature. He chose Ronda in Spain and created the Casa Moro and Prado. The latter is a great open air restaurant

Geoffrey & Hilary Herdman

overlooking the gardens. We had a celebratory tincture and drank to Midnight Haze and Kim Bailey, his trainer.

A girl needs to shop, but requests for Ferragamo met with blank stares and we were directed to Fashion Valley instead. TomTom knew about Ferragamo but the nearest was 26 miles North. Anyway Fashion Valley proved satisfactory and we then set out for Coronado Island driving over the bridge just as the sun was setting – v picturesque.

And back home for dinner once again at Arrivederci.

Meals in N America always seem to cost the same i.e. $120. Sometimes this includes tip and sometimes not but wherever we have eaten we end up with the same sort of bill. For tipping one is expected to add 18%. There is a curious system where you give them your credit card, they bring back the slip for signature and addition of tip. The credit card is not required again to validate the tip. They could add anything really!

TOTAL MILEAGE: 11,360

ROUND THE WORLD WITH 10DPG

N

UNITED STATES OF AMERICA

MEXICO

BELIZE
HONDURAS
NICARAGUA
COSTA RICA
Panama City

GUATEMALA
EL SALVADOR
PANAMA

León

Mexico City
Guadalajara
Mazatlan

La Plaz

San Diego
Tijuana

map is not drawn to scale, for illustrative purposes only

CHAPTER 2
Central America

DAY: 101
12/11/10   DRIVING IN MEXICO
The border is only 16 miles south of our B&B, but we had over 4 hours to drive, once across, with no idea of how long it might take to clear the frontier. Thus it was that we were on the road by just after 09:00. In the event this proved fortuitous.

The approach to the border is a six lane highway, which was absolutely solid. It must have taken 30 minutes just to get to the barrier.

Everyone had told us NOT to go into Tijuana, the Mexican border town. We had thought we didn't need to, as the road now goes straight through it. BUT we had to buy insurance and a permit for the car, and so were directed to a grubby back street in downtown Tijuana wherein lay the Banjercito, issuer of required documents.

Crossing the border is a huge culture shock as one is really going into a different world. For $2 a taxi navigated us to the Banjercito and an hour and a half later we had settled the Mexican debt and bought all necessary papers.

Immediately on leaving the frontier you drive absolutely along the border for several miles with huge fences to the right and views of San Diego in the distance.

The road then follows the coast to Ensenada. Where there are no building sites the scenery is spectacular. But it took about half an hour to grind our way through Ensenada, which as seen from the Ruta 1 is the most awful dump, and then things got worse! We hit 8 miles of roadworks and for the most part were driving over incredibly bumpy dirt and sand.

We finally arrived in San Quintin as dusk was falling. Very, very relieved not to be driving at night. En route we had been through two military road blocks. The trouble is you can never be entirely sure if they are genuine military or not. Whilst I was sorting paperwork in Tiuana, H struck up conversation with a delightful Mexican who told her that the drug barons were not interested in our car as it wasn't 4 wheel drive. Lets hope he's right!!

We passed several cyclists with all sorts of trailers and saddle bags, who presumably were doing the Baja Peninsula – over 1,000 miles long. One was sporting both a French and a Canadian flag. If he had cycled from Canada he was doing very well!

Filled up in San Diego 14.3 gallons 11,361 miles
TOTAL MILEAGE: 11,565

Geoffrey & Hilary Herdman

DAY: 102
13/11/10   TO GUERRERO NEGRO   Guerrero Negro is approximately half way down the Baja Peninsula and 260 miles South of San Quintin. TomTom says it will take us 6 hours 45 mins. In the event we knock an hour off that.

We leave at 09:45 – indecently early some might think!

Once clear of San Quintin the road is wonderful. For the first half the surface is absolutely new. It twists and turns and climbs and falls through bleak but spectacular mountain scenery. We are surrounded by cacti.

We overtake one truck an hour and are overtaken by perhaps twenty cars all day.

In the other direction there is a steady stream of vehicles heading for the start of the Baja 1,000 next week. This is a race with three hundred entrants, both dune buggies and bikes, on dirt roads from Enseñada to La Paz. It is not actually 1,000 anything – but the name has stuck. The distance is approximately 1,100 miles driven non stop, apart from fuel and crew changes for the buggies. Some of the bikes have the same rider for the whole distance. The winners will complete it in about 18 hours. Bikes used to be quicker but nowadays 4 wheel buggies with 36" spring travel are just as competitive. Apparently spectators create artificial and unexpected jumps to see the vehicles fly!

This morning as we were having breakfast we saw five truck loads of army heading North. The trucks are all open and at the front the lead soldier is equipped with a formidable looking sub machine gun.

We are stopped at two army check points. Both want to know where we come from and make polite conversation about the car. We also have to go through sanitation; 20 Pesos and an undercar spray!

Our hotel, the aptly named Desert, is situated on the 28th parallel, which is where the clocks change. Theoretically the front of the hotel should be an hour behind the back! but in fact the whole hotel has moved forward one hour. At least it will be dark at 18:00 rather than 17:00 from now on.

Fill up in San Quintin 11,565 miles 38 litres
and again in Guerrero Negro 11,832 miles 45 litres.
TOTAL MILEAGE: 11,835

DAY: 103
14/11/10   CROSSING BAJA   The Baja California Peninsula is the same size as England with a population of just over three million. Today we cross from West to East, from Guerrero Negro to Loreto, which used to be the capital of all the Californias from 1697 to 1777.

But first things first. One woke up not in the best of health as sadly one got into bad company yesterday evening. After dinner we tried a variety of tinctures; T&T (Tencate, the local beer, with a Tequila chaser), a Margarita (Tequila, Cointreau and lemonade), and finally straight Tequila. Mrs H ought to have looked after me better!! Instead she had to pay the bill.

We set off in perfect weather 10 minutes earlier than yesterday, but as clocks

CENTRAL AMERICA

have gone forward we have an extra hour of daylight. The distance is the same as yesterday; 260 miles.

The weather is absolutely glorious without a cloud in the sky. It is a little on the cool side at first but we have the top down until about midday when the sun is too hot.

The road is sensational in all senses. The surface is superb, and many parts must have been relaid within the last six months. En route, about eight gullies are being traversed by new bridges under construction, but the deviations are on perfect tarmac.

For the first 70 miles the scenery is totally flat and arid and there are just four bends in all. Otherwise the road is dead straight. Around midday we pull off onto the dirt and have a coffee. Soon we are climbing in the hills with the bizarrely named Volcano of the Three Virgins on our left. At the summit we see the sea in the distance, an absolutely amazing blue with picturesque islands, and then we are down at the coast at Rosalia, which is about half way to Loreto. From there on South sometimes we are by the sea and sometimes back in the hills. It is all incredibly beautiful. Today has been one of the great drives. A little more traffic than yesterday, but nothing to hold us up. The speed limit is 80 ks most of the way, and we potter along at a little over that but not much.

Two army check points and one set of police but they all wave us by.

G probably does not remember very clearly (see above,) but last night in the bar we were talking to one of the drivers in the 1,000 mile race. He has been doing it for the last 8 years, and explained that he was doing the second section (through the area we have driven through today,) assuming that his boss, the owner, makes it through the first section. He had been testing, in a replica car but with a smaller engine, the section he will drive. I thought of him during the extraordinary landscape of giant cacti we have been driving through; sometimes like cypress trees providing an exclamation mark to the scenery; sometimes whole forests of them. He said that the whole point of the race for him is driving at 100 mph at night along the dirt roads, weaving through the cacti, and seeing their fantastic shadows cast by his lights.

We are staying at the Posada de Las Flores, which is an old colonial Spanish building – absolutely charming and now with the addition of a pool on the roof.

TOTAL MILEAGE: 12,099

Geoffrey & Hilary Herdman

DAY: 104
15/11/10   BOATING IN THE SEA OF CORTEZ

AM: The colours really are like this. Captain Grigo took us for a morning's idyllic boating – and yes that's his boat – to Coronado Island, which is a) volcanic and b) a marine reserve. Despite 'a)' it has the most dazzling white sand.

The view is of the mainland from the island, about 5 miles away.

First we made a circumnavigation and saw Boobies with blue feet – only seen here and in the Galapagos – pelicans, sea eagles and a large colony of sea lions all barking away and swimming for our benefit.

Once we landed Captain Grigo attracted about five pelicans with some fresh fish and pretended to throw it to them. Each time he raised his arm they would raise their wings expectantly in unison, with a mad scramble when the fish was finally thrown. Then some gentle snorkelling over masses of yellow, black and orange fish, until abrupt retreat when stung slightly by minute biting things. The effect fortunately wore off after about half an hour.

Around midday we set out for home sated with sun, sea and brilliant white sand.

PM: G stayed home to wrestle with his Paxos book. As the Mision de San Francisco Xavier was said to be up 40 k of dirt road, 10DPG had a well deserved rest, and I set off at vast expense in a taxi. The first 12 k were along a beautiful well engineered sealed road, so I began to feel very extravagant. However the succeeding 25 k more than justified the taxi fare; taxis must have a short life span in these parts, and the Bristol would not have liked it.

Today is a Bank Holiday celebrating the Revolution, when Mexico gained independence from Spain. So it seemed somehow appropriate to travel from the old Spanish capital to the second oldest Spanish Mission, established at the end of the 17th Century. The mountainous countryside was very arid as they have had no rain at all this year. However the Mission is in an oasis, high up in the mountains, with palms, huge mango and orange trees and an ancient olive tree said to have been planted when the Mission was founded. The Church is a beautiful stone building, very well preserved. The little town has a wide cobbled street, full of children playing football. Children come to the school from the mountains and live there five days a week.

The race practice was in full swing on our journey back; this will presumably mean changes next year, when the tarmac is complete. Will the Mexican govt. leave 1,000 miles of dirt road for them to play on?

CENTRAL AMERICA

DAY: 105
16/11/10

TO LA PAZ The picture is meant to illustrate secure parking Mexican style. In Loreto we parked on the street. At least it was a dead end, about 50 yards away from our hotel. The poor car is very dusty but there wasn't so much as a paw print on it after two days. When loading this morning a small crowd gathered. First question is always "Where do you come from?" I had an offer of a clean as well but as we were about to set out on an equally dusty road I sadly declined.

We are parked outside our hotel; the Posada de las Flores in La Paz. It is situated on the sea front with the main drag going right past it – great Mexican parking! Anyone with remote common sense might put the cover over the car, but we have had nothing but kindness thus far.

Our room is fortunately at the back, and so hopefully not too noisy. We have a palm tree growing through the middle, painted to match the decor.

Our drive has not been the most exciting today. We were very sorry to leave Loreto, which is enchanting. We even found a blindingly good restaurant last night called Mita Gourmet and both had superb Sea Bass – in one case (guess) washed down with a Margarita! complete with salt rimmed glass.

The first hour of driving was most attractive along the coast and then through the mountains, but thereafter the road was dead straight for mile after mile with very boring countryside. The surface however continues to be superb. The only problem is the Mexican habit of putting a series of sleeping policemen of increasing ferocity before any possible place where one is required to slow down. Fortunately they were the only sort of police we saw all day. Just as well really as at the only road junction of the whole route, (222 miles), I managed to turn left up the wrong side of a dual carriageway. A very obliging truck stopped whilst I did a U-turn. Can't imagine that happening on the M1!

La Paz reminds us both of Igoumenitsa.

Filled up in Loreto 49.6 litres at 12,099 miles
TOTAL MILEAGE: 12,311

Geoffrey & Hilary Herdman

Our roof top balcony in La Paz

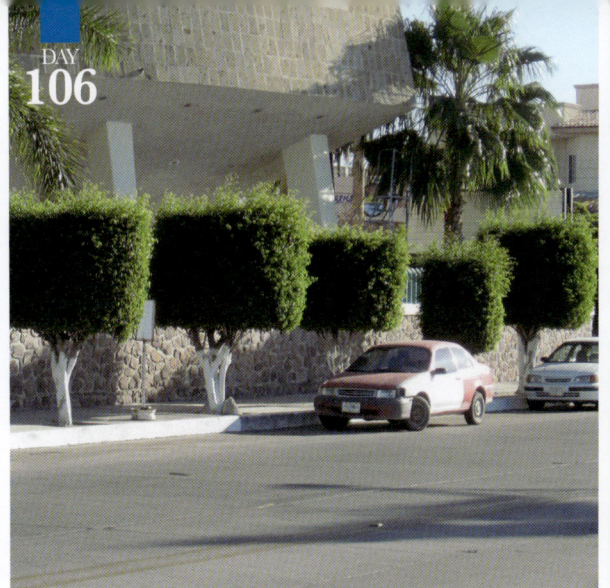

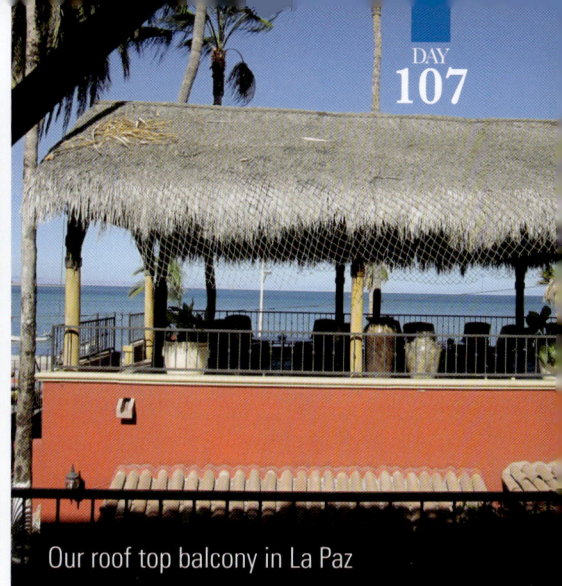

DAY: 106
17/11/10   LA PAZ   The picture is of neatly pollarded trees in La Paz. The town is growing on us.

AM: Clean car.

PM: Ticked off by hotel manager for cleaning car on street. V lucky the police didn't come along or there would have been a fine. I promise not to do it again.

For hotels in Mexico, as we didn't know until the last moment if we would actually cross the border, we have used an agency called Condor Verde, where a very helpful girl called Kathrin fixed up four weeks in Mexico, with about 6 hours notice.

In the evening to excellent restaurant called El Patron where we sit outside and have delicious fish, by the water's edge.

DAY: 107
18/11/10   CROSSING TO THE MAINLAND   Kathrin from Condor tells me she has made the reservation for the ferry so all we have to do is go along 3 hours before departure with no reference other than our name and the tickets will be ready....

I did think we should perhaps drive there during the daytime as 3 hours before the ferry departs is 17:00 (18:00 in Ciudad de Mexico) by when she will have gone home if there are any problems.

Instead we have a very leisurely day and for lunch walk to the Palmira Yacht Club where we find an excellent restaurant called La Panga. We sit "pieds dans l'eau" or "pie en agua", over the water surrounded by bougainvillea and yachts.

We order a Caesar salad for two. Juan comes to our table with an empty wooden bowl, a tray full of ingredients, and proceeds to make mayonnaise from scratch. Garlic is crushed into the base of the bowl, then lime is rubbed around it. An anchovy comes next. An egg is delicately cracked, the white drained off and the yolk added. Then the olive oil, and some Worcester sauce, salt and pepper.

CENTRAL AMERICA

Finally the lettuce and croutons. The whole thing costs £7 and we give him a round of applause and 50 Pesos. Needless to say it is absolutely delicious.

We wander back and pack up 10DPG. The port is rather further from downtown than we had thought and we don't arrive until about 17:15. I check in to the ticket office and a very pretty girl tells me she has no knowledge of the reservation, but her colleague will keep looking. Other punters come in and out. I even have to translate for some backpacking Brits. They only speak Spanish in the ticket office. After an hour or so when the office has cleared I suggest we start again. I will pay for a fresh set of tickets and recover the money from the agency. After another half hour the process is almost complete when somehow they find the reservation!! All very wearing.

The good ship Chihuahua Star is rather like a Minoan Lines ferry, same size and same sort of customers. Many truck drivers and a huge amount of tourists sleeping rough. We have an extremely comfy cabin and an excellent dinner, with the dining room practically to ourselves.

The ferry is supposed to leave at 20:00 but doesn't cast off until 20:30, then hangs around for another 30 minutes about 100 yards from shore while a small boat circles round us. This turns out to be the boat for the pilot, who swings down the side of the ferry, and raises his arms in acclamation when he is safely on board. No idea why he was needed for that first 100 yards! We finally get under way at around 21:00.

TOTAL MILEAGE: 12,325

DAY: 108
19/11/10 THE DRIVE TO GUADALAJARA

The distance from Mazatlan to Guadalajara is 295 miles and TomTom estimates it will take 6 hours 30 minutes. It gets dark around 17:30.

The ferry crossing is listed as being 12 hours, so having left at 21:00 we anticipate arrival for 09:00. Unfortunately it was not to be. They need a Greek crew to run their ship.

We eventually, and with the aid of two tug boats and a pilot, tie up at 11:00 and I am not called down to the car deck until 11:45.

Mrs H is not allowed to accompany me but has to walk a considerable distance. Whilst doing so she meets a charming Swiss girl, who with her husband – both in their early 30s – has bought a new Land Rover, which they shipped to Canada, and plan to spend about 2 years driving through North and South America, before settling down to have a family. It is not a long wheel based vehicle, but they can raise the roof, cook and sleep in it. The Land Rover is white, and being Swiss is spotlessly clean!

Eventually just before midday we are off. The traffic and roads in Mazatlan are awful. By the time we clear the town TomTom is giving an arrival time of 18:50. At least an hour and a bit of driving by night.

We fill up with petrol in Mazatlan. There are very few petrol stations between towns. Coming down Baja we passed one sign saying next petrol in 195 ks. You

Guadalajara Cathedral

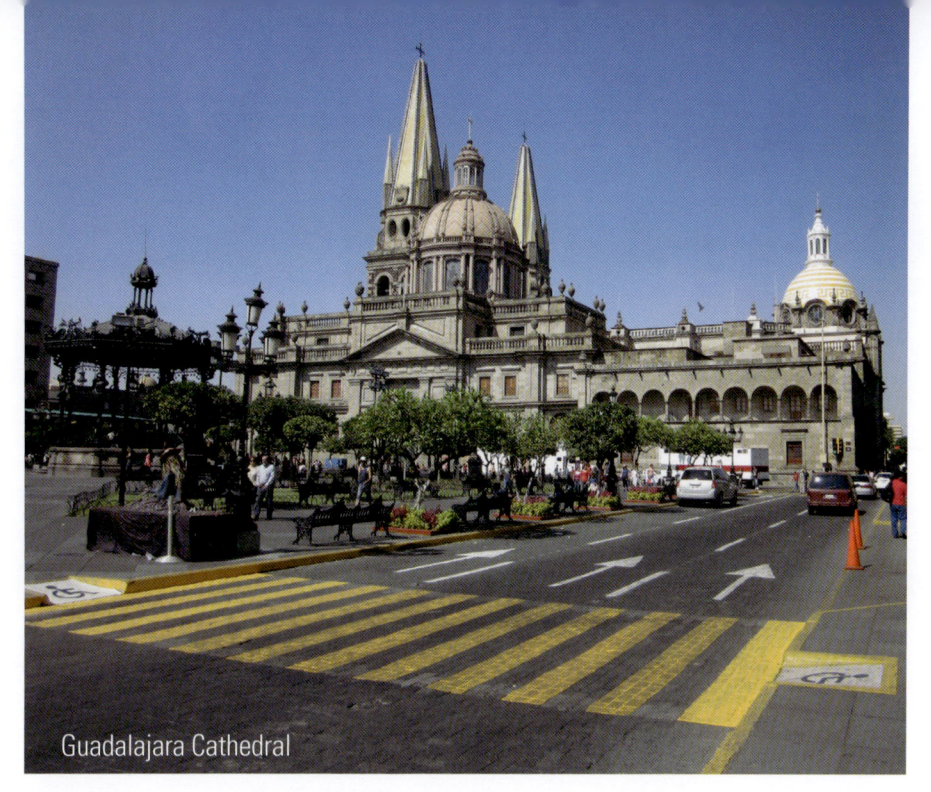

don't want to run out of petrol in Mexico, or you could be very lonely! Petrol, Pemex almost universally, which is a Mexican government monopoly, is 10 Pesos or 50p a litre and 10DPG seems entirely happy on it.

Twenty miles from Mazatlan we make a sharp left for the Via Cuota or toll road. This is still not dual carriageway but the surface is very good and mercifully traffic free. It ain't cheap, which is probably why there is so little traffic. The journey costs us at least £30. We lost count of the tolls.

Until about 30 miles before Tepic the road is flat and not far from the coast. It is lovely, after the desert of Baja, to see rivers flowing, and lush vegetation.

We then start climbing and by Tepic are at 850 metres. The Tepic bypass is not much fun as we have conflued with the Via Libre and both the surface and the traffic are awful. Once clear of Tepic we pick up speed. We also start climbing again and at one point there is a speed restriction to 70 ks (normal is 110 k on the toll road) as we wind through dramatic mountainous country. TomTom shows the free road just to the north of us, which looks spectacular with its twists and turns but hardly fast.

Guadalajara is 1,500 metres above sea level and the second largest city in Mexico with a population of four million. It is Friday night and everyone is coming into town. Tomorrow is a national festival. It is also very hot. One roundabout alone, the size of Hyde Park corner, with traffic lights at every entrance AND exit, takes half an hour to negotiate. We take 90 minutes to do the last 5 miles, and it was 19:45 by the time we reached the hotel. 10DPG has behaved impeccably, with electric fan running constantly and no overheating. But we needed a beer or two! and at long last were able to sit on the hotel terrace and watch the world go by.

Filled up at 12,329 miles 40 litres
TOTAL MILEAGE: 12,620

CENTRAL AMERICA

DAY: 109
20/11/10   SIGHTSEEING IN GUADALAJARA

20th November 2010 is both the 100th and 200th anniversary of Mexican Revolutions. In 1810 the first declaration of independence from Spain was made. On 20th November 1910 a revolution started against the dictatorship of Porfiria Diaz, who had been president/dictator continuously since 1876.

Actually most other days of the year could probably qualify as the anniversary of one revolution or another!

The main square is decorated with garish skeletons, but the whole town is clearly warming up for a monumental party.

Downtown Guadalajara is most attractive and well laid out. The town itself is reckoned to have the best climate of anywhere in the N American continent. Guadalajara was officially founded in 1542, but all the buildings are 18th or 19th Century and none the worse for that. Earthquake or fire has destroyed anything earlier. The style is taken from 16th C Spain, although the French were in occupation for 3 years in the mid 19th C and introduced the Mansard roof and crème caramel. Both of which were regarded as being very chic!

First things first though, one has a Mexican hair cut. Cost £4.50 and an extra quid for doing the eyebrows! Meanwhile Mrs H has her nails done.

Then it's culture. We visit the Governor's Palace with its striking murals painted by Oroczo in the late 1930s, the Theatre Dollgado, the most amazing Hospital founded in the early 19th C by the Church as an orphanage, with a wonderful lantern roof; the whole site is absolutely vast. After a chequered career between orphanage and military barracks it is now a museum with nothing inside except several brides being photographed against a romantic background. Next stop, the market complete with bird sellers with ten cages piled high on their backs, and finally the Cathedral.

In the evening we dine in a converted convent, which again has had a very chequered history of nuns being evacuated, allowed back in, evacuated, allowed

Geoffrey & Hilary Herdman

back in etc. until they finally gave up and moved voluntarily to new quarters in 1977. We are given an antiseptic handwash to use as we check-in, but eat well in the cloisters with a distant piano playing.

DAY: 110
21/11/10 **STOPPED BY THE FUZZ!** Today we are off to Guanajuato – 3 Stars in the Michelin Guide, 2,000 metres above sea level and 171 miles to go.

In the back of my mind I seem to remember once reading that the Solex carburettor as fitted to the Bristol engine has an altitude compensator, which kicks in around 6,000 ft? What does it do?

Exiting Guadalajara is a piece of cake, although the traffic coming in is solid. Once out we take the Via Cuota and for the first half of the trip drive on probably the best road we have driven on in all of N America.

We see a police car at the side of the road. About 5 minutes later he is behind us with lights flashing and loudspeaker requesting us to pull over. One of them comes over with automatic rifle by his side, while the other hovers by the car. He is confused by our placa (licence plate). We explain it is English. He wants to see the car papers and H's driving licence. I point out that it is me who is driving. He can't believe it until he sees the steering wheel on the right hand side and laughs. Having checked the papers he wants to know all about the car and our trip and then we are waved on with much hand shaking. As he goes he calls over his loudspeaker "Goodbye"! Subsequently it occurred to me I should have asked if we could take a photo, but that might have been pushing it!

We arrive in Guanajuato around 15:30. The hotel is a little out of town and up a particularly steep cobbled street. The car park is a sharp left turn at the top on the steepest part. 10DPG refuses and we have to roll back a long way to have a run at it. At this point a group of revellers come out from lunch. First they want to take photos of the car. Then they dawdle up the hill blocking one's run, while an impatient Mexican hoots from behind. Eventually the road is clear. With no good being done to the clutch we make the parking lot. Getting out is going to be another story!

Petrol 59.6 litres at 12,625
TOTAL MILEAGE: 12,788

DAY: 111
22/11/10 **GUANAJUATO** Our well travelled friend Bernard describes Guanajuato as his favourite city in Mexico. In a word it is sensational. Silver was first discovered here over 300 years ago and there are still mines in production, making the city enormously rich.

Topographically it is amazing. We are staying at the bottom at around 1,925 metres but it is built into the side of a hill and rises to over 2,100 metres, a climb of some 600 ft.

The centre is densely packed with buildings and there is really only one main

CENTRAL AMERICA

road. But out of old mine shafts and a dried up underground river they have created a most amazing network of tunnels, and even a couple of underground cross roads! No traffic lights of course.

All the streets are paved with cobbles, spoil presumably from the mines, and there are frequent reminders of the source of the wealth, with mining trolleys being used for floral decorations and statues of miners hacking the rock with hammer and chisel and also pneumatic drills.

We thought that the trees in La Paz looked attractive, but the topiary there was but as nothing to here. We start in the Jardin Union, sitting under an elegant awning having coffee, with a line of laurels shaved to make a dense wall from about 7 ft up. The garden has an impressive bandstand and well preserved wrought ironwork. We might think we are in Paris except two coffees cost about £4.

We admire the Teatro Juarez and discover that there is to be a ballet performance this evening. At a fiver a ticket it is too good to miss. There is what appears to be a very good university and the town is full of young people, all enjoying themselves. There seem to be very few tourists. We debate whether to climb the stairs to the statue of Pepilla, a local hero. I point out that next time we are this way we probably won't be able to! so up we go.

To walk round this enchanting town in glorious weather takes only 2 - 3 hours and we return to our hotel to brush up for the evening's excitements. I discover to my joy that the incredibly steep, narrow, and cobbled hill up which we struggled yesterday is in fact two way, so tomorrow will, after all the panic, be a matter of rolling down it.

Opposite our hotel is a very well presented Colonial style house with sixteen different types of garden, formerly belonging to one of the richest of the mine owners.

We return downtown in the evening in time for a Margarita and guacamole at another of the superb cafes in the Jardin. One of us, while not liking a whole glass, loves the salt lick and a quick sip or three, washed down with a glass of dry white wine.

The inside of the Nineteenth Century, French style theatre is magnificent and in wonderful repair, exuberantly decorated in a Moroccan style. Sadly there are no more than sixty or so in the audience, but the performances are a mixture of classical and modern and excellent.

Afterwards we repair to an Italian restaurant next door, where we have effectively our own balcony on the first floor overlooking the Jardin with a full moon above. We almost feel the H (happy) word creeping up, but have to fight it back.

Today has really underlined H M Tomlinson's observation that; "The best things in travel are always unexpected." (Our thanks to Carol Nishiker for this)

Geoffrey & Hilary Herdman

DAY: 112
23/11/10
SAN MIGUEL DE ALLENDE

Parish church of San Miguel Archangel. Pollarded trees in foreground. The 19th C stonework facade of the church was created by one master mason as his interpretation of a French cathedral, based on photographs he had seen; pink Gothic!

San Miguel is only about 53 miles from Guanajuato. We stop for petrol, and as there appear to be airlines at every pump I test the tyre pressures. Having set them at 27 psi at sea level some weeks back they are now at 32. Of course a reflection on the reduction of external pressure. We decide to leave them as is.

We venture onto a cross country road, but there is plenty of traffic on this part of Ruta 2010, so no need for alarm, and in not much more than an hour come to San Miguel. We are booked in to the Puertecita, a boutique hotel. TomTom is not very good on Mexico. He claims to know every street in Mexico City and Guadalajara but outside the main towns he is a bit sketchy. He has never heard of the hotel. The previous night we checked it on the internet and their map could best described as vague. However we do get onto the ring road and at the roundabout where we had expected we do see a sign for the hotel, but it is not exactly clear.

We ask a taxi driver, who tells us the hotel has changed its name and to follow him along the most appalling cobbled roads. Every 100 yards or so with the road getting narrower and narrower there is a huge but invisible sleeping policeman made from the cobbles. Thank goodness for a 14 gauge steel chassis! We arrive at the Bicentario, who tell us that the taxi driver is completely wrong and we have to reverse our steps back over the same cobbles and then some, and eventually we arrive at the Puertecita, which certainly lives up to its boutiqueness.

The last half hour has been rather wearing on driver and car. When the poor car gets really hot and bothered the electric fuel pump starts rattling noisily, and the engine seems to struggle and run very raggedly. Vapour lock? I stop and change over to the mechanical pump and all is well. I too have developed a vapour lock but a couple of Indio beers on the hotel terrace fixes that.

San Miguel was put on the map by an American artist in the 1930s. Now it is full of wintering Americans and Canadians with some impressive follies, and really rather splendid houses, but to us it lacks the charm of Guanajuato. It has been a

National Heritage site since the 1920s, and has a rather unlived-in atmosphere. It does have yet more impressively toped trees though in the main Plaza.

Filled up in Guanajuato 29 litres 12,789 miles
TOTAL MILEAGE: 12,843

DAY: 113
24/11/10   MEXICO CITY – PHEW! Six o'clock in the evening and we still can't quite believe we are here.

As we were setting out from the hotel this morning 10DPG pulled yet again and a charming Mexican stopped to talk. He told me that there is in fact an old car club in San Miguel and probably one hundred or so English families living there, not to mention many more Americans and Canadians. His great, great, great grandfather had been ambassador to the Court of St James in the mid 19th C and had had an affair with a notable society lady. This had been frowned on and the ambassador was sent home, followed some years later by the offspring, who was despatched loaded with furniture and cash, and became the great great grandfather of Guillermo, my new acquaintance.

Mexico City is only 160 miles down the road. En route we climb to over 2,600 metres (8,500 ft). 10DPG purrs.

As we approach the air becomes darker and darker with a thick smog (see photo!). Until about 10 miles from where TomTom says the hotel is we are really doing quite well, but then we hit the traffic. The last 5 miles takes about an hour. We are in a three lane dual carriageway. Overhead they are building additional roads to celebrate the 2010 bicentenary but they have some way to go by 31st December. All along street vendors are standing between the lanes peddling their wares; nuts, fried bananas, cool drinks etc. etc. The police seem to be urging one of them to move on but we must have passed at least fifty of them.

We are staying at the Melia on the Paseo de la Reforma. TomTom has never heard of the Melia so we head for the Paseo only to find we are at the wrong end, need to do a U-turn across a wide dual carriageway and that it is 5 ks in the opposite direction. Mercifully the Paseo is reasonably traffic free, but we do have one interesting moment when we are caught in the middle of a huge dual carriageway by the lights. A wonderful policeman stops all the traffic and waves us on against the red light. Who said Mexican police weren't friendly!!

Our eta was originally 14:44. We actually arrive at about 16:00, by which time 10DPG and driver are feeling just the teensiest bit ragged, and passenger quite faint, but hopefully four day's rest for the former and a large reviving beer/tea for the latter will restore the inner men.

TOTAL MILEAGE: 13,009

DAY: 114
25/11/10 SIGHTSEEING IN MEXICO CITY

The photo is of the view from our bedroom window at 10 in the morning on a fine sunny day. How do people live here?

A morning sightseeing and an afternoon on essential body maintenance. The doctor had the temerity to tell me there was an imperfection in the way I was made, and I was out of warranty!! An impressive grasp of English for a Mexican doctor.

In the evening a trip to the newly restored Sala des Belles Artes, only just refurbished and superbly. The tickets were worth it to see the interior alone, including an extravagant Tiffany glass curtain designed before the First World War, but delivered many years later, owing to political uncertainties in Mexico! It was a very good performance of Onegin, the ballet. However it started an hour late with the audience slow handclapping and so didn't finish until 23:00, by which time the hotel restaurant had closed. Fortunately they were able to offer superb room service complete with a Margarita! so we had a TV dinner at midnight.

DAY: 115
26/11/10 PEOPLE WHO LUNCH.

A very leisurely start to the day. We were due to meet Bernard for lunch in Condesa, which he describes as the Kensington of Mexico. He had just finished an intensive course of one to one Spanish.

We met him outside his school and then walked back to his apartment to collect Luger, a delightful 4 year old miniature Schnauzer, who was looking after him.

And then a splendid lunch, washed down with perhaps more wine than was strictly necessary, sitting outside on the pavement. On arrival the restaurant was empty but by the time we left at around 16:00 it was absolutely packed.

After a little retail therapy a much needed walk back to the hotel, where we more or less collapsed at 18:30!

CENTRAL AMERICA

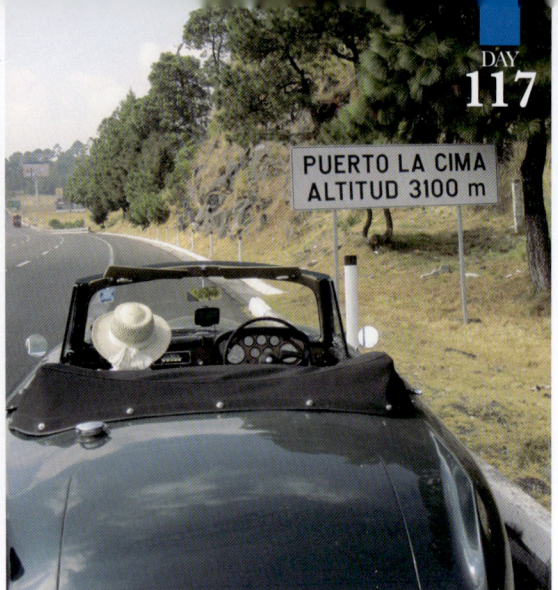

DAY: 116
27/11/10 **XOCHICALCO** Our dear friend Lucia, whom we had first met in France in 1986, and was hostess to many memorable weekends on Le (not La) Loir, came and picked us up from the hotel at around 09:30. She hasn't changed a bit!

The idea was to visit one of her favourite tourist spots outside the city. By the time we had had a coffee or two we found all the streets were closed and when we made it to her car were only just in time to make a hurried exit 100 yards in front of a huge procession.

It still took us over an hour to find our way out of the city as most of the main roads were closed.

Xochicalco, the X is pronounced as an S, was a huge settlement from the 7th - 9th Century AD. Nobody is really sure why it was abandoned but the surmise is that after 4 years of drought the people turned on the priests, despising their rain Gods, and anarchy broke out.

The magnificent site is in a beautiful mountainous setting, with lovely views over the golden maize fields. Vast and with very few visitors, a wonderful Museum, and a UNESCO World Heritage Site.

We didn't leave the site until about 15:00 and then found a delightful road side caff, which was doing a roaring trade.

Lucia had suggested a concert in the evening by the university orchestra. We made the campus by 18:30 in time for a quick dinner to find the restaurant, being part of the university, was dry – shock horror.

The concert hall, part of the university facilities, was absolutely stunning and the quality of the orchestra magnificent. A mixed programme of Beethoven, Schumann, Grieg, Revuelta – who he? and de Falla. A rousing and entertaining evening.

Geoffrey & Hilary Herdman

DAY: 117
28/11/10

LEAVING MEXICO CITY It has to be said one was in a slight stew at the joint prospects of getting out of Mexico City, and climbing to over 10,000 ft.

The Paseo de la Reforma, where the hotel is located, is closed on Sundays to all but cyclists, which I had anticipated would add to our difficulties.

In the event we left at just after 10:00, and were clear of the city half an hour later. The traffic was a doddle.

As soon as you leave the city you start climbing. 10DPG never batted an eyelid, or carburettor butterfly. The high point, as will be seen from the photo (opposite), is 3,100 metres or something over 10,000 ft. At idle the engine hunted slightly, but climbing was no problem. Temperature normal – of course it gets cooler with altitude, but not that cold. We had the hood down and were in shirtsleeves – and we even managed some of the climb in overdrive. There is an alarming red line on the precipitous hairpin descent, with an accompanying sign that cars without brakes should follow that line, and cars with brakes should avoid those without!

As soon as we had gone over the top we dropped back to 1,000 metres and then climbed again to reach Taxco, 1,900 metres.

Our hotel is called Monte Taxco. As we entered the town we saw an impossibly steep cobbled street leading up to it. Poor 10DPG. We started well, managed a hairpin bend, and then totally ran out of steam. This was a little trying as it meant backing down the hill and doing a seven point turn on a hairpin bend with traffic coming from both directions. H had wonderfully commandeered a VW beetle (the original type) taxi, who directed us to a car park at the lower level and then casually took us and our luggage back up the hill. Where is my new engine?? (Note from ED.: Both car and driver deserve a medal for retaining their cool, in all senses, under trying circumstances.)

The VW beetle reigns supreme here. None of them can be a day younger than 20 years old.

From the hotel there is a Swiss built cable car with cabins into the most gorgeous town.

Taxco, like Guanajuato, is a silver producing town, built into the side of several hills, but without the advantage of most of the traffic going in tunnels. The views however are spectacular. A visit to the beautiful church of St Prisca and St Sebastian, followed by a Margarita – to soothe the shattered nerves, and all was right with the world.

Filled up at 13,021 miles, 51 litres
TOTAL MILEAGE: 13,134 miles

The hairpin bend where we had to back and turn in the face of oncoming traffic in both directions!

CENTRAL AMERICA

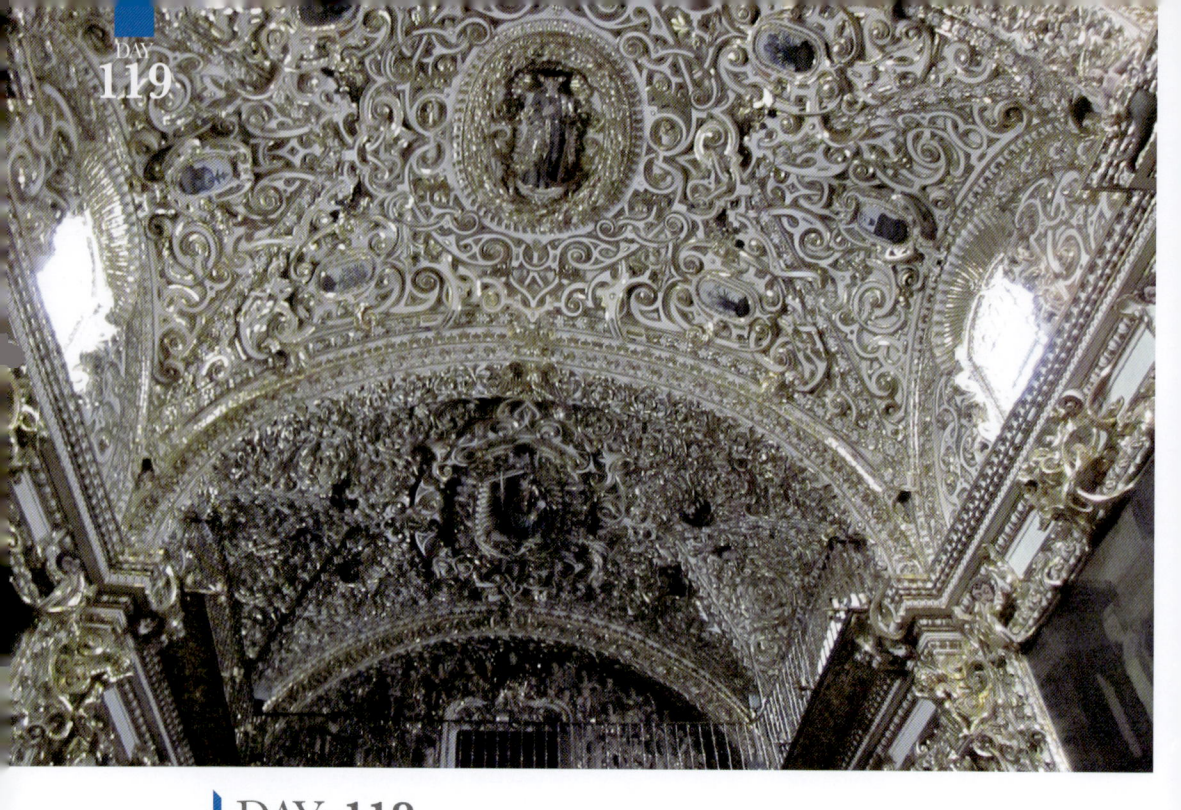

DAY: 118
29/11/10 **TAXCO TO PUEBLA** We asked our taxi driver from yesterday to come and collect us at 10:30. Instead his brother came, also in the ubiquitous beetle with the front passenger seat taken out. I was wrong about them being at least 20 years old. Hugo told us his was made in 2001, and apparently the last Mexican proper beetle was in fact produced on 30th June 2003!

As well as being a taxi driver Hugo is a football commentator and he gave us a running cabaret of an imaginary commentary, punctuated at frequent intervals with either a high pitched and rapid "Goal – Goal – Goal – Goal – Goal", or a long drawn out and lower voiced "Goooooooooooooal".

He also took us on a mini sight seeing tour of Taxco which is utterly irresistible.

Having collected 10DPG he finally led us through tortuous narrow cobbled streets to the main road out.

Taxco is at 7 o'clock from Mexico City and Puebla is at 4. We thus had to go cross country from one to the other. All was well to start with, but having changed drivers H suddenly found she was in a monstrous traffic jam in Cuernavaca, with a dreadful road surface and vicious "topés" (invisible sleeping policemen) every 100 yards or so. The only way one could see them was by watching the car in front. Unfortunately things did not get much better until we reached Cuautla some 30 miles and an hour and a half later.

Puebla more than made up for it though. The city is laid out on a grid with streets being named either 5 North South or 5 East West etc. It is flat and the road surface is excellent. In about 10 minutes we had found our hotel.

Puebla has been home for more than 40 years to a huge VW plant, which

Geoffrey & Hilary Herdman

can do no harm for the local economy. Downtown is gorgeous and frankly my favourite Mexican City thus far. We sat under awnings at the Royalty Hotel on the Zocola or Plaza Mayor and had Margaritas. Well, some of us did.

TOTAL MILEAGE: 13,280

DAY: 119
30/11/10   SIGHTSEEING IN PUEBLA   The roof of the Capilla del Rosario in the Templo de Santo Domingo (pictured opposite), a Baroque masterpiece.

First impressions from yesterday were totally confirmed by today. Puebla is magnificent. Christmas decorations were being installed and all the municipal flower beds planted with Nochebuena or Poinsettia, which is the symbol of Christmas in Mexico.

An excellent dinner back in the Royalty hotel.

DAY: 120
01/12/10   TRAVELLIN' LIGHT   A demonstration of what makes a 405 Drophead such an ideal travelling car. Seven large suitcases, toolbox, printer, and car washing kit on display. Total weight about equivalent to two adults. In addition hidden in the side bays of the boot are cans of petrol, set of spare parts, jump leads, tyre inflator, emergency battery etc., etc.

Today was not a good day! Not knowing where our hotel was in Oaxaca I printed out a map before we set out. Trouble was there is a Hotel Mision de los Angeles and a Calle Mision de los Angeles. Guess which one Google hit on?

It was also our coldest day so far with a chill wind and we had to have the roof up for most of the way. The drive through the mountains was beautiful, with a mixture of lush valleys and stands of cactus on the mountainsides. We had good views of the snow-capped Pico de Orizaba, to compensate for the three volcanoes surrounding Puebla having been shrouded in cloud.

Having set out rather later than we should we arrived on the outskirts of Oaxaca around 18:00 just as it was getting dark. With enormous difficulty and driving over the most atrocious potholes we eventually found the Mision de los Angeles as highlighted by Google, to find we were in a back street slum on appalling roads.

We headed back downtown to find a taxi and ended up in the main bus station, which was stationary with wall to wall buses, people and taxis. However a taxi said he would take us to the hotel for 70 Pesos, about £3.50. I told him that he

CENTRAL AMERICA

couldn't miss me as I had three lights in front. It took us about half an hour to do the first quarter of a mile, with cars trying to shove in between my St Christopher and 10DPG at every road junction. But we persevered and 2 hours after reaching Oaxaca made it to the hotel. We have to think of a better way of doing these things!!

Come dinner time we were thirsty. The wine reminded one of us of that sublime nectar of Antipaxos. The other still thinks nothing approaches that!

Filled up at 13,284 56 litres
TOTAL MILEAGE: 13,499

DAY: 121
02/12/10   OAXACA

Oaxaca is both a city and a state, one of the thirty one that make up Mexico, excluding the Federal District of Mexico. The state is about 3/5s the size of the UK and has a population of approx 4 million. There are some sixteen different tribes, of whom the predominant are the Zapotecs. 30% of the population speak no Spanish, which ergo means that they don't go to school, as all schools teach in Spanish.

The city is completely different from Puebla. The buildings aren't so beautiful, but the whole place buzzes with activity. Everywhere there are street vendors, musicians and dancers. The main square has three separate bands in different parts, all playing at the same time late into the night, whilst street vendors are still plying their trade, with children fast asleep on rugs.

Passing any doorway there will be music emanating of one sort or another. One of the most popular items for sale is a gas balloon and the vendors have huge arrays of them colourfully blowing about in the wind.

It was a tourist day today. In the evening we ate in the main square (Zocola), on the first floor, with a grandstand view of all the comings and goings. The only problem is that I had been recommended to try grasshoppers, a Zapotec speciality. You spread some guacomole on a tortilla and then ladle your grasshoppers onto the mix. They have their revenge!!

DAY: 122
03/12/10   MONTE ALBAN AND AN OIL CHANGE

A.M. A trip to Monte Alban, 10 ks out of the city. Hector drove us out there. He spoke wonderful English and having been born in a hill village won a scholarship to University in the UK to study English. Sadly, or otherwise, the Bank which had made the offer subsequently changed it to a scholarship to Madrid for 2 years, which as his friends said, would improve his Spanish!

During our 15 minute taxi ride in a mixture of Spanish and English he told us all about Oaxaca. We also covered religion. For about 100 years from the 1860s to the 1960s Christianity was banned in Mexico. When it was first banned the State seized all church properties and even today the church buildings are owned by the government. It has to be said that in many cases they have done a wonderful job of restoration.

Geoffrey & Hilary Herdman

Monte Alban was constructed between 300BC and approx. 800AD by the Zapotecs. It is huge and massively impressive, although the present site is probably 65% reconstructed. Once the Zapotecs had abandoned it, succeeding generations venerated it, and it was largely unspoilt by man. In the 1930s Tomb Number 7 was discovered with treasures from a later burial in the 12th Century, the equal of any other major tomb anywhere in the world. Some of these are on display in Oaxaca, gold, pearls, obsidian, and silver jewellery but the major part is in Mexico City. Some of course was looted in the 30s.

P.M. Time for an oil change, and just round the corner from the hotel was a very friendly garage. The proprietor had lived for 10 years in Austin Texas and spoke excellent English. Once on the ramp we noticed that the offside strap holding the silencer was broken. On the 405 Drophead the silencer runs transversely under the boot rather than longitudinally, so the nearside strap had the full weight of the exhaust swinging precariously.

An hour later oil changed and two new exhaust straps. Cost 830 Pesos, about £45.

In the evening, on Hector's recommendation, we tried La Catrina de Alcala and had the best meal we have had in Mexico, with a live trio playing Beethoven et al. excellently.

Changed oil at 13,499 miles.

CENTRAL AMERICA

DAY: 123
04/12/10
HEADING SOUTH

The bane of our and all Mexicans' lives. Warning for a Topé or speed bump. It is most unusual to have a warning. They are mostly blind.

Tehuantepec is only about 150 miles from Oaxaca, but Hector had warned us that the road was twisty and hilly. Additionally he had told us that there is a refinery near our destination, so the road is usually full of oil laden trucks. I thought that as we were heading towards the refinery they might be empty going our way and thus faster.

Oaxaca is about 1,500 metres above sea level. We climbed to 1,800 metres, dropped to 800, back up to 1,200 and so on. The road is absolutely beautiful, twisting and turning through glorious valleys, surrounded by mountains and distant snow capped volcanoes. We were probably the slowest car out, but were in no hurry. My prognosis about the tankers proved to be correct and those coming towards us ground up the hills, whilst we were overtaken rather shamingly by a couple of empty double articulateds.

En route we passed through the world centre for the production of Mezcal. Very like tequila and made from the agave plant. Tequila is made only from blue agave. The agave looks like a cactus but has a pine about the size of a football. This has to be crushed to extract the juice, which is then fermented and distilled. Along the roadside we saw and smelt several plants in the process of manufacture including one where a donkey was turning the millstone to extract the juice, just like the old Cider mills. Sadly no photo!

After our hotel locating disaster in Oaxaca we took extra care in Googling the hotel Calli. But Google had misplaced it by over 2 miles and on a totally different road. The hotel could best be described as moonlike – no atmosphere, but it was comfortable and we had an adequate dinner. After which I thought I should try a back to back comparison of Mezcal and Tequila. Someone, who shall remain anonymous, urged me not to finish them, but it was like Everest – they were there. Tequila won hands down. To drink either you rub your index finger on a lime – lick it, then dip it in salt – lick it, and then drink the drink. (The Mexicans have a more elegant way of savouring the lime and the salt! ED.)

Filled up outside Oaxaca 13,511 miles 48.4 litres
TOTAL MILEAGE: 13,659

DAY: 124
05/12/10   TO THE GUATEMALA BORDER

A good bit of dual carriageway. Note foliage on the left, dividing the lanes.

Yesterday the horn stopped working. This has been happening intermittently for some time, due Charlie says, to 50 amp fuses being a bit dodgy. No amount of fuse wiggling this time sorted matters and I discovered the wire going over the flexible coupling on the steering column had broken.

The washer connector having been removed I was amazed at the thickness and strength of the copper and it took a while to clean it up.

This morning up at 07:00 for the refit. All went well until I turned the steering wheel and nearly broke the thing on one of the "one shot" pipes. Clearance is minimal. Anyway we now have a working horn.

Before we set out, we had a friendly telephone call from Hector, who had remembered where we were staying, and was concerned to know that we had made it safely.

Our destination is Tapachula on the Guatemala border about 260 miles away. Tehuantepec is at sea level and all the driving today was at not more than 100 metres above – so it was HOT. It was also incredibly windy and we passed three huge wind farms with literally hundreds of windmills.

The countryside is pastoral, with plenty of water in the rivers. Ranches with cattle and horses line the route, against a background of mountains, all very refreshing to the eye. Although the Spanish introduced both cattle and horses, the villages and the people are very much Indo-American; it all seems a long way from Mexico City, and we wonder how such a vast country can be governed. *Continues overleaf*

CENTRAL AMERICA

Two army check posts today, looking thoroughly at the lorries, but we are waved through with smiles.

Once into the State of Chiapas the map showed the road as being dual carriageway. It was for large sections. Bizarrely when they built the second carriageway they just put it on the other side of the village, so frequently villages were in the middle of the road. We also had tricycles and pedestrians coming towards us in the outside lane. But the main problem was the road surface, the worst we have had in Mexico. In many places it was being repaired and we had to drive for long distances over the most appalling dirt roads. This unfortunately showed up a problem with my friendly garage's handiwork. They had made the new exhaust straps too long and there was a lot of scraping and rattling.

We are now in the Casa Mexicana hotel in the middle of Tapachula. It is an absolute gem, very small and calling itself, justifiably, boutique. As I write we are sitting by the pool in an enclosed courtyard. The hotel is painted in Rameses Red and the rooms are – well, boutique.

Filled up at 13,672 31 litres.
TOTAL MILEAGE: 13,920

DAY: 125
06/12/10   INTO GUATEMALA

First sights of Guatemala are spectacular. Driving along a tropical road with palm trees on either side out of Tapachula one suddenly sees Tajumulco, the first of thirty two volcanoes, some still active. In Tapachula we are more or less at sea level. Guatemala is mountainous. Tajumulco – see photo – rises to 13,485 ft.

But first things first. The helpful hotel manager at the Casa Mexicana told me of an excellent exhaust shop three blocks away from where we were staying. A quick trip to their premises and 30 minutes later they had replaced the exhaust hangers, put on in Oaxaca, with much more secure brackets and raised the silencer 2″ in the process – all for about £20 or it might have been only £10. I do hope the Oaxaca oil change was more satisfactory!

With one thing and another we weren't on the road until after 10:00. This proved to be unwise!

The border at Talisman is only about 20 minutes drive away, but there the trouble started. Three hours later and having revived the local economy singlehandedly we were at last properly into Guatemala. Not however before having three in the car (two sharing the passenger seat, but also cosily sharing the mandatory safety belt, which seemed to satisfy the numerous police) for some distance to clear customs.

While Geoffrey was wrestling with customs, H was talking to the group of boys surrounding the car, and congratulated one on his English. He replied modestly that he had learned it in the course of a 14 month prison sentence in

Geoffrey & Hilary Herdman

Atlanta, after a 9 year stay in the US, and then been deported. Needless to say it was a trumped up charge, but at that stage his English was so poor that he could not resist the police... On reflection a 14 month sentence in Atlanta is pretty mild, but we were glad to move on!

We were heading for Lake Atitlan – not a great distance but there are two roads, one by the coast and a shorter road inland. When we asked which was the quicker there was much sucking of teeth. "The short road was indeed shorter but I needed a strong motor and a good radiator". I said I had both and off we set, but not until gone 14:00.

Our drive took us through Malacatan, where we stopped to collect some money. The Guatemalan currency is the Quetzal named after the national bird. There are no sign posts anywhere in the towns and we had difficulty exiting. The driver even resorted to asking the way! several times!

Having left Malacatan we immediately started climbing, mostly in first gear at 3,000 rpm. The terrible thought came to me that as the hairpin bends were so steep if at any stage we couldn't make it we would have to drive all the way back down and take the coastal road. After a couple of hours we peaked at over 10,000 ft and started the descent to San Marco. Again there were no signs and we were hopelessly lost. A kind "collectivo" or local bus told us to follow him.

The next town was Quetzeltenango: again no signs. TomTom doesn't work in Central America, and the maps are small scale. At least we were joining the motorway, which comes down from the North, and is the Pan-Am highway. By the time we left it was pretty well dark and we thought about staying the night but the hotels looked pretty uninspiring.

Once on the motorway we had two problems. The first was the most appalling mud slides, after the disastrous Summer floods, which in many places had completely wiped out one half of the road. The second was that having come down to about 5,000 ft we started climbing again. As the road was wide and not quite so twisty we managed mostly in 2nd, again climbing to 10,000 ft. There was the most magnificent sunset as we climbed up the ring of volcanoes.

CENTRAL AMERICA

However it was soon pitch dark and the first rule of driving in Central America is NOT to drive in the dark.

Around 20:00 we came to the turn off for lake Atitlan, where H fortunately noticed a sign saying the road was blocked. We rang the hotel, who told us to drive along the motorway to Trappas and follow the signs, but because of the deviation we were still about an hour away!

In the dark we slightly overshot the sign and at that stage the driver gave up. (Understandably: ED.) Driving on the so called motorway in the pitch dark was one thing. Getting lost on minor country roads was another. By the side of the "motorway" was a hostelry called the Posada de San Miguel. We must have been their first guests in weeks. We were at 8,500 ft and the place was bitterly cold. They said they only had eggs, but H showed them how to make omelettes.

Accommodation cost $40, rather overpriced, and supper the same, but that did include a litre of beer and a bottle of Chilean wine. There was no hot water and the room was unbelievably cold, but we had a bed, and for that we were profoundly grateful. Every truck in Guatemala changed gear climbing up the hill that night, but we didn't care!

Mileage on leaving Mexico 13,970. Filled up at 13,920 41.9 litres
TOTAL MILEAGE: 14,087

DAY: 126
07/12/10   ANTIGUA GUATEMALA

Breakfast turned out not too badly, but was over and above the room charge!

It was still very cold and we kept the hood up. There had been a heavy dew on the car and probably frost earlier on.

Our rather exiguous map showed possibly a motorway going from Chimaltenango to Antigua G. By comparison with yesterday we managed today without getting too lost, but the fact that there was theoretically only one road through may have accounted for this!

We even found a signpost for Anitigua G and followed the RN 14 through Parramos. At the exact moment when I had said to Mrs H "what an excellent road it was" we ran out of tarmac. After about a mile of dirt road, albeit with spectacular views of volcanoes, we turned round and headed back to Chimaltenango, where we picked up a rather better road. Needless to say there were no signposts on this and we were by now getting rather adept at asking our way. The diversion on the RN14 went through beautiful agricultural countryside; masses of wild flowers that cost a fortune in UK garden centres, and very Indian villages, including a busy communal washing tank.

We filled up in Vieja Ciudad, which was the original Spanish capital, before being wiped out by a dreadful flood in 1541. The capital then moved 5 miles up the road to Antigua G, which in turn was largely destroyed by an earthquake in 1773, and was finally established in present day Guatemala City.

Petrol is sold in US gallons rather than litres but seems to be much the same price as in Mexico. There are only 8 Quetzals to the $ as opposed to 12 Mexican Pesos. A gallon of super costs 30 Q.

And so finally to the Casa Santo Domingo. It is absolutely gorgeous, built in the ruins of a vast earthquake-stricken Dominican convent. By night we are candle lit. Our bedroom has a fireplace. Despite being at about 15° North we are still 5,000 ft above sea level and we are extremely grateful for a warming wood fire. Yesterday we were definitely travellers; this evening we have happily reverted to being spoilt tourists!

Filled up at 14,164 15 US gallons.
TOTAL MILEAGE: 14,169

DAY: 127
08/12/10

ANTIGUA GUATEMALA

A Guatemalan bus. All are ex US school buses. They have all been modified slightly and painted garish colours, but are spotlessly clean. They drive like Jehu!

The morning is taken up with car cleaning and paperwork. In the afternoon we visit the local agency handling the Central America part of our trip. They advise us to buy a fire extinguisher before entering Honduras! as that is a standard requirement when clearing customs.

Reading the Rough Guide it appears that for many years the country has really been run by the army and armed gangs. We ask the agency to tell us in 30 seconds how are the politics. In 2008 Presidente Colom was appointed. We are told he is good but cannot stand up to the army.

CENTRAL AMERICA

Last night there was a firework display in town with huge crowds. I woke up at about 03:30 and there were still bangers being let off. Or were they bangers?

The weather is cloudy and en route to the agency we hear thunder. They tell us it is Volcan Fuego rumbling!

DAY: 128
09/12/10 HELLO & GOODBYE EL SALVADOR

The plan for today was to cross into El Salvador, and then drive to San Miguel near the Honduran border.

The Central America "expert" at our UK agency had told us that from Antigua G to the border would take us 2 hours. The local agency thought more like 4, and were to be proved right – what a surprise. We were on the road by 08:05 and the other side of Guatemala City, with only one wrong turn, by 09:40, which was actually rather good going.

The drive from the City to the border is beautiful, and we descended the valley to the frontier. Having fought off the touts we cleared Guatemala in about 20 minutes and crossed the river into El Salvador. After 2 hours of paper being shuffled around and a phone call they told us we couldn't enter El Salvador because the car is right hand drive. We could see the head honcho, who by then was at lunch and half an hour later she confirmed that it was impossible to enter El S.

Back to Guatemala. The only alternative was to drive through Honduras, which does connect Guatemala to Nicaragua, but the drive through El S is much better and the roads are mostly dual carriageway.

The helpful local agents suggested we head for Esquipulas on the border, 100 miles away. By now it was 14:45, clearly we were not going to get there by daylight.

Once again the roads were completely unsignposted but we made the hotel Corchi by about 18:30. It had been a long, rather trying day and even Mrs H resorted to a whole Margarita!

TOTAL MILEAGE: 14,384

Geoffrey & Hilary Herdman

DAY: 129
10/12/10

BORDER CROSSINGS Central American frontier crossings are NOT for the faint hearted! nor for the impatient.

As we couldn't enter El Salvador the plan for today was to enter Honduras and drive more or less up to the Caribbean coast before heading South through the capital towards Nicaragua. It would be a long drive.

The crossing into Honduras was only about 20 minutes away. We set out at a little after 09:00 and having filled up in Esquipulas were at the border by 09:30. No touts – Oh joy, and we were out of Guatemala in half an hour. Entering Honduras was a different matter.

At all the frontiers the procedure is as follows:

You clear customs and immigration on leaving one country and 500 yards later reverse the process. Simple really. It does of course involve copious photocopying, queues, and usually a horde of touts hassling to be of help.

There is a no-man's land of about 500 yards between each post, so the enchanting little 3 wheel communal taxis, and bicycle rickshaws, ply busily to and fro, laden with passengers and their luggage, who pick up a new bus on the other side of the border.

At customs in Honduras there was only one official and he was trying to sort out an American who wanted to bring in his trailer home and dune buggy. (This was part of a complicated saga, involving renewing his visa, as he had been working as a volunteer in a hospital in Honduras for over 3 months. He had accordingly gone to Guatamala, not realising that there is a union between the four countries for access arrangements, so he was heavily fined in Guatamala for outstaying his Honduran visa! It seemed very harsh in the circumstances!) This took 2 hours before officialdom was able to even start on me. Richard, the American, had been on our route in Honduras and said it was very mountainous in the North and he would seriously recommend trying to head South and see if we could get into El Salvador again.

So having taken 3 hours to clear the frontier we then spent about 30 minutes in Honduras before reversing the process and retrying El Salvador, with out hearts in our mouths.

Whilst I was talking to customs H met some cheerful Swiss boys who have been touring the globe in a Land Rover for the past 2 years, and plan to continue for about another year. Needless to say, the Land Rover was spotless. It made our trip pale by comparison; however the Land Rover was much younger than 10DPG.

Fortunately nobody took much notice of the right hand drive. We purposely had the top up, and an hour and bit later we were into El Salvador. The roads were pretty good and we even had dual carriageway around San Salvador, the capital.

The currency is the good old US Dollar and gas is measured in US gallons. We headed to San Miguel and with slight difficulty found the Tropico Inn. Car parking was in an attached multi storey, of which more tomorrow.

Filled up in Esquipula 14,386 12.6 US gallons
TOTAL MILEAGE: 14,507

CENTRAL AMERICA

DAY: 130
11/12/10 THROUGH HONDURAS
In the car by 08:05! It felt very heavy getting out of the multistorey. When I parked in front of hotel reception the guard pointed out that my nearside rear tyre was flat. He also pointed out that someone appeared to have taken a jemmy to the wheel rim as a small part was completely bent up. Not good news for a tubeless tyre!

I pumped the tyre up and left it for 5 minutes. It seemed o.k. so we thought we would give it a go and were on the road by 08:20. At 09:00 we stopped to check and found that pressure was down. On repumping we heard air escaping, so it was wheel change time.

Most fortunately we still have the repaired inner tube from Boone all those months and thousands of miles ago, so will see if that works, plus a little gentle treatment on the rim with a hammer!

On arrival at the El Salvador/Honduras border we were absolutely surrounded by touts, including one cleverer than most who said that right hand drive might be a problem in Honduras and he could fix it. We were rather sensitive about this and so a couple of hours later and having once again semi relieved the national debt we were on our way.

The part we were crossing is the narrowest part of Honduras at about 90 miles. Despite this we were stopped by the police six times, of which two were police helping charity girls collecting by the road side. We said quite truthfully that we had already contributed three times to the charity.

The last police stop wanted to see both my red triangle and fire extinguisher. Christophe from our local travel agents in Antigua Guatemala had warned us that this might be the case and for $6 we had bought an extinguidor. If the policeman was disappointed that he couldn't have his $20 "fine" for non production of either he didn't show it, and thus we managed without fines in Honduras.

The last 20 miles of road to the Nicaraguan border were truly awful with pothole after pothole. It was a matter of weaving our way. The trees were by now casting shadows and it was sometimes difficult to spot the problems. At one particularly savage hole we lost a hub cap, sadly irretrievably due to the undergrowth.

At the Honduras/Nicaragua border we managed to fight off the touts, but they were not particularly persistent. I asked Nicaraguan immigration if they had stamped our passports. It's all in the computer was the reply.

Geoffrey & Hilary Herdman

We were also sold insurance – phew, the first time it had been possible since leaving Mexico, what a relief!

For the first 20 miles the Nicaraguan roads were very good, but then we were back with the potholes for another 20 miles. The countryside was totally different from Honduras. Altogether more kempt, huge tree lined estates and all very orderly and green. The standard means of transport is still the horse or cart, horse, or even bullock drawn – see photo opposite.

And so to Leon. As usual arriving about an hour after dark. Leon is the old capital and still the main university town. The roads are all cobbled and in very bad condition. We were surrounded by bikes, with no lights, coming in all directions, usually with the girl friend sitting side saddle across the central bar. Most uncomfortable, not to mention unstable we thought. Hot and tired we eventually found a friendly taxi to guide us.

We were staying in El Convento, which was an absolute oasis of peace and quiet, in the centre of town, and with a fountain and palm trees in an inner courtyard. However we were just beginning to relax over the 2nd or 3rd beer when this paradise erupted into the most earsplitting cacophony. They had set up a disco/dance band, grossly overamplified, and reverberating through every corner of the hotel. When we asked reception what time it would stop we were blithely told 2 in the morning.

Sleep was out of the question until 01:17 when the guests must have finally left, completely deaf I should think.

Filled up on en route 12 gallons US
TOTAL MILEAGE: 14,741

DAY: 131
12/12/10   NICARAGUA & COSTA RICA

Despite the rural charm of Nicaragua, as we drove out of Leon we found rubbish piled high on the street sides and the roads in dreadful condition. Once on the highway though things improved dramatically.

We more or less bypassed Managua, stopping only for petrol and the police! In one village where there was very slow traffic a 4 wheel drive stopped in front of us and father and son jumped out, son posing against 10DPG whilst father took his photo. They then jumped back in and drove off. If we had a $ for every time 10DPG has been photoed this trip we would be very rich.

A little later we were again stopped by the police who told us we had been speeding and that the limit through urban areas was 30 ks. At first they wanted $50 and when they saw we had more increased the amount to $60. Before setting off they then asked for another $10 for a drink. But as we by now had all our documents back they were out of luck.

It was slightly galling to be relieved of cash in Nicaragua, whereas we had passed through Honduras, which we had heard was the most corrupt country, scot free. Another 10 miles down the road we were again stopped and all our documents taken and recorded. One was becoming a little sensitive about speeds, and we drove very slowly to the border.

CENTRAL AMERICA

On our left we passed Lake Nicaragua, which is the largest lake in the Americas after the Great Lakes. The Spanish thought they had found the Pacific when they saw it. We turned off to the Playa de Virgenes to look at the Isla Ometepe, which boasts two volcanoes. See photo. Just after we had stopped a Triumph bike pulled up alongside us and Ian, the rider, said he had been on the same ferry as us from Baja California to Mazatlan. Small world!

There is only one border crossing between Nicaragua and Costa Rica. We had been warned that it would take at least 90 minutes. In fact it took us over 2 hours. The exit from Nicaragua was easy, about half an hour; the entrance to Costa Rica slower. The place was absolutely swarming with trucks and one had to be very careful not to get boxed in. When we had our final piece of paper we thought we had been, but Mrs H charmed half a dozen truckees, who managed to make way for us.

Whilst queuing for our customs permit we talked to a Nicaraguan and told him about the police. He was outraged and said we had set a bad example by paying so much. He never paid more than $2 and if necessary was prepared to go to court, which he admitted could take four to five days. We rather felt that for the sake of the hassle $60 wasn't too bad, as we had undoubtedly been doing more than 30 ks through a village.

And so to Liberia. We arrived for the first time for a long time by daylight, around 17:00. Poor 10DPG was absolutely filthy. As well as the dust and dirt of travel, and scores of greasy fingermarks, where touts had lounged against the car, we had had to go through a filthy looking spray for sanitation, which covered the whole car.

We were guided by the Rough Guide and stayed at the Siesta Inn in the centre of town and had an excellent dinner at the Paso Real overlooking the Parque. The rather alarming bill came to C28,680, but we were relieved to find that there are about 500 Colones to the $!

TOTAL MILEAGE: 14,930

On rereading I note we filled up in Managua. No record of mileage or fuel taken on! Say 13.5 US at 14,820

Geoffrey & Hilary Herdman

DAY: 132
13/12/10 — LAGO AND VOLCAN ARENAL We should have spent two nights at Lake Arenal in a very touristy tropical hotel, but with the delay getting into El Salvador it has turned out to be just one, and just as well. Per the original plan we would have been driving along very bad country roads for a couple of hours by dark. One probably feels safer in Costa Rica than anywhere else in Central America, but one's night vision is not what it used to be!

We are only 1,200 ft up but it is cool and we need a sweater. In the evening we have a very heavy shower, our first rain since California, and just after cleaning 10DPG. But the poor car did need and deserve it.

Whilst I slaved over poor 10DPG, H went for v expensive but interesting bird watching walk, which turned out to be a very private tour, with a group of one. As a result I had to pay not to go! Wonderful toucans so I understand. Remember the old Guinness advert about what "one or Toucan do"?

We are staying at Arenal Nayara, near Volcan Arenal, which is usually active. However it has been dormant now for six weeks and is wreathed in heavy cloud, so we would have been unaware of the fact even had it been smoking. H tells me that she was in fact able to see it for a little while on her walk.

The hotel is made up of a series of beautifully appointed chalets, complete with outside baths and showers and I think we are the only non Americans staying here.

TOTAL MILEAGE: 15,014

Roadside coatimundi approaching lake Arenal.

DAY: 133
14/12/10 — ARENAL TO QUEPOS The photo (overleaf) was taken at a humming bird garden at about 3,500 ft above sea level, above Arenal.

As we were checking out H idly perused the Guest Book to find the following entry: "We have had such a wonderful time here we are going to come back next year to make our first baby!" Pass the sick bag Alice!!

Costa Rica is unlike any of the other Central American countries. Everything is in English, as well as Spanish and frequently only the former, including countless unbelievable real estate opportunities. We have certainly passed from third world countries and for much of the time could be in Europe. Even the tap water is said to be "potabile". The first time since San Diego.

It is the most stable of the Central American countries and disbanded its army in 1948. At the moment there is a disputed border with Nicaragua, which does have an army, but I am sure they will resolve it. The President won the Nobel Peace Prize for ending the Nicaraguan civil war in 1988.

CENTRAL AMERICA

Having left Arenal we climb to 1,200 metres and near the top come to a large agricultural estate with a butterfly and humming bird garden; entry $2 each, but that's only for the humming birds. Mariposas (butterflies) are an extra 3 bucks, but we pass on that one.

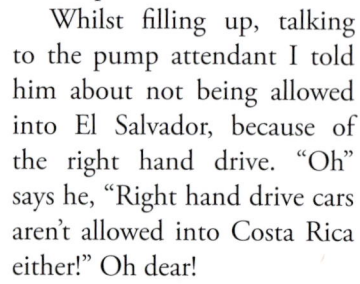

Whilst filling up, talking to the pump attendant I told him about not being allowed into El Salvador, because of the right hand drive. "Oh" says he, "Right hand drive cars aren't allowed into Costa Rica either!" Oh dear!

After a certain amount of discussion about the route in Esparza we take a pretty, but slow road to San Mateo and shortly afterwards join a brand new road which takes us to Quepos. This is on the Pacific Coast and grossly overdeveloped, including a "Gentlemans' Club". I was informed that I was busy that evening! The developments for the moment are low key affairs, but doubtless in a few years the place will be wall deep with condos.

We are staying at the Makanda hotel, down a small private road and with what should be spectacular sunset views, but almost as soon as we arrive so does the rain.

To cheer us up the food is quite extraordinarily good.

Filled up at 15,062 48.4 litres
TOTAL MILEAGE: 15,160

DAY: 134
15/12/10 LAST TRAIN TO SAN JOSÉ

Having been on the road with only one night in any one hotel for six nights we were very much looking forward to spending three nights on the Osa Peninsula. However no-one was really sure how long it would take to get there.

The UK travel agents said it was 60 ks from Quepos to Palmar Sur, our meeting place. The hotel in Arenal said it was 165 ks and our Costa Rican agents thought something in between.

Our instructions were to be at Palma Sur airport (see tomorrow's picture) by 10:00. Thus it was that we were en route by 07:30. It wasn't actually raining but very damp and cold and we kept the roof up. In the event we made the airport by 09:15, the distance being about 100 ks on pretty good roads.

In the middle of Palmar Sur we found this poor abandoned engine, and not far away the wreck of an old railway carriage. The gauge is 3′ 6″ and the railways

Geoffrey & Hilary Herdman

packed up in the late 60s or early 70s. I think they were mainly for the banana trade, but there was also a passenger service from Punta Arenas to San José.

Four more guests were flying in and eventually we all set off with us following their minivan to Sierpe, a small but attractive and undeveloped town on the banks of the Sierpe river. We parked 10DPG under a car port and transferred to an open boat with skimpy awning for the 2 hour transfer to Corcovado. The river is most impressive, but the clouds were ominous. We had a beautiful journey for about an hour down the river, including a side trip into the mangrove swamps, where we saw cayman, having seen an enormous crocodile on the bank of the main river. Once out to sea it started raining, and we all put on heavy duty ponchos. The rain became heavier and heavier. The boat had no side awnings and we were absolutely drenched. Then it started thundering. The journey was made slower as we had had to take another boat in tow, and by the time we arrived we were all soaked. It was also cold. The journey was enlivened by the tow rope snapping just as we were passing through a very narrow and rocky channel, with high surf; fortunately the other boat still had a little power, and managed to get through the rocks without disaster.

The bungalows are beautifully appointed, but everything was incredibly damp, not improved by continuous rain for the rest of the day. With dinner over by 21:00, I think we had the lights out by 21:45.

TOTAL MILEAGE: 15,246

CENTRAL AMERICA

DAY: 135
16/12/10   R&R ON THE OSA PENINSULA

The Osa Peninsula is the hook and bay in the South East corner of Costa Rica just to the West of Panama. The only place of any significance is Drake's Bay with a handful of tourist resorts. The peninsula is home to the Corcovado National Park, 100,000 acres of protected tropical rain forest. We are staying at the Corcovado Lodge, with fourteen cabins built in 1994 by a Chicago businessman. Ecotourism is an important part of Costa Rican culture and economy, and the lodge certainly makes every effort to comply.

We are up at 06:30, but having had the lights out pretty early last night this is not a problem. After breakfast we go for a 6 hour geriatric potter through the forest. Occasionally we see a blur in a tree, which with the eye of faith may be something interesting. Having been driving for six days, more or less non stop, it is good to have some gentle exercise. Even I see howler and spider monkeys, and a couple of brilliant red macaws. Some of us swam in a pool at the foot of a waterfall, very refreshing! The lodge had kindly lent us gumboots, and we now know the technique for fording rivers, namely to take off your socks, replace your boots, and empty them on the far side, resuming socks. It works surprisingly well; less squelchy than we expected. We also saw a large basilisk, and a sloth, very idle in a tree, where I think it had been for several days, making life easier for our excellent guide. "Three toes on either foot have I, and half a doz on both. Swinging gently upside down, its hard to be a sloth!" (With thanks to Flanders and Swann.)

But it's early dinner and early to bed. There are no communications with the outside world, so the blog is written, but unpublished.

The main terminal building / customs / air traffic control for Palmar Sur airport

Geoffrey & Hilary Herdman

DAY: 136
17/12/10 **MORE R&R AT CORCOVADO** We were woken at dawn by the sound of heavy rain, so G had a lightning change of plan, and decided to go no further than the lodge today. H however stuck to the 'programme', and was rewarded by a boat ride to Caño island. This is a marine reserve about 15 km out to sea, charted by Drake. She was escorted for part of the way by dolphins, and then some exhilarating snorkelling in deep Pacific waters, followed by a picnic lunch on a white sand beach. No rain!

In the afternoon we went for a walk on the beach back at the resort, and met our charming and hard-working host, who has created this place and its beautiful gardens over the past 16 years, having first dreamed of doing so when he came here on a gap year 35 years ago. We then staggered up the incredibly steep hill to the sunset bar for some reviving Margaritas.

Macaws at Corcovado

CENTRAL AMERICA

DAY: 137
18/12/10 **THE LAST FRONTIER** The first mosque we have seen in five months, bizarrely in the City of David! (pictured above)

Alarm at 06:00 and breakfast at 06:30, but as there is nothing to do in the evenings it has been lights out at 22:00, so this is really not too much of a hardship.

We wade to the boat. Stephen Lill, the owner of the resort, will not put in a jetty as it then becomes public, and will show from the sea. Once out to sea we can see nothing of the hotel or the owner's house. We set off at 07:00. We have half an hour at sea and then an hour motoring up the Sierpe river. It is most attractive and lined with mangroves. We are strongly reminded of the Kinabatangan river in Borneo. It is still the highway, and full of small craft en route to the market in Sierpe. We only saw one small crocodile this time!

Thanks to the electric fuel pump 10DPG starts instantly. Seventy miles and 2 hours later we arrive at the Costa Rica/Panama border, which is total mayhem. A huge sprawl of duty free shops, people milling everywhere, very hot, very dusty, with potholed roads, and every passing car and truck throwing up a huge cloud of dust over poor 10DPG.

Exiting Costa Rica takes an hour and a half. A friendly tout takes pity on us and guides us through the procedures for immigration to Panama. We actually wouldn't have managed without him, and he is entirely unavaricious, but the process of immigration takes 2 hours, including another disinfectant car wash. Having arrived at 11:15 it is 14:45 before we are finally on our way. The last frontier Yee Haaa!

David is only 40 minutes up the road. We then turn left for Boquete, a further 25 miles, and 3,500 ft above sea level. Unlike earlier climbs this one is dead straight and a gentle incline taken in 4th gear all the way. In David we pass the above mosque, part of the Panamanian/Arabic institute.

We find the hotel Panamonte by about 17:00. It is glorious. Being high up the climate is perfect. The hotel has been in the same family of Swedish coffee planters since 1914. The rooms are superb, the gardens lovely, the atmosphere relaxed and

Geoffrey & Hilary Herdman

welcoming and we eat extremely well. After the remote but expensive rigours of Corcovado it is a joy to be back in well appointed comfort. [Don't forget that everything has to be brought by sea to Corcovado, and we were really remarkably comfortable in what is effectively a luxurious campsite of extraordinary beauty in a very special place. ED.]

On arrival I wash the dust and disinfectant off 10DPG in huge gratitude. Our fellow guests are Americans and all the staff address us in "English." We answer in our execrable Spanish. We call this "Spingles", the Spanish equivalent of "Franglais". [G is being unduly modest about his rapidly improving Spanish; it's amazing what stress at a frontier can do! ED.]

Boquete is still a coffee growing town and every January they have a Festival of Flowers to celebrate the successful gathering-in of the coffee harvest. I regret to have to report that much drink is taken during the ten day Festival!

Filled up in David 15,345 miles 13.5 US gallons
TOTAL MILEAGE: 15,377

DAY: 138
19/12/10 BOQUETE TO PANAMA CITY

The photo opposite is of 10DPG approaching the bridge over the Panama Canal. As will be seen the weather is heavily overcast.

From Boquete to Ciudad de Panama is a shade under 300 miles. The hotel tells us we will do it in 6 hours. We leave Boquete at 10:15.

Until Santiago we are on single carriageway. Various cars flash us as we drive. We have had a lot of this and it usually means Hi, but just in case... and lo and behold we pass a couple of police radar guns with a shining conscience. We are also stopped by police checks a couple of times but are becoming quite blasé about them. They either want to know where we come from, and show gratifying astonishment, or how old the car is and ditto. "Muy linda" and "classico", come tripping off the tongues.

In Santiago we hit dual carriageway, but with a very poor road surface for the rest of the drive to Panama City. The weather is not looking too good and when we see cars coming the other way with headlights, we stop and put the top up – just in time – as the rain is soon so heavy we have to stop, as do most other cars for about 5 minutes, to let the worst pass over.

It has to be said that from David to Panama the drive is not particularly interesting. We see a few horsemen riding by the side of the dual carriageway, and one bullock cart but otherwise it is just a long drive. Panamanian driving is just as bad as anywhere else in Central America. They NEVER indicate, and usually stick in the outside lane at about 40 mph. Traffic merges into the fast lane of the dual carriageway, and U-turns are permitted.

The approach to the Canal causes a frisson of excitement. It is rather like driving up the West side of the Hudson and seeing the Empire State Building across the river bathed in evening sunlight. Sadly the weather was very overcast and so the picture is a bit gloomy.

Entering the city the whole place is absolutely lined with people. We are gratified, word has got about! but we soon discover that there is a huge Christmas parade and all the streets, especially where we are staying, are closed off. We resort to flagging down a taxi, who tells the police to move the barricade to one side as we wish to pass. Surprisingly the police comply and we arrive at the Hotel Bristol, downtown Panama, very very relieved for both ourselves and 10DPG.

We are staying in the Bristol for a whole nine nights – bliss!

This is really the end of Part 1, but as we have yet to finalize the onward shipping the diary will continue until 10DPG is safely en route for Buenos Aires.

TOTAL MILEAGE: 15,674

DAY: 139
20/12/10 PANAMA CITY

We are enormously taken by Panama City. There is building going on everywhere, and the skyline is of high rise office and apartment blocks, some very attractive. They are interspersed with old colonial style houses and gardens, presumably whose owners are holding out for a yet higher price for their real estate. But it makes for an attractive mix.

There are also hills and parks, and of course the Pacific Ocean bounding the Southern side. The old town, now called San Felipe, is full of character, and real estate very expensive. We meet a Brit who is about to become an expat and come and live here, so he can afford to send his precocious 11 year old to Eton. Every magazine extols the virtues of retiring to Panama. Personally we would probably choose Boquete, but the city is one of the most vibrant we have visited. Where we are staying is said to be completely safe to walk around at night, and like Costa Rica the tap water is drinkable more or less everywhere.

Most of the day is taken up with trying to sort out shipping. In 2006 the return fare for the cars UK – Buenos Aires – UK was a little over £2,500. We are now being quoted about $6,500 one way Panama to Buenos Aires, of which $1,700 is port handling fees in Buenos Aires. To add to the avariciousness we are told we can't leave any luggage in the car. As we have eight cases this is rather trying. I rather think the spare tyre, which is allowed, will find its way into the boot and the heaviest case into the bomb bay!

10DPG is currently due to go into the container this Friday.

Geoffrey & Hilary Herdman

DAY 139

Forecourt of the Bristol Hotel, Panama

CENTRAL AMERICA

Carless Days

DAYS: 144-181
25/12/10 - 31/01/11

PANAMA, SAILING, AND THE GALAPAGOS ISLANDS

After several days wrestling with notaries, and our bank, in order to complete elaborate paperwork and pay the agents, 10DPG was safely boxed and launched to Buenos Aires. We then had four weeks in Panama, and loved it.

Highlights:

- Christmas lunch in the restaurant beside the Canal, overlooking the Miraflores lock, with vast container and passenger ships passing within feet of the balcony; a really surreal sight.
- The coffee growing highlands near Boquete, one of the loveliest places we have seen.
- The romantic ruins of the sixteenth century Spanish fort at San Lorenzo, on the Caribbean side, built to protect the gold route.
- Ten days over New Year, sailing in a 34 ft Benetteau, in the San Blas islands; shallow and potentially treacherous Caribbean waters, with an alarming quantity of quite recent and visible wrecks. These semi-autonomous islands belong to the Kuna Yala people.
- Next, a week in the Galapagos islands; after the rigours of 34 ft, the seven cabined Samba (ex Dutch fishing boat) hot water, and a 3 ft shared bunk seemed luxurious!
- The abundance of unconcerned Iguanas and giant tortoises.
- A feeding frenzy of birds; hundreds of boobies diving at about 40 kph, before folding their wings at the last moment to plunge like arrows into the sea.
- We had a couple of nights in Quito, en route to Buenos Aires, and remember: The Equator Museum, where experiment proved the water really does run straight down through a plughole on the line, while swirling clockwise or anti-clockwise if moved one metre South or North respectively.
- The magnificent Spanish colonial architecture of the steep old city, set high in the Andes.

CARLESS PHOTOS OVERLEAF...

CENTRAL AMERICA

128 Geoffrey & Hilary Herdman

Carless Days

CENTRAL AMERICA

129

map is not drawn to scale, for illustrative purposes only
BOLIVIA
PARAGUAY
BRAZIL
ARGENTINA
Purmamarca
Salta
Amaicha
Catamarca
La Rioja
Cordoba
Mendoza
San Rafael
Buenos Aires
Neuquen
La Serena
Cerro Allegre
Santiago
Curico
Panguipulli
Puerto Montt
San Martin De Los Andes
San Carlos de Bariloche
El Calafate
N
ROUND THE WORLD WITH 10DPG

CHAPTER 3
South America

DAY: 182
01/02/11 REUNITED WITH 10DPG What a difference between 2006 and 2011.

In 2006 10 Bristol owners spent nearly three torrid days in the docks, wrestling with, and bribing customs to get their cars released. In 2011 our agent relieved me of the log book and passport yesterday, and having warned it could take up to four days for clearance, rang this morning to say we could have the car this afternoon if I cared to make my way down to his warehouse at about 16:00.

This was also the day when Anthony and Iris Spooner were arriving to join us for a couple of weeks and we had arranged to meet for lunch in the Brasserie Pétanque. It was lovely to see them and bless them they had brought me a new hub cap and inner tube!

Lunch was rather abstemious, and then off to the rendezvous. No sign of a container or 10DPG but we were assured they were on their way.

On arrival the container was precariously off loaded by forklift. Huge croppers were produced to break the seal, one end of which struck the cropper handler quite a blow on his forehead. He was very lucky it wasn't his eye. And there was a very grubby 10DPG. Not only grubby but the first sight – as I had backed in – was of the steering wheel covered in mildew, as was all the leather.

Embarrassingly we had a non start situation and had to be pushed out. The battery was fine but not a flicker of life from the engine. We tried pushing and eventually took a jump from the enormous battery on

Geoffrey & Hilary Herdman

the delivery truck. Even this took an awful long time. I wonder if the fuel, when it evaporates completely, leaves a sticky residue? Next time entering a container must remember to run engine until carburettor is drained!

Once started 10DPG ran like a bird and it was a lovely topless drive back to the Estacionamiento, just round the corner from our hotel. TomTom is quite good on Buenos Aires, and even the mildew just wiped off without leaving a trace.

DAY: 183
02/02/11   TIGRE AND ARGENTINIAN TRAINS

We had always planned to leave Buenos Aires on the 4th and were waiting for various pieces of paperwork to fall into place, so today was for sight seeing.

We took the train out to Tigre on the delta. The train was absolutely packed, stopped at every imaginable stop, rattled atrociously over rails probably laid by the British in the 1920s, and took an hour to do 20 miles. But the return fare cost 2.70 Pesos or about 45p. Having had a complete Nemesis in the early 1990s, Argentinian trains are on the up and more and more freight each year is very sensibly returning to the tracks.

Tigre and the delta were absolute gems. The little town had its heyday in the late 1890s/early 1900s, with Edward VII a visitor to the Tigre Club, now a museum. The architecture was reminiscent of Henley, on a larger scale, with some impressive rowing club buildings, sadly not affiliated to the RAC. We took a catamaran for an hour up the Sarmiento river passing by Summer houses for Porteños, all on stilts. There are no roads and everything has to be delivered by boat. Depending on the direction of the wind your land is liable to flood – hence the stilts. The delta is unsurprisingly a huge market garden. Being naturally fertilized with river silt must make for wonderful soil.

For the return trip we decided to take the Tren del Costa, which theoretically runs along the coast. However we missed our turning trying to find the station, and were picked up by a charming Argentinian, José, who walked us the 10 minutes to it, rattling away in Spanish the whole way, with us nodding wisely.

An excellent dinner in Puerto Madero with Anthony & Iris at Rodizio.

SOUTH AMERICA

DAY: 184

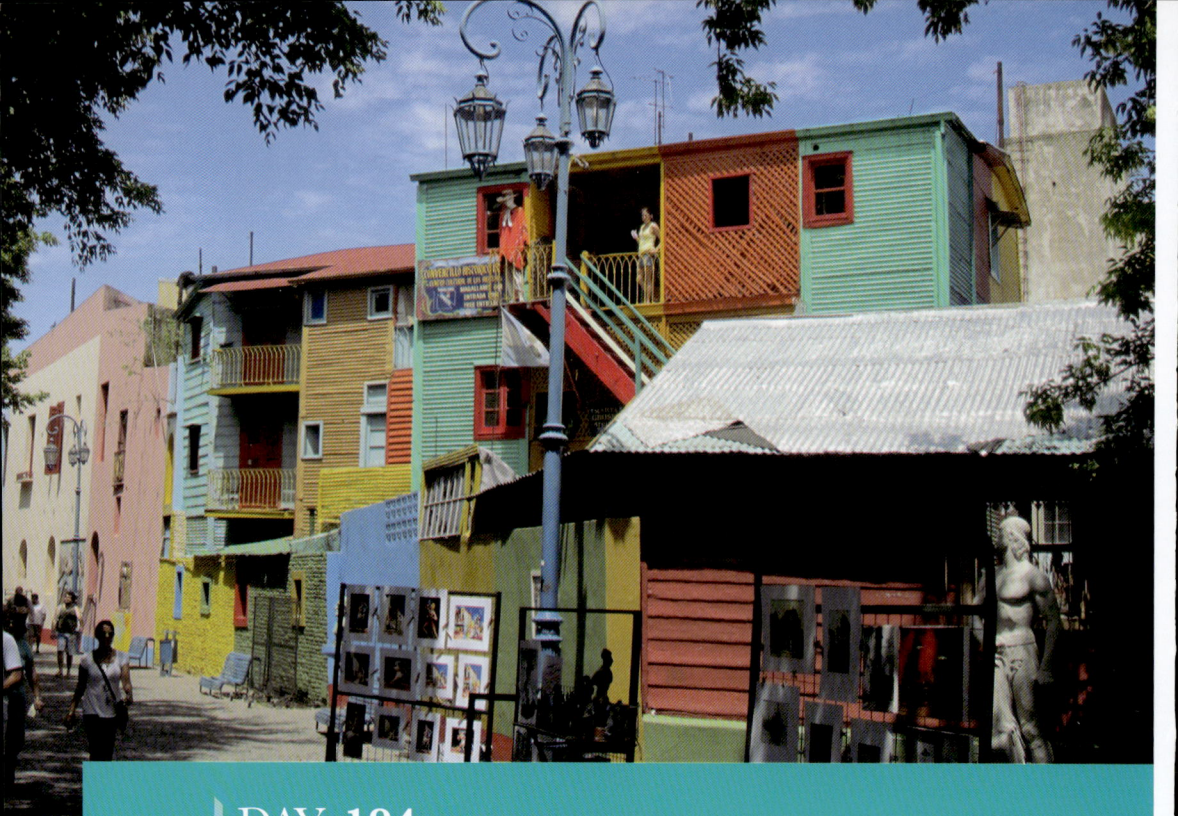

03/02/11 **ADMIN** The photo is of La Boca in Buenos Aires. I never tire of it!

The morning was spent collecting insurance, settling the usurious bills for transporting 10DPG, and trying to pay our travel agents. The latter involved poor H in a 2 hour marathon at the headquarters of HSBC, with the manager, assistant Manager and charming PA going to immense trouble to enable us to transfer not a huge amount of money from our HSBC account in the USA to our travel agent's HSBC account in that B A branch. American banking can be time consuming! But at least H is now very well informed on Argentinian exchange regulations.

PM: I asked the people in the estacionamiento where I could get the wheel repaired. Diligent readers may remember that in El Salvador we found the rim of the nearside back wheel to be sufficiently badly bent that it would not seal properly on a tubeless tyre and thus needed changing. Since El Salvador, more than 1,000 driving miles away, we have had no spare!

They sent me to a wonderful gomeria, who removed the tyre and straightened the bent wheel and told me that if I came back next Tuesday they could do a complete repair on the wheel, but even so it would be o.k. without the new inner tube. Fortunately they placed the tyre in a water bath and found that they did in fact need the tube and we now have a working spare – Hooray! Charge about US$10.

They in turn sent me to a car wash, where five boys set to with a will and 10DPG was cleaned and hoovered from top to bottom. As they had to move the car around and I had sloped off for a coffee I think most of the garage had had a go driving the eengleesh right hand drive car!

Anyway on my return 10DPG was looking immaculate. They also advertised that they did oil changes so I got them to check the level in the diff, which was fine. With five boys cleaning and taking about 40 minutes plus checking the oil the bill was 55 Pesos or about US$14.

As I was leaving, 10DPG ran out of petrol but one of the boys took my spare can and ran to the garage and back, before coming as passenger to guide me there. It was actually slightly alarming that I ran out of petrol as the car only took a total of just over 60 litres. Maybe the reserve is also playing up? Must remember to refill the spare can!

Excellent dinner again in Puerto Madero at Marcello. The busiest (and most expensive, but everything is relative!) restaurant we had been to. Dinner for four with propina (tip) came to 1,060 Pesos or just over £200.

TOTAL MILEAGE: 15,692
Filled up at 15,692 59 litres.

DAY: 185
04/02/11

TO CORDOBA A drive of 431 miles today and depending on whom you talked to it was going to take between 7 and 9 hours. Bang up to date maps showed dual carriageway under construction for large parts.

Anthony and Iris were staying in a different hotel, about 3 miles from ours and rather than trying to rendezvous at one or other hotel we each determined to leave at 09:00 and meet en route. In one case 09:00 actually meant 09:15 and apart from Simon (aka TomTom) having a problem with the Buenos Aires one way system we satisfactorily exited the city and were on our way.

If two separate cars are both using TomTom, then a quick phone call to establish how far each is at that point in time from the destination gives a precise indication of where they are relative to each other. And thus we did indeed meet up and we are indebted to Iris for the above photo.

SOUTH AMERICA

The road from B A to Cordoba is in fact now completed, and is dual carriageway all the way. It is by far the best road that H and I have driven, probably since Manitoba. We did have one superb stretch of near motorway en route to Guadalajara, but it was probably a fifth of the length of today's road. Even better – having paid a couple of tolls at the beginning they were still building the rest of the toll stations and thus not collecting any money, and the tolls we did pay were only a few Pesos.

The weather was hot and having started out topless by midday we were frying so put the hood up. Anthony told us it was about 30°C per their car.

The drive was chiefly notable for the vast amount of agriculture. Each field must have been 1,000 acres and they went on for the whole of the journey. The end of January in Argentina is of course the same as the end of July in the UK when crops are browning nicely. Here in Argentina everything was amazingly green. The pampas stretches for ever. It is a quite magnificent country.

Cordoba came up at around 18:30, but we had stopped for a primitive lunch and driver changes, so the driving time was probably around 8 hours.

We stayed in the Azur Real, bang in the centre of town, a beautifully converted couple of town houses. We asked where to eat to which the reply was "the hotel of course, but just in case we wanted something else there was Faustino's."

H and I went walk about and knocked off Cordoba in about an hour, and then had an excellent dinner in the aforementioned Faustino. It turned out to have been a wise move!

TOTAL MILEAGE: 16,123
Filled up at 16,012 53 litres. Super costs Pesos 4.60/litre. Also a litre of oil.

DAY: 186
05/02/11 HEADING NORTH TO CATAMARCA

Or San Fernando del Valle de Catamarca to give it its full title. Here in Argentina a double L is pronounced as a J so Valle becomes Vaje.

Bizarrely we had the complete opposite to yesterday. As soon as we left Cordoba we had to pay a toll for a road, which was neither dual carriageway nor completed. But having said which today's roads would be dead straight for mile after mile, although traffic was heavy for the first half of the journey, which apparently caused some anxious overtaking!

We stopped at a Jesuit Estancia at Jesus Maria – see photo opposite. It was gloriously sited on the old Camino Real but in what could easily have been an English park, walled and wonderfully green, with a willow tree, the smell of fresh mown grass and the distant sound of a mower. At one time the estancia had extended to 9,000 hectares and had produced the first wine from the New World to be drunk by the royal house of Spain. It had a feeling of great tranquillity, but of course had involved fantastically hard work. The reason for these estancias was that funds from Spain were cut off to the Jesuits in the late 17th C, so they set up estancias to fund their educational projects, in this case Cordoba University.

Shortly after Jesus Maria we turned off the 9, the main road North onto the 60,

Geoffrey & Hilary Herdman

passing huge salt flats. The drive, it has to be said, became slightly monotonous. At one stage the 60 makes a sharp left for Catamarca, whereas the continuing road to Tucuman becomes the 157. Once we had made the sharp left we had absolutely no traffic and could see the road as straight as a die for perhaps 10 miles ahead.

Slightly worryingly "Simon" did not agree with the Argentinian mapping and we found ourselves, according to Simon, completely off piste and scrabbling to get back. As the roads today were very straight and very obvious this was of no account but tomorrow it would matter!

Catamarca is the poorest province in Argentina, and its capital was no great shakes, but the Ameria hotel was wonderfully air conditioned – we had had 35°C today, and the top up most of the way to ward off the sun. In the evening H and I ended up in the main square, after a couple of false starts, for a Moroccan dinner!

TOTAL MILEAGE: 16,397
Tried to fill up but as they had no V Power put in 21 litres (100 Pesos) en route.

DAY: 187
06/02/11 HELPING THE FUZZ WITH THEIR ENQUIRIES
The original plan for today had been to stay at Tucuman, but Gaston, from our agents Aliwen, had second thoughts, on the grounds that Tucuman is rather a depressing place and unbearably hot, and so instead elected for the Estancia Las Carreras near Tafi del Valle. The address was K13 on the Ruta 325, but Kilometres13 from where?

The distance was not great, and it was 11 before we were on the road, with H travelling with Iris and Spoons coming with me. In glorious weather we set out topless and filled up in Catamarca, but then things deteriorated.

Neither of our TomToms had the first idea where we were, and although leaving Catamarca meant picking up the road by which we had come in, it was a slightly fraught process. The scenery however was wonderful with a spectacular ridge maybe 2,000 ft higher than we were to the East.

SOUTH AMERICA

We turned onto the 307. It was somewhere along here that we were pulled over by the police, who wanted to see my insurance. This accomplished they then wanted to know all about the car and pose with it. They were also completely relaxed about being photographed with me by Anthony.

It was shortly after this that the road became spectacular, very very twisty, climbing by a small rushing torrent, which plunged down for thousands of feet. The road surface was pretty well broken up. Hairpin after hairpin and much changing down into first on same. At one stage we stopped by a viewplatz and were much photographed including by an exceptionally pretty bikee in red leather, who posed at the driving wheel to her boyfriend's delight. We asked where was the estancia and she told us to turn off for El Mollar, but warned that the road was not paved. We continued climbing to over 7,500 ft with the road surface deteriorating by the minute. We had also had rain and were putting the top up and down.

El Mollar was no problem but where from there? Actually Anthony had worked it all out but we stopped and asked a couple of gypsy girls, both in their late teens and with two teeth between them – how sad. The road now became dirt, and then mud, and then very wet mud with the occasional stream pouring across it. Traction was not good!

And eventually to the Estancia, an oasis of peace and quiet and the manufacturer of a very good cheese; queso M. We were surrounded by cows being milked, and newly born calves, with clouds rolling in towards us, and still at over 7,000 ft. We felt we had arrived in Shangri La, in a secret and beautifully verdant valley, with brilliant red and blue flowers by the roadside, cattle of Channel Island stock grazing, and lots of horses. The cheese was delicious, and the farm claimed to be part of the National programme to eliminate both bovine TB and brucellosis. We had tea, with milk straight from the dairy, and a delicious dinner, which of course featured the homegrown cheese. A lovely place where we would happily have stayed for longer.

TOTAL MILEAGE: 16,551
Filled up in Catamarca 46 litres

DAY: 188
07/02/11   NORTH TO SALTA The photo is of the central courtyard of our Estancia at Las Carreras – ridiculously pretty. The address was K 13 R325, which meant 13 kilometres along the R 325 from Tafi del Valle, all of them dirt. We had also been warned that for the first part of our trip North from Tafi to Amaicha del Valle the road was unpaved, a distance of 56 ks. What they hadn't told us was that we also had to climb to just under 10,000 ft and the roads were VERY twisty! Poor 10DPG found the going hotmaking – ditto his driver!

On leaving Amaicha we had been told to look out for the ruins at Quilmes 21 ks north. Quilmes as well as being an Argentinian beer was a tribe living here, who quite unreasonably refused to be evangelicized, or enslaved by the Spanish – so were slaughtered instead. They left behind a most impressive stone settlement, built into the side of a hill – doubtless by slaves of their own – where some 3,000 people lived from the 11th C onwards. The site has been extensively restored, but is absolutely worth a visit.

From Amaicha onwards, although the road surface was good, every 3 or 4 miles there would be a gully with a fairly large stream running straight across. These are called badenas.

Approaching Cafayate we were into vineyard territory. The region is set to rival the more established Mendoza as the major wine producing area. On our return South we are staying at a wine lodge there for a night, and need to determine whether they deserve to succeed!

And then the scenery became seriously spectacular as we drove along a gorge surrounded on either side by huge cliffs of differing shades of red mud, with fantastic patterns, and names such as The Devil's Throat, and the Amphitheatre which has perfect acoustics. We were running late so had no time to stop, but on the return South we should be able to explore further.

We were booked into the Legado Mitico, a brand new hotel in a beautifully converted private house and all thought we had died and gone to heaven. Dinner was taken in a nearby elegant restaurant, served by a Uruguayan waitress. One of us had Llama. Gwynneth I hope you are not reading this! The same one of us narrowly missed eating cuy or guinea pig in Ecuador a couple of weeks back!

TOTAL MILEAGE: 16,753.
Filled up at 16,591 46 litres

DAY: 189
08/02/11   ARGENTINIAN RAILWAY ENGINE! Sightseeing in Salta, which is a lovely town. It is built on an absolute grid and for the most part there are no traffic lights at intersections, but it seems to work.

AM: H and I visited the standard tourist attractions and took the cable car up to a rather good look out.

PM: The excitement was too much for H but I visited the railway station, which is still in very good order. Sadly there are no regular trains other than the Tren a las nubes – Train to the clouds. This runs from March to November and climbs to 4,220 metres from a start of 1,200 metres without using rack and pinion. For purely useless information it consumes an average of 2 gallons per mile of diesel, hauling ten coaches. H and I very keen to return to Salta when 10DPG is being shipped to Oz and take the train. Apparently they have supplies of oxygen and even a doctor. More importantly they have a restaurant car. The return journey takes 15 hours and current price is Pesos 630 or US$160. Can't wait!

There used to be a regular service from B A on 3′ 6″ gauge, but that died with most of the other services in the early 90s. Most of the track and signals are still in place as apparently is one of the engines – see photo!

An excellent dinner with the Spoons being serenaded by guitar and drums. Alas the wine flew perhaps a little too freely!

DAY: 190
09/02/11 HUMAHUACA AND PURMAMARCA

We were booked into Purmamarca for the night, which is on the junction where the road to Chile branches off from the road to Bolivia, about 100 miles N of Salta.

There are two roads out of Salta and we opted for the 9, on which we had started out from B A, and which goes to the Bolivian border. Until La Caldera 20 miles N of Salta the road is excellent, climbing gently. North of La Caldera you are warned that it is sinuoso – twisty, and angosta – narrow for the next 30 ks and they aren't kidding. It is also absolutely gorgeous, with a very good surface but many places which are wide enough for one car only with a warning "Una por vez" or one at a time. We did manage one rather risky overtake but it is NOT recommended.

Having arrived at Purmamarca at about 13:30 we decided to head on up the valley to Humahuaca. The valley here is wide and we are following the Rio Grande all the way, with the remnants of the old railway line still beside us climbing all the while. The road surface is excellent and by the time we had reached our destination we were once again at 10,000 ft.

The town was larger than we had expected, laid out in a grid of cobbled streets with single storey adobe colonial houses, and a predominantly Indian population. It was quite different from anything we had seen so far, and flourishes in a remote and desolate area.

Despite its small size the simple and beautiful church has now been declared a cathedral and is the See for a huge area. Bells were ringing and fireworks exploding. We had an excellent lunch – one of us even having the "LL" word before touring downtown somewhat lightheaded from the altitude.

Returning South we stopped for a photo opportunity at the tropic of Capricorn. By the roadside a farmer was ploughing the bright red soil with his horse and free range pigs rooted in the verges.

Purmamarca is chiefly known for a fantastic rock formation towering over the village with seven different hues of red and purple. The town also seems to be quite a hippy hang out. It is on the main road to Chile and despite the pass being 4,480 metres there was a surprising amount of traffic, both tourist and commercial.

Filled up at 16,919 62.4 litres
TOTAL MILEAGE: 16,935

DAY: 191
10/02/11   THE AXE HEAD (see introductory page for photo)

The start of the run to the South. On the road at about 11:00 but with no great distance to go. Our goal was once again Salta, but to a new hotel – House of Jasmines – Relais et Chateau.

Setting out we were still at over 8,000 ft at Purmamarca and needed sweaters and scarves. On rejoining the main road we were pulled over by a rather attractive police lady. We had forgotten our headlights, which are obligatory in Argentina. That seen to, with profuse apologies, she cheerily waved us on.

H elected to return by the sinuous 9, which was just as gorgeous going South as North and as always seemed much shorter on the return. At one stage I pulled over to let two cars pass, only to find them stopped a couple of miles on, with cameras out waiting for us. Once again 10DPG posed prettily whilst we answered the usual

SOUTH AMERICA

questions. For some reason everyone wants to know not only what type of car but also what model!

Our hotel lay South West of Salta and driving on the very bumpy ring road I noted a YPF gas station which advertised servicing. 10DPG was in need of an oil change and we determined to return tomorrow.

The hotel was gorgeous – a mini estancia set in about 100 hectares. We needed to stretch our legs and so walked down to the river. Along the path I spotted what I could only imagine was a flint axe head. The land here is flat with a river and mountains in the distance and I imagined people must have lived here for centuries. The estancia also boasted an ancient dyke of sorts.

H kindly thought I needed a massage, which was delicious, but sadly I couldn't remember the Spanish for "Do you do extras!"

TOTAL MILEAGE: 17,010

DAY: 192
11/02/11 **TOBACCO COUNTRY** I took the poor manager, who was on his last legs with flu, to show him my axe head. Bless him he was quite excited and pocketed it.

We returned to Salta for an oil change. I asked the efficient mechanic to check the diff and he thought it could do with some oil but only sold 140SAE in 4 litre cans so we now have an abundance – handy for the one shot!

For the first 30 miles South of Salta the road is not in terribly good condition, rather bumpy and far too many traffic lights, presumably to make up for lack of same in Salta itself. However we are in tobacco country and it is harvest time. Ready for harvest the leaf looks pretty depressing – see photo – but we passed truck after truck of the stuff, not to mention drying and curing houses.

Nearer to Cafayate, or Cafajate as we say hereabouts, we returned to the glorious red soil and cliffs. We had thought we would stop for a photo opportunity and there in the same spot were Iris and Spoons. Their rentacar had sprung a hydraulic leak and so they had a new one, but the old one was to be repaired and driven down to them in Cafayate tomorrow. When they set off we were just about to follow when a small car pulled up in front of us with hazard lights going frantically and two largish Porteñas or ladies from Buenos Aires leant on either door of 10DPG and wanted to know our life history.

The red cliffs boast various named geological features e.g. The Devil's Throat, and The Amphitheatre. We had rushed past them en route North but determined to visit them on the way South. Having inspected The Devil's Throat we returned to find 10DPG surrounded by people having their photos taken and it was quite some time before we could escape.

And so to the Cafayate Wine Resort along 2 ks of unmade and very dusty road. Poor 10DPG was in urgent need of a clean and once again pulled some admirers. This time English, Paul Parsons and Tim Jackson-Stops. Paul was a quondam Bristol owner, 411 and Beaufighter, before children intervened.

The wine resort itself was gorgeous, very new and surrounded by vines, with hills and a waterfall in the distance.

TOTAL MILEAGE: 17,182
Filled up at 17,180 48 litres, oil change at 17.056

DAY: 193
12/02/11 DIRT ROADS, FORDS AND LONDRES

The plan had always been to drive to Mendoza, nearly 700 miles to the South in two days, if for no other reason than there appeared to be only one town of any size, La Rioja, en route.

A rather leisurely start after Tim and his wife had tried the driving position of 10DPG. He has a Porsche 356, which she describes as most uncomfortable and was complimentary about our seats. In fact I can, and have slept with the hood down! H does it all the time. Some retail therapy on the outskirts of Cafayate for some beautifully engraved wooden boxes and rather belatedly we were on the road by 11:15.

We were lulled into a sense of false security on our old friend the Route 40. This runs for over 5,000 ks from the North to the South of Argentina and is one of the longest roads in the world. Mrs H tells me she wants to drive the whole route – but not in 10DPG!

For the first few kilometres the surface was beautifully tarmacced but we were then diverted through Amaicha, as the road was being repaired. Sign posts ran out, the surface became worse, and we drove through endless small rather depressing villages, before rejoining the 40. Just before Los Nacimientos we saw the dreaded sign Fin de Pavimiento and we were on dirt road for 30 miles.

Not only were we on a dirt road but we were in Badenes country. Badenes are dips in the road across which streams or rivers run, what we would call fords. One of these must have been a couple of hundred yards wide. We saw a car

SOUTH AMERICA

parked at the beginning. Worse, a biker had made his bikee wade in her leathers and to our horror saw that she was up to her knees. But there was no other route, so 10DPG took the plunge and was given a thumbs up and big smile by the bikee as we climbed out.

Whenever we are asked – about five times a day – "de donde viene?" where do you come from? we have always answered Londres. It was somewhat of a surprise therefor to find ourselves actually driving through Londres, which looked to be a pretty town, but sadly involved the most massive pothole, which I hadn't seen, at the Plaza Mayor. Londres is in fact the second oldest city in Argentina and was named in honour of the marriage of Bloody Mary to Philip II of Spain.

And so to La Rioja and the Naindo Hotel for the evening.

TOTAL MILEAGE: 17,494

DAY: 194
13/02/11 BACK IN WINE COUNTRY

360 or more miles today and the whole team was actually on the road earlier than planned – just before 09:00. We were rather impressed!

La Rioja has the "enviable" reputation of being the hottest place in Argentina with temperatures regularly reaching 50°C. We were lucky at around 30°C but the countryside is more or less desert and very bleak.

At our lunch stop Spoons pointed out that my trafficators weren't working and I found that not one but both leads had come loose from the back of the timer. Rubbish workmanship – mine – back in Lenox! Anyway whilst they all had a rather dubious looking steak and eggs at an even more dubious Comedor, by a filling station I took the switch out and reconnected. Needless to say the wrong way round first time!

We tried to take the San Juan bypass, but both TomToms had completely given up by this stage and their mapping bore very little relationship to reality. At one stage the "short cut" disintegrated into a dirt road at which stage we beat a hasty retreat.

San Juan is the second most important wine growing area, about 100 miles North of Mendoza. Having rejoined the tarmac we found ourselves on gorgeous tree lined avenues with vines as far as the eye could see. Everything was a wonderful lush green. The bypass, successfully circumnavigated, we were back onto our old friend the 40 for an easy run down to Mendoza.

As in 2006, with the BOC tour, we were staying at the Park Hyatt, where famously Eva was courted by Juan Peron. It has the most perfect location on the Plaza Independencia and we were soon sitting outside with badly needed liquid refreshments.

TOTAL MILEAGE: 17,864
Filled up in La Rioja 61 litres 17,495 and took on 36 litres at 17,742.

DAY: 195
14/02/11   **CONCERNING THE EQUATOR** Valentine's day was spent sight seeing in Mendoza, so I thought I would put in a word or two about our trip to the Equator.

Whilst 10DPG was transitting from Panama to Buenos Aires, amongst other things we had a wonderful trip to the Galapagos. This involved a couple of nights in Quito, capital of Ecuador, both before and afterwards.

On our last day in Quito we took a taxi to El Mitad del Mundo or "The Equator", which is only about 20 miles from the old part of Quito. There is a small ethnographical museum as well of course as the Line itself – well marked and with various experiments.

The first was a basin with a plug hole. Two feet to the North of the line when water was poured into the basin it rotated anti clockwise when draining out. Two feet to the South it rotated clockwise. On the line it drained straight down.

Our guide then asked me to stand to one side of the line and place finger and thumb together in the Italian sign for a cuckold whilst she tried to pull them apart without success. On retrying the experiment absolutely on the Equator she had no trouble in prising them apart.

We then repeated the experiment with me intertwining the fingers of both hands whilst she tried to push my hands down. Two feet from the Equator she couldn't – on the Equator she did it with ease. Hilary and I then repeated both experiments with exactly the same results.

SOUTH AMERICA

DAY: 196
15/02/11 **MENDOZA STATION** The train on platform 2 has been delayed – indefinitely!

Spoons and Iris sadly left this morning at 07:30. We were NOT there to wave them off – pathetic – they had been very good company.

The main railway line out of Mendoza station ran down the middle of one of their busiest streets, Avenida Belgrano; gauge 5′ 6″. The signals are still all there, but when Menem privatised the railways in 1992 effectively the train service died. By the end of the second world war there were 30,000 miles of railtrack, now practically none working.

In Mendoza it has all been dug up and the Provincial Government proudly announces that it is introducing a light tramway called the Metrotransvia to run 12.5 ks along the old route. They also proudly proclaim that it will open in 2011. No chance!

In an earlier entry I suggested that rail freight was on the increase but a very knowledgeable Argentinian told me that the Truckers Union was massively powerful and would resist any such move. He also told me that there had been plans for a high speed rail link between B A and Cordoba but corruption had put paid to that. How sad!

In the evening we were recommended to try a seafood restaurant called Praga. When we found it we thought it was probably where we had eaten in 2005, with vaguely "cod" Picasso pictures. The next door table was occupied by French Canadians, but when I tried to talk to them the French came out as a hopeless mixture of French and Spanish and so we settled for English! This may have had something to do with the first Margarita for a long while! not to mention the bottle of wine thereafter!!

DAY: 197
16/02/11 **CAVAS WINE LODGE** The photo opposite is of Martin, the owner of the Cavas Wine Lodge.

The drive should have been about 30 miles – however in 2006 exiting Mendoza we managed everything correctly first time. In 2011, alas we went round and round in circles and a 30 mile drive became a 40 mile drive, but Boy was it worth it.

The Cavas Wine Lodge is probably the most expensive hotel we have ever stayed in, but also one of the nicest; Relais et Chateau with fourteen individual and rather strangely designed, but very sybaritic lodges. The evening view across the vineyard to the snowy Andes and the tiny clouds, golden in the sunset, left Mrs H almost dumbstruck. We struck especially lucky in that Wednesday was Tango night and we were treated to the best looking Tango dancer either of us had ever seen. One of the musical stays of Tango is the bandoneon, which is a type of button accordion, designed in Germany at the beginning of the 19th C for churches which couldn't afford a proper organ. It had come across with late 19th C immigrants to Argentina and its plaintive sound, nearly always in the minor key, is the backbone of Tango music.

The Wine Lodge only has 20 hectares of grapes and they are processed under contract and mainly used for house consumption. Dinner was a barbecue of outrageous proportions and we sensibly drank by the glass rather than the bottle!

TOTAL MILEAGE: 17,906

DAY 198

DAY: 198
17/02/11 **ARGENTINE ECONOMICS** The snow capped Andes floating above the trees on the ruta 40 from the Cavas Wine Lodge to Zapata.

A long chat with Martin, our host, at breakfast. His family are tea producers in Corrientes; Té Taragüi. At the height of the 2001 financial crisis his wife Cecilia and he bought 16 hectares of derelict vineyards and built a hotel, which opened in 2005. The hotel has fourteen rooms and forty seven staff! Martin freely admitted that if he increased the number of rooms to twenty he would only have to take on perhaps three extra housekeepers and could then afford to have a full

SOUTH AMERICA

time manager. Actually he and his wife were doing brilliantly and gave the hotel the personal touch which is one of its many fortes.

He told us that inflation was running at 25% in Argentina. We had seen reports of the IMF being worried about their rate but had no idea it was so bad. Cristina Kirchner has to restand for presidency this Autumn. He thought and hoped she wouldn't be re-elected but also said there was no credible opposition. The trouble is that the government is printing money.

I said I was interested in an apartment in B A as it seemed to be about one tenth of the price of flats in Marylebone. He thought Recoleta real estate was US$3,000 per square metre. In London it is £10,000 or five times as much. Actually, prices I have seen suggest less than $3,000. He thought that it was unlikely one could go wrong investing in B A. We do love the country – watch this space!! (We'll see, ED.)

We asked him about water management, as we understood the basic system of dykes was pre Columbian, from the Huerpes people. He confirmed that it was still working perfectly and was the mainstay of water for most of the Mendoza vineyards, coming from the Andes. Mendoza itself has over 500 ks of open ditches, between road and pavement, all with running fresh water. Not good for reaching a pavement with oncoming traffic in a tight skirt – so I am told!

We had planned today to go riding – for the first time in 2 years – but the weather was looking ominous in the mountains, so that was cancelled and instead I cleaned a deserving 10DPG.

Finally around 13:15 we set off for San Rafael about 130 miles to the South. The photo (previous page) doesn't do justice to the spectacular backdrop of the Andes, we were both in love! Up to Zapata ruta 40 is either dual carriageway or they are busy building it. As we drove the road was lined with weeping willows and poplars, with every kind of agricultural product growing behind.

South of Zapata we were in barren desert, but the weather has been strangely cool today. In 2006 from San Rafael to Neuquen, which is the route tomorrow, we were in the desert and a sand storm with temperatures around 100°F. Lets hope the cool weather continues for another day!!

Overnight in San Rafael.

TOTAL MILEAGE: 18,036
Filled up at 18,036 65.5 litres

DAY 199

DAY: 199
18/02/11 **SOUTH TO NEUQUEN** A long easy day's drive, 366 miles. Immediately on leaving the hotel H noticed a sign to the right for the 143. Simon was intent on going straight on, thus probably completing two sides of a triangle.

In 2006 we visited the Canon de Atuel – stunningly beautiful and miles of dirt roads – before flogging through the desert in 100°F and water temperature over 100°C. John Hamshere did suggest at the end of the day that I check the water level, which could have been quite a bit higher!

Today we started with rain and it was cool for the whole of the journey.

A stop in Santa Isabel for petrol – gas stations are few and far between in these parts! – followed about 80 miles North of Neuquen by the sight of nodding donkeys, or Vicunyas as they are called over here, before hitting the "fleshpots" of Neuquen.

We had been booked into the Casino Magic Hotel, which turned out to be very comfy with an excellent swimming pool. We had one of the best meals we had had in Argentina and chef justifiably did the tables. H wants to set him up in B A in his own restaurant! They even made a superb Margarita!

After dinner we wandered into the casino, which was frankly sad. Flashing, flashy lights in all directions; most of the usual casino ways of depriving punters of their money and seven hundred slot machines. About 90% of these were occupied by depressed looking people – but then they do live in Neuquen!

TOTAL MILEAGE: 18,402
Took on 27.4 litres in Santa Isabel

DAY: 200
19/02/11 **SAN MARTIN DE LOS ANDES** GPS navigators – don't you love them? Simon was convinced that we had but just over 200 miles to drive. All the signposts suggested differently. It transpired that Simon was going to take us on one gravel road that the map did acknowledge, and one that the map didn't, which would have meant swimming a river.

One of Neuquen's biggest industries is hydroelectricity. Despite the desert bleakness of the scenery we are also driving by huge artificial lakes of dazzling blueness.

In 2006 we drove due west to Zapala, at one stage stopping for a dinosaur museum. We were alarmed that the car didn't seem to be going very well but when we stopped we found the head wind was so strong we could only just open the doors. Very windy in Patagonia.

Today we took the diagonal along the 237 before heading North back up our friend the 40. And the wind was gentle by comparison.

San Martin is the playground for Buenos Aires, built around Lake Lacar. It could be Alpine, and many of the houses are wooden. In the evening we ate in Torino, as recommended by the hotel. It was packed and our waiter told us everyone else was from B A.

TOTAL MILEAGE: 18,665
Filled up outside Neuquen 18,428 40.7 litres

SOUTH AMERICA

DAY: 201
20/02/11 **10DPG PULLS AGAIN!** (see photo opposite). Actually today was a catching up and exercise day in San Martin. In the afternoon a pleasant walk of a couple of miles with a climb of 500 ft to a viewplatz overlooking Lake Lacar. Just before the entry to the mirador we passed into Mapuche territory and were dunned a very reasonable 2 Pesos each from some very cheerful locals. The track was incredibly dusty and the bath on our return looked like a sand pit!

DAY: 202
21/02/11 **INTO CHILE** When preparing the BOC Tour of Argentina I visited the Chilean consul in London, who told me that I couldn't take a right hand drive car into Chile. This, as it happened was a blessing as the original plan had been to drive from Mendoza across to Santiago. The frontier crossing is at 3,834 metres. Having been up to 3,100 metres several times now, I think that is quite enough to expect of poor 10DPG.

However now we needed to go into Chile, as the plan is to ship from Valparaiso to Adelaide at the end of March.

Time is a great healer and we had forgotten how bad, though beautiful, the road of the seven lakes is. For the first 20 miles out of San Martin we were lulled by excellent tarmac but then for the next 36 miles the road is unsealed, very dry with clouds of dust and very very bumpy. It took 3 hours to do the 56 miles to where we joined with the 231 from Bariloche. This was a total contrast, with a superb surface. They were actually starting to tarmac the road to San Martin but thus far have only done the first half mile.

The Argentinian and Chilean frontiers are 41 ks apart. In 2006 we did drive through the Argentinian frontier and across the border into Chile, which is at a lowly 1,340 metres. The Chilean frontier post, is still another 25 ks on, and we decided then not to tempt fate.

Geoffrey & Hilary Herdman

DAY 201

DAY 202

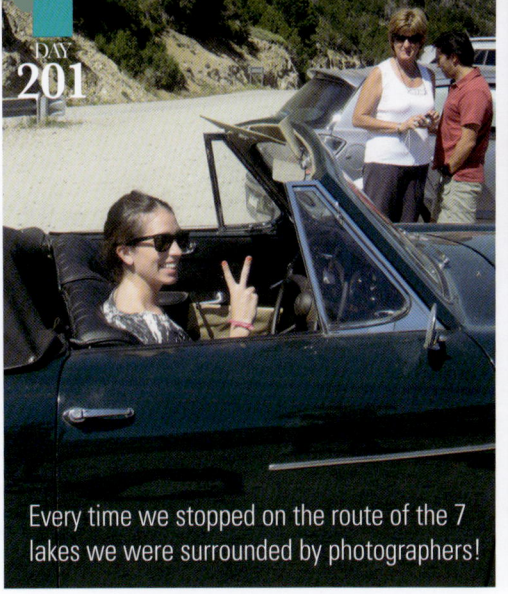

Every time we stopped on the route of the 7 lakes we were surrounded by photographers!

Today we were testing to see if we could cross over. There was quite a queue exiting Argentina and the now familiar procedure of clearing immigration and customs took the better part of an hour. At least the weather was perfect and we weren't surrounded by touts.

On breasting the peak between the two countries we descended into cloud and the temperature must have dropped by at least 15°F.

At the Chilean frontier we had three processes. Immigration, customs, and health and sanitation, of which the last was by far the most time consuming. A very efficient girl examined each of our eight suitcases in great detail; sniffer dogs were in attendance. Customs were in an inner office and never even looked at the car, but just handed out an entry permit with a little help from me explaining the DVLA certificate. And we were into Chile proper.

The first hotel along the route turned out to be the enormous and expensive Termas de Puyehue. However we were mollified to find that there would be a substantial reduction if we stayed two nights and then that everything was included – even wine at dinner. This proved to be a slight own goal. I have never tried wine smelling of tinned sardines before and we quickly upgraded!

The plan is to go back into Argentina in two days and repeat the exercise in a couple of weeks. Masochists, us?

Filled up in San Martin 18,666 miles 35.5 litres.
TOTAL MILEAGE: 18,774

DAY: 203
22/02/11 MODEL A (pictured overleaf). A day of R&R at the Puye Hue Resort and Spa. It is absolutely vast, full of families and all rather serious.

We managed our first game of table tennis in probably 30 years, which Mrs H won (just! ED.) and table football, which got us both very overexcited, (and G won convincingly.)

SOUTH AMERICA

DAY: 204
23/02/11

MODEL B 10DPG pulls yet again! at the border going back into Argentina. A very suitable travelling companion – but out of bounds!

We managed the Chilean frontier, for us, rather well. Whilst H queued for passport control I queued for customs. Having signed us out the customs lady realised that I had broken the rules and hadn't previously cleared passports. She was clearly about to give me a ticking off but with the language barrier thought better of it. All in all we were through in 30 minutes – something of a record.

For old time's sake we stopped for a photo opportunity at the actual border, 15 ks from one frontier control, 25 ks from the other. In 2006 we had the place to ourselves, apart from an itinerant 406 Zagato. In 2011 it was crowded, and 10DPG instantly acquired a coterie of photographers.

The Argentinian frontier was not such a success and took over an hour due to the amount of holiday makers returning home. However we were parked in front of a model A Ford and… another type of model!

The drive continued through Angostura and round the most gorgeous lake Nahuel Huapi. As we were heading some 15 miles to the South of Bariloche, along the Ruta 40, we bypassed the town itself.

The Peuma Hue turned out to be one of the great hotels. More like walking into a private party. Beautifully designed log cabins overlooking Lago Gutierrez. Communal drinks before dinner, and two dining tables with "mine host" Reuben presiding in the absence of his partner and owner Evelyn.

TOTAL MILEAGE: 18,910

Geoffrey & Hilary Herdman

DAY: 205
24/02/11   MODEL H

The perfect travelling companion!

The original plan had been to drive down to Ushuaya. This was then amended to driving to El Calafate. However by route 40 El C is over 800 miles from Bariloche and going via Commodoro Rivadavia, to keep on paved roads, over 1,000 miles each way. So we abandoned that for a more modest schedule of leaving 10DPG at Peuma Hue and flying down instead.

But first things first! A two hour ride through the grounds on a fabulously comfortable and responsive horse with Chris, who is universally known as the "horse whisperer". She has around ten horses in her charge, does all the shoeing herself and told us she had only needed the vet three times in 9 years and one of those was for a gelding! She talked to, listened to, and understood her horses and they instinctively knew what she wanted. We can think of a couple of race horses in the UK with whom we would like her to have a little chat!

The gardens are lovely; there is a long avenue of mountain ash, with brilliant red berries that would have seemed rather autumnal, but for a full midsummer of roses. We have seen the most beautiful rose gardens ever since Mendoza, often old fashioned ones with wonderful scent.

Then a visit to the airport as that seemed to be the only way of acquiring tickets for Aerolineas Argentinas. They told us there was no availability until 1 March, which suited us very well.

Next the bus station to buy tickets for Peter and Fran to go into Chile. This proved impossible as you cannot buy a ticket without an original passport showing you have validly entered Argentina, and they absolutely will not take reservations – even fully paid! Our new best friend instantly became the manageress of the rather good Italian restaurant at the train station, who said she had friends who would fix everything. All we had to do was turn up with P & F on 7th March and she would sort it all out. We will see.

Surprisingly there is still one train a week from Bariloche which goes some 500 miles across to Viedma on the Atlantic coast. It even has sleepers and a dining car. Subsequent reviews were a little mixed, but an idea is twinkling for a diversion during the 2012/13 trip!

Finally a ride on the Gondola to the top of Mount Otto at the back of Bariloche. Tickets were exorbitant at 100 Pesos, but being very old we had a reduction to 70. Incredibly there was not a breath of wind at the top and a clear blue sky. We watched with fascination a hang glider, possibly motorized,

SOUTH AMERICA

thermalling to a prodigious height, before flying to the far side of the lake and back again, and then make a perfect landing in his exact landing area. It must have been a flight of well over 40 minutes.

TOTAL MILEAGE: 18,974
Took on 42 litres at 18,944 not full.
And back to our gorgeous hotel.

DAY: 206
25/02/11   SOUTH TO ESQUEL
As we don't have photos from today here is one of a very rare occurrence, from yesterday!

Our agent had assured us we could confirm our flights on line, but it proved beyond me, so we started off by going back to the airport, 20 or so miles in the wrong direction. We were slightly gratified to find it took him a good 15 minutes!

Then South along the good old Ruta 40 for Esquel. In 2006 South of El Bolson we took the 71 along wonderful lake country and dirt roads, but today, as time was getting on, we stuck to the 40 all the way. One thing which has really surprised us has been the amount of traffic. In 2006 we were here in November, just before the holiday season. Now we are right at the end of it. In 2006, once South of Mendoza, we often wouldn't see another car for 15 or 20 minutes. Now it could be a real pain overtaking trucks as there was so much coming the other way, but everything is relative. The roads are not that crowded and the driving for the most part a joy.

Esquel is a strange town in the middle of nowhere with a population of nearly 30,000. Its streets are on an absolute grid and only the central ones are paved. We have no idea how the people support themselves economically.

We had booked into Las Bayas bang in the centre of town. On arrival the prop told us that they were having a Sushi evening, a first for Esquel and surprisingly the Herdmen too, but it turned out to be rather good. She had dressed the part and managed to fill the restaurant. The hotel itself was eight months old and very comfortable.

TOTAL MILEAGE: 19,176

DAY: 207
26/02/11

A NEW CAREER? The Old Patagonian Express or la Trochita (meaning narrow gauge) is a 75cm 2′ 6″ gauge railway, which when completed in 1947 ran 402 tortuous kilometres from Esquel to Ingenerio Jacobacci, where it connected with the main line to Bariloche. The journey was always slow and usually unreliable. As it was primarily meant as a goods train the advent of better roads and reliable trucking signed its death knell. However the provincial (Chubut) government took it over as a tourist attraction in the mid 90s.

Now trains run over two short sections. Ours was from Esquel to Nahuel Pan 19 ks up the track. One of the big problems is keeping the engines going. Having started with twenty two Henschels and Baldwins they are down to four, as the rest are cannibalised to keep the four going. The engines are oil fired, burning waste oil, which has to be preheated. They consume 20 litres of oil and 100 litres of water per kilometre. As reported earlier the modern Tren a las Nubes uses about 6 litres of diesel per kilometre, which apart from the difference in ages shows graphically the difference between internal and external combustion. But nothing can compete with the romance – or smell – of steam, and we had a wonderful trip. No smuts of course being oil fired. We had been allocated a 2nd Class carriage shock horror. The seats were wooden, as opposed to leather, and the wash basin, still in place but not working, zinc rather than china. Both classes still had their ceramic hole in the floor loos!

For the afternoon we took another trip down memory lane and drove to the infamous Hosteria Futalaufquen, which in 2006 had been run by a concentration camp Kommandant, who managed to lock poor H inside as we were leaving. It was built by Alexandro Bustillo, Argentina's most famous architect, on the shore of the Lake of the same name and has the three Ls of real estate. To our joy we found it had changed hands only 3 months previously and we promptly booked for the next night. Another revelation was the road, which in 2006 was dirt for most of the 35 miles from Esquel. Now only the last three were dirt and the rest brand new.

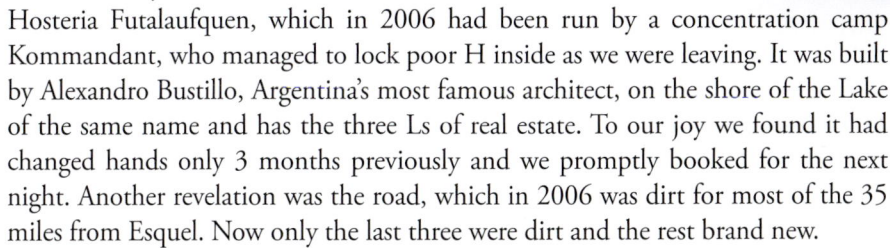

En route back to Esquel we had to change to reserve and were alarmed to find it working at best intermittently. There have been reports before of porous reserve supply tubes sucking air. A prominent member of the BOC's father and uncle supplied all those tubes to Smiths or was it Lucas? Fortunately we had a spare can, but must remember to claim on the warranty!

TOTAL MILEAGE: 19,240   Filled up at 19,240 68 litres

Petrol is cheaper in Patagonia. Pesos 3.90 against 4.90 elsewhere. In 2006 the respective figures were 1.30 and 1.60!

SOUTH AMERICA

DAY: 208
27/02/11   HOSTERIA FUTALAUFQUEN   The route of the lakes between San Martin de los Andes and Bariloche somehow gets the rave reviews, but for our money the lakes in the Parque Nacional de los Alerces knock spots off it. The photo is of one of them.

We had booked a 5 hour boat trip on Lake Menendez which meant 20 miles of dirt road. We rather underestimated how long that would take, not to mention the 20 minute walk to the jetty. In the event we left Esquel at 9:10 and reached our boat at 11:35. Bless them, it should have started at 11:30, but they had a full passenger list – impressive – and waited for us. Our destination was a walkway past a 2,600 year old Alerce tree, known as El Abuelo (the grandfather). These ancient trees look similar to the Californian redwood, and were almost lost through logging as they grow very slowly, to produce wood that is resistant to rot and insects. They have a flaking bark which provided ready-made shingles for the early settlers.

On arrival at our destination, which was actually the turning point for an out and back trip, the captain seemed to be having great difficulty parking. After an hour's walk about, we were alarmed on our return to see the crew stripped to their waists in the water, 4°C, manhandling the boat, but they got us back again successfully and we had to renegotiate the dirt road. Average speed 16 mph with clouds of dust.

In 2006 when we arrived at the Hosteria I was told by the manager that it was most inconvenient having us and they weren't ready. We had made the booking some months in advance so it wasn't as if they weren't warned. Dinner was fairly revolting, culminating in Angel Delight for pudding – and we were required to give the chef a round of applause. It was somewhat muted! There is only one entry for the hotel in Tripadvisor from an Argentinian in February 2010, who called it Estafa or swindle – so nothing much had changed by then.

As already mentioned the concessionaire has changed, but only in December 2010 and this time the staff were cheerful and the food excellent.

TOTAL MILEAGE: 19,308

Geoffrey & Hilary Herdman

DAY: 209
28/02/11

BUTCH CASSIDY When life became too hot in North America for Butch Cassidy, the Sundance Kid and his wife Etta Place, they fled to Patagonia in 1901 and bought a ranch just north of Cholila. For about 5 years they led peaceful lives farming, but by 1906 were on the run again. The Sundance Kid was probably shot dead in a bank robbery in Bolivia. Etta Place returned to the States for "appendicitis" or possibly because she was pregnant by a neighbour, whilst Butch Cassidy almost certainly died of rectal cancer under an assumed name in an old people's home in Washington State in 1937!

Anyway here is a photo of "Etta Place" outside the heavily restored Patagonian homestead.

We were back on unpaved roads for about 50 miles or 3 hours, to the junction with the 40. The dust to start with had been settled, partly by dew and partly by watering, but soon dried out and we once again had a trailing cloud. O.k. when on our own, as it was all behind us. Not much fun when being overtaken.

Just South of El Bolson we stopped for a spot of lunch in a superb mirador overlooking a very fertile valley and had the most delicious, locally produced, pure raspberry juice, for refreshments. Our host Dario told us it came from the valley. He was most interested in 10DPG and cleared up one little mystery; why everyone wanted to know "what model it was". In Argentinian "que modelo" usually means "what year". No wonder people looked blank when we told them 405!

Tonight we were going back to Peuma Hue. Rather vulgarly we had asked for, and been given a discount and somewhat to our surprise were upgraded to the best suite in the place, which was absolutely gorgeous. There must be a moral here!

The track up to the estancia is unpaved and after miles of pounding the gravel on the route 71 a final stone led to a strange tinkling sound. On examination we found one of our exhaust brackets, from Tapachula in Mexico, had given up the unequal struggle and was trailing along the road. With some handy wire the bracket was tied up out of harm's way, to be fixed by a local "taller des escapes" or exhaust shop at a later date.

TOTAL MILEAGE: 19,468
Filled up in El Bolson most northerly point for cheap petrol!

SOUTH AMERICA

DAY: 210
01/03/11   SOUTH TO EL CALAFATE   El Calafate is at latitude 50° South. London is at latitude 51° North. Our hotel, Los Notros, some 50 ks to the West of El C, overlooks the Perito Moreno glacier, which is 20 miles in length and one of the few glaciers in the world not retreating. The front floats in the Lago Argentina, the largest lake in the country. Huge chunks crash spectacularly and noisily into the water as we watch. It has taken them about 500 years from formation to dissolution. The ice we are seeing is pre Hispanic – just.

10DPG has been abandoned, as we have run out of time.

One of us had considered taking the bus from Bariloche to El C but it is a trip of about 30 hours, albeit in de luxe Pullman seats, but there was a distinct whinny from the other half. The plane takes 1 hour 25 minutes and was only 25 minutes late. Apparently something of a triumph for Aerolineas Argentinas.

DAY: 211
02/03/11   EAT YOUR HEART OUT FERRAGAMO   The latest must have footwear, but brilliant for walking on glaciers. An hour's trekking culminated in rounding a corner to find a table laid out with glasses and bottles of Famous Grouse. Our guide hacked off pieces of the glacier to add to it. Scotch never tasted better!

Geoffrey & Hilary Herdman

DAY: 212
03/03/11 ESTANCIA CHRISTINA

In 1914 a Scotsman, Percival Masters, with his wife and young children, having worked their way round various sheep estancias, settled near the Upsala glacier, next one along from Perito Merino, on a holding of 12,000 acres. The Argentinian government gave him a lease with the proviso that after 30 years they would give him the freehold. After 25 years his land was incorporated into the new national park so he lost out, but was allowed to stay there for the rest of his and his heirs' lives.

In the early 20th C sheep underpinned Argentina's wealth and he was a workaholic. More or less single handed he built his own homestead with attractive garden and water supply from a curious but effective water wheel. In his late 60s he built a 60 ft cargo boat, and lived to be 99. But everyone in Patagonia seems to live to a ripe old age. The cynic might think that with the climate it seems even longer!

[We had lovely weather. ED.]

The estancia has now, like most others, been turned over to tourism under government control – his son having died without issue. It is in a wonderful setting and only accessible by boat. We had a glorious cruise past the Upsala glacier and its spectacularly blue icebergs.

For one photo opportunity I had to lean out of the window and the wind whipped the sacred hat away, much to the relief of someone who shall be nameless. It has to be said it is getting a little on the manky side, but there is a God and it blew back onto the stern where it was caught by a kind passenger!

SOUTH AMERICA

DAY: 213
04/03/11 — **R&R IN LOS NOTROS** Whilst H went riding I opted out for the day. However in the evening we walked to the balconies overlooking the Perito Moreno glacier about 7 ks away from the hotel. There must be 3 to 4 miles of beautifully constructed and recently finished passerelles and we climbed several hundred steps. It costs 100 Pesos ($25) to enter the national park but certainly the money has been put to good use here. To give better access the roadway from El C has now been paved all the way to the glacier.

DAY: 214
05/03/11 — **FISH WEIGHT** Time to go back to Bariloche. However, as the plane was not due to leave until the evening one was dragged, hardly kicking at all, back to the estancia where H had ridden yesterday.

My horse was called Dos Coppas (two glasses). One of us thought this rather appropriate! We rode for about 10 ks across the estancia in glorious weather, not a cloud in the sky and even rarer for Patagonia, no wind. Estevan, our host, told us that the Indian people had lived here for thousands of years and picked up a stone with a groove around its middle, which he swore was at least 10,000 years old and used as a weight for holding down fish nets.

Under the shade of some poplars we dismounted and Estevan produced home grown steak and buns, and even beer from his saddle bag. Having kindled a small fire he then produced a frying pan. Steak never tasted better and we lingered rather longer than time allowed over this magnificent repast, which meant a fairly quick return. It certainly shook down lunch!

Aerolineas Argentinas now lived up to their reputation and I think we were 1½ hours late, arriving back at Peuma Hue at 23:00, but bless them there was an excellent cold collation waiting for us. This time we were staying in one of the chalets.

Geoffrey & Hilary Herdman

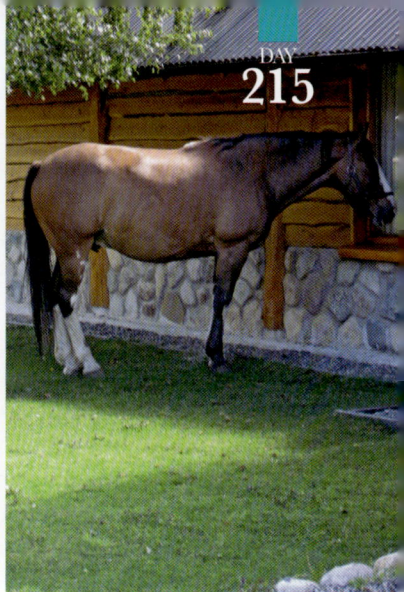

DAY: 215
06/03/11   BARILOCHE   We woke to the wonderful sound of munching! and on looking out of the window found we were surrounded by horses, one with nose up against the window. Evelyn the owner once found one of them in her living room.

In the afternoon a trip into Bariloche. Despite it being Sunday there was a lavanderia operating. Hotel laundries the world over are grossly overpriced, so this was exciting!! How sad is that?

Bariloche, or San Carlos de Bariloche to give it its full title, is well situated on Lake Nahuel Huapi. It is the largest Andean ski resort, has a population of 150,000, and is a total dump. Most of the central streets are still dirt roads, and the architecture is universally depressing. We headed for Cerro Catedral, which is the main skiing area. There is a hugely impressive array of ski lifts, of which the gondola and one chair lift were working, allowing us with not too much effort to climb almost to the top. Inadequate shoes and a slight uneasiness at heights by one of us, prevented the last 100 metres or so.

Seen on a brilliant blue Summer's day the buildings of the ski resort have taken their style from Bariloche and were frankly underwhelming, but the ski slopes did look fantastic and the views astounding.

TOTAL MILEAGE: 19,518

DAY: 216
07/03/11   PETE AND FRAN ARRIVE   The plan had been to take 10DPG in to an exhaust shop, BUT as Wednesday is Ash Wednesday, Monday and Tuesday are Carnival and nothing was open. Gonzalo, the estate mechanic said he would see what he could do.

At 10:00 I headed over to his workshop where he had a pit! albeit with very rickety ladder and no light, but the well equipped 405 Drophead comes with a

SOUTH AMERICA

large maglite. He foolishly asked if there was anything else I would like done, and kindly checked the oil in the diff, and most importantly, cleaned the air filters which were last done about 12,500 miles ago in Canada.

Gonzalo did a superb welding job on the exhaust and was suitably impressed with the amount of filth which came out of the K & Ns. It was with the greatest difficulty that I was able to press any cash on him.

Pete and Fran, like the Spooners, 405 Drophead owners, were due in at 18.25 from Buenos Aires but flying LAN Chile. At 18:25 the plane touched down and in perfect weather. Whilst H was riding up and down near vertical cliffs, on impossibly narrow tracks, with astounding views of the lakes from the summit, we drove back to Peuma Hue. Having company we hope will save the marriage for another two weeks!

The wonderful "horse whisperer", when the summit was reached, told H to go and look at the view, while she "prepared the horses for the descent." This turned out to involve verbal instructions and encouragement, before setting off, with the horses virtually sitting on their bottoms as they slithered down. H thought best not to interfere with any decision on the route taken!

TOTAL MILEAGE: 19,575

DAY: 217
08/03/11

BACK INTO CHILE Pete and Fran were booked onto the 14:30 bus from Bariloche. As we had no idea how long customs etc. would take – let alone if we would be allowed into Chile – we set out at midday under clear blue skies.

We stopped in Villa Angostura for petrol. On a sunny day nestling on the side of the lake it looked most attractive. I had naively thought that this was where the bitters came from but it is a very common place name in Spanish meaning narrows, the equivalent of the French Detroit, although there is only one of them!

And so on to the Argentinian frontier. There was absolutely no-one around and we were through both immigration or should that be emigration? and customs in 10 minutes.

The border control is at 800 metres and the distance to the actual boundary between Argentina and Chile, which is at the high point of 1,320 metres, 10 miles further on. Two weeks ago as we started the climb we could see cloud ahead and then fog and rain. Today the weather stayed perfect – a cloudless blue sky.

Another 13 miles from the boundary and we were at the Chilean frontier. Again there was no-one here – hardly surprising if there was no-one at the previous one! This time clearance took 15 minutes and only because they wanted to examine all the cases in the boot to ensure we weren't importing fruit, seeds or flowers. Despite a distinct bulge under the tonneau all our cases on the back seat were ignored! and we were back in Chile.

The countryside is very different from Argentina; very green and European with much smaller fields, often tree lined. Were it not for the distant snow capped volcano we could have been anywhere in Germany or Switzerland, which is probably because so many of the Chilean population originated from there.

The route was turn left in Osorno and keep going – easy. Well it should have been but we managed to drive straight over the Panamerica, which is an enormous dual carriageway, and had to do some interesting navigating in Osorno. Once reunited with the road we were amazed to find it was motorway all the way to Puerto Montt and paying at that. We had no Chilean Pesos and credit cards were not accepted. Most fortunately H had her last US$20 and all was well.

Puerto Montt is not the sort of place to go for a holiday but it is the capital of Chilean fishing, which in 2003 was worth over US$1 billion. We ate very adequately in the Yacht Club, which isn't a club at all, but most attractively built on stilts over the sea.

Pete and Fran had a very different experience at the frontiers. Despite there being a manifest of all the passengers with passport numbers, clearance at each frontier took the better part of an hour.

Filled up in Villa Angostura 19,644 miles 54.7 litres.
TOTAL MILEAGE: 19,818

DAY: 218
09/03/11   CHILOE A trip to Puerto Monnt airport for Peter to pick up his rentacar. The airport was finished a year ago and is splendid. However there were eleven flight departures listed for the day, of which nine were to Santiago. It will be a long time before it recovers its costs!

Having retrieved the girls we set out for Chiloe.

Chiloe is the second largest island in S America after Tierra del Fuego. The Panamerica runs down through it and

SOUTH AMERICA

terminates in the South at Quellon, rather than going down the mainland.

For the Chile part of the Tour we are using a travel agency called Chile Protours. Carolina, the rep, rings us every day to see how we are getting on and give us advice on what to do – what service! Today it was a diversion to Ancud to see the penultimate fort built by the Spanish in S America and a spot of lunch in a recommended restaurant.

What is going on? We don't do lunch – and we certainly don't drink during the day. We put it down to Pete and Fran's influence!! They thought it was the other way round.

After lunch a diversion to Dalcahue. We had planned to take the ferry to Isla Quinchao but time forbad. However the wooden church, one of the sixteen Chiloean churches designated by UNESCO, was outstanding.

Our destination was Castro and the hotel, Palafito 1326. A palafito is a fisherman's house built on stilts over the water, at high tide, and the mud at low tide. Many of the houses were destroyed in the 1960 earthquake, but those that remain, formerly slums, are rapidly becoming gentrified. Ours had been beautifully rebuilt on the site of two old disintegrating houses, and we had gorgeous views over the bay. The Spanish did colonize Castro but found the harbour to be insecure and the town has had a torrid history of fire, earthquakes, not to mention being sacked twice by the Dutch, when the men were killed and the women sold into slavery. I wonder if that would have been the case if it had been the other way round!

An excellent dinner at Mary's restaurant, complete with piano accordion accompaniment. It was absolutely packed.

TOTAL MILEAGE: 19,948

DAY: 219
10/03/11

IT'S CHILLY IN CHILE – WET TOO! Today we clocked up 20,000 miles since leaving Miami in July last year. What a great car in which to do them.

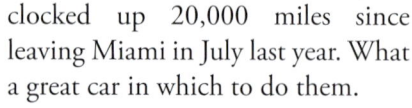

Weather cold and wet as we do the sights of Chiloe. The photo is of the port captain's offices at Chonchi. Surely one of the more beautiful places in which to work.

We attempted a walk in the Parque Nacional but rain set in and so yet again had lunch. This has to stop! At least we kept off the sauce!

After lunch to Chonchi, probably the prettiest town in Chiloe, where we took the ferry across to Lemuy

Geoffrey & Hilary Herdman

island and were delighted to find the road for the first 5 ks tarmaced. The countryside is SO English – apart from the wooden houses and churches. The weather too! We happened upon a curious retreat set up by an engineer who had dropped out of the Santiago rat race at the age of 52 and had set up an ecological walk through his grounds. This involved a precarious rope bridge spanning about 100 metres and definitely for one at a time only, not to mention a couple of collapsing planks on other bridges. The object was to view some rather good cascades. This meant squeezing through overgrown bamboo tunnels and passing magnificent displays of fuchsia. Our host enjoined us to have tea on our return, as there was much more that he wanted to show us. Perhaps fortunately he wasn't around, but as we walked back up the dirt road to 10DPG we heard distant hollering, which I am afraid we ignored.

Dinner in Castro at Octavio's, a most splendid wooden building.

TOTAL MILEAGE: 20,035

DAY: 220
11/03/11   **THE BLOGGIST!** At breakfast we met the delightful José Antonio, another guest, who told us he was heading up to a hotel he owned at Frutilla, near our destination. We invited ourselves for drinks in the evening and he was too polite to refuse. He was there to inspect a salmon farm, which he uses to produce very special salmon to export to Tokyo for sushi in the best restaurants. His story of how he has carefully and patiently built up this trade, and the extreme quality control that is required, coupled with the loyalty of his customers once they were convinced that his product was produced to their required standard of perfection, was fascinating and instructive.

The plan was to go and see a penguin reserve before crossing back to the mainland, but reports started coming in of the terrible earthquake in Japan, and the subsequent Tsunami. Our faithful agent was on the phone and assured us that the wave was not due to reach us before midnight.

We therefore headed off for the reserve about 20 miles beyond Ancud. First however we stopped in downtown Castro for some shopping. I stayed with 10DPG and was besieged by photographers, including one Chileno who said "Ah Bristol made by the Bristol Aeroplane Company after the second world war". I was seriously impressed and we shook hands.

Having seen a penguin before I opted to bring the blog up to date in

SOUTH AMERICA

a splendid caff overlooking the sea. The others however were soon back. All boats were cancelled, as a precaution. However, they had been able to see some from the shore. Another lunch, but this time very light, and then we thought we ought to head for the ferry quam celerimae. Fortunately it was running normally and we were soon motoring up to Puerto Varas on the shores of Lake Llanquihue, the third largest lake in South America.

On arrival we crossed the road to the offices of Protours where we met Carolina, our delightful agent. She told us that Puerto Montt, being by the sea, was evacuating the whole of the shore area. Our hotel there had been just over the road so we would presumably have been homeless had we been staying there tonight.

To complete the day's entertainment we drove out to José's hotel, on the side of the lake. It was almost opposite a brand new theatre, built over the lake, which had been bequeathed by a German national for whom Chile had been good, and was according to José even more beautiful inside than out. Sadly there was nothing on for a week.

We declined dinner but then found we were being plied with vast quantities of salmon, wine and postres, and in fact had the most wonderful hospitality. José most unwisely gave us his address in Santiago!

Filled up in Puerto Varas 20,170 62 litres
TOTAL MILEAGE: 20,171

DAY: 221
12/03/11 THE TAJ MAHAL OF VOLCANOES

Volcan Osorno, just round the lake from where we are staying is apparently known as the above, due to its almost perfect conical, snow capped shape. It was one of the most active volcanoes in S America with eleven eruptions between 1500 and 1869, the last thus far. Despite this there is an excellent road up it to a ski resort. Skiing is possible from July to December.

You can take a 7 hour hike, but we climb into Pete's rented Yaris and drive to the

Geoffrey & Hilary Herdman

resort where, quite exhausted from the drive, we have refreshing hot chocolates et al.

We then drive to Petrohue, where we had considered staying, but are very thankful we didn't as the road is awful, although they are working on it. The Yaris copes manfully but 10DPG would not have been happy.

And finally back to Puerto Varas for some excellent tea. We are even able to sit outside. There is a semblance of sun, sadly a rarity these past few days. Mrs H and I go for a geriatric stroll and I become very overexcited at the sight of a railway track, 5′ 6″ gauge, still clearly in use, but the receptionist in the hotel tells me that from Temuco to Puerto Montt it is for freight only.

DAY: 222
13/03/11   TO VALDIVIA

The photo is of Puerto Varas church. In the mid 19th C the Chilean government encouraged German people to come and settle in this part of Chile and both Lake Llanquihue and Valdivia were to become the homes of people on the wrong side of the 1848 upheaval. Everywhere one goes signs are still in German and the local beer, Kuntsmann's, from Valdivia, was at the end of the 19th C the largest brewery in S America. Puerto Varas was founded in 1854 and the church is clearly of German design.

But first things first. Peter was woken at 02:00 to be told that someone had smashed the window of his car. Outside he found four cops looking on bemusedly and wisely went back to bed. Apart from his dark glasses there was nothing inside, and they were still there. After breakfast a trip to the police station to make a report, followed by a drive to Puerto Montt airport for a car exchange. He was rewarded with a Chevrolet Corsa, which was in an even sorrier state than his clapped out Yaris!

And so to Valdivia, where in 1820 the admirable Lord Cochrane, by now in charge of the independent Chilean navy, surprised and sacked the strongly held Spanish fort, causing the Spanish to retreat to Chiloe. Cochrane was one of the models for both Hornblower and Jack Aubrey of O'Brien fame.

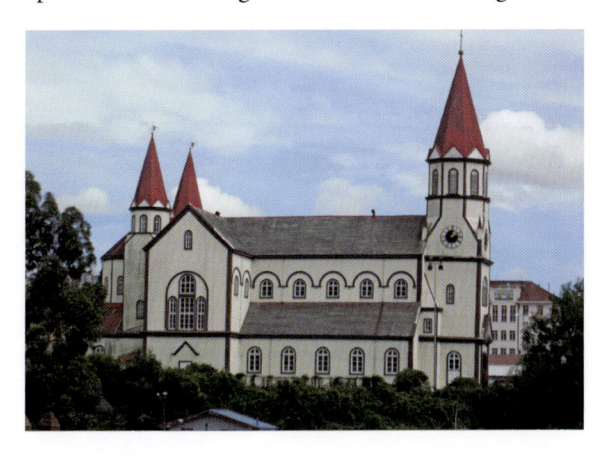

We were staying in a rather curious hotel called the Melillanca. H & I walked to Teja island, home to most of the German settlers and also the aforementioned brewery. Here we toured a quite excellent small museum, the 19th C home of the original brewers, which even had a "Cochrane Room" downstairs, and a Mapuche museum with some interesting silver upstairs.

TOTAL MILEAGE: 20,321

SOUTH AMERICA

DAY: 223
14/03/11   HUILO-HUILO   The photo doesn't do justice to the most extraordinary hotel at Huilo-Huilo. Apparently built entirely of wood, the main accommodation block is cylindrical and access to the bedrooms is by a spiral walkway. As the hotel has the equivalent of eleven floors a couple of quick trips up and down the spiral has one puffing!

There is a secondary building called the magic mountain, which is in the form of a moss covered wooden cone with windows peeping out and a waterfall cascading down its sides.

Lunch was in the attractive town of Panguipulli. We are in timber country where in the early 20th C timber was hauled out by traction engine to a branch railway line. It seems that most of the traction engines are still around as we see them all over the place in various conditions of rust.

Our last 10 miles or so approaching the hotel were on very bad gravel road, but for the most part the roads have been excellent.

TOTAL MILEAGE: 20,408

Geoffrey & Hilary Herdman

DAY: 224
15/03/11

EIGHT MEN AND A DOG

On our return from the Huilo-Huilo waterfall there is a request from the park ranger to take a photo of, and then to be photoed in the car! Shurely shome mishtake here. Not nearly as good looking as the usual clientele! The keen eyed will note that the bomb bay door has lost its securing catch, somewhere on a rock. I do have a spare but lacking WD40 am finding it quite impossible to remove one of the screws holding the broken one in place. Engine oil is not doing the business. (We continue to be amazed at 10DPG's capacity for meeting new friends and admirers. ED.)

Today we are driving to the Monte Verde hotel on the South shore of lake Villarica near Pucon – no great distance. BUT having driven back up the nearly 10 miles of gravel from our hotel, a little later we come to another 15 miles of unpaved road. We pass an impressive hydro setup, and at last reach Conaripe at the end of the gravel, where we stop for petrol. Conaripe it has to be said is a one horse town, but with a fairly major road passing through. Immediately after filling up we find a large labrador fast asleep in the middle of the road. He looks up at us but doesn't move. Actually this is unusual. Chile seems to have a massive dog population, certainly compared to Argentina, and they are mostly car chasers. Soft hearted Brits drive slowly to avoid causing canine distress – not to mention Bristol distress. Chileans drive faster. We have seen quite a few dead dogs!

A little further along the street we find a farmer, also in the middle of the road, leading his cow home.

On our visit to Chile in 2005 we stayed at the Villarica Lake Park Hotel, a vast thermal spa on the edge of the lake, run with teutonic efficiency. We stop for tea and find the management is now French and of a much gentler disposition.

Tonight's destination is set in a lovely garden at the Monte Verde and we dine locally in Pucon.

Filled up in Conaripe 55.7 litres 20,456 miles
TOTAL MILEAGE: 20,508

SOUTH AMERICA

DAY: 225
16/03/11

VOLCAN VILLARICA – SMOKING! Not quite sure why Volcan Osorno is the Taj Mahal of volcanoes. Admittedly my photo has some cloud round the top, but you really can't beat Villarica (see photo – and as featured on the cover) which is smoking and looking utterly gorgeous.

At last the weather is perking up and today we are heading North, where it is always better (or at least in Chile). We set out for the volcano and, as will be seen have 9 ks up, and 9 ks down – curious that – of gravel road. The sky is more or less cloudless and the road stops at the main ski resort at 1,360 metres; low by European standards. Today there must be twenty empty buses waiting for intrepid mountaineers, who need gas masks as well as all the other paraphernalia for the 7 hour climb. The view over Lake Villarica is superb with other volcanoes in the distance.

Our schedule tells us that our drive is about 387 ks, mostly up the PanAmerica or ruta 5. I was once told that the trouble with the PanAmerica in Chile is that although Chile is a narrow country, the road runs down the middle, so instead of seeing either the sea or the Andes you see truck after truck. Ruta 5 is now motorway, certainly all the way from Santiago to Puerto Montt, and paying at that. The four tolls in about 200 miles cost 7,800 Pesos or £10.

Today we are in luck and the snow clad peaks of the Andes are spectacularly visible to our right. At times we can see five different peaks. It seems we were also quite lucky with the trucks, although being on a motorway they are no problem.

What is a problem is our instructions. Admittedly we weren't paying attention at one crucial stage, but we end up driving up and down the motorway and I regret to say covering nearly 387 miles rather than kilometres. At one point I needed to do a U-turn on a narrow country road, and misjudged the drop from tarmac to kerb. This resulted in poor 10DPG rocking gently about the nether regions with wheels spinning and nose in the air. A very kind Chilean stopped and H, the Chilean, and his girlfriend managed to push me back with terrible graunching sounds, as chassis scraped tarmac.

We arrived rather tired and cross at about 20:30 at Vina Chillan, run by a very loud Swiss immigré, surrounded by acres of fairly recently planted Pinot Noir. Dinner was a time warp back to the days of Boeuf Stroganoff, thick with cream, onions and mushrooms, followed by quite delicious walnut ice cream. The Statins will be working overtime!

Filled up at 20,756 53.3 litres
TOTAL MILEAGE: 20,876

Geoffrey & Hilary Herdman

DAY: 226
17/03/11 TROUBLES WITH THE FUZZ – AGAIN!

Having set out in convoy in good time we were both stopped by the police 2 miles up the road. Neither of us had our headlights on – slapped wrist, but then it was pointed out that I had a right hand drive car and right hand drive cars are not allowed in Chile. Oops! I told the police that I had an import permit, which he read through very slowly, and having done so handed both it and my driving licence back. With a "Que lindo auto" or "what a pretty car" he waved us on – Phew! The import permit is only a standard customs document allowing temporary import and they didn't even check to see which side the steering wheel was on!

We wanted to pay homage to Chile's favourite hero, Arturo Prat. At the battle of Iquique in the war of 1879 between Chile and Peru he was commanding the Esmeralda, a wooden ship with 40 lb cannons. Caught between the ironclad monitor, Huasca, with 200 lb cannon, a shore fort, and then rammed by Huasca, he leapt onto his attacker sword in hand, but was slaughtered, at the age of 31. Sadly his home, now a national shrine, and museum was closed for renovations. As it was up 2 ks of gravel we drove on, but Pete and Fran in their "rentacar" made the pilgrimage and said the house and grounds were lovely.

We then drove the route of the Conquistadors, through Cauquenes, along brand new and superb country roads with very little traffic apart from the occasional logging truck. We were surrounded by forestry both newly planted and mature.

Cauquenes was in full fiesta with a school band and massed school children in the square. We tried Churrascos, which turned out to be rather large baps filled with beef, avocado and tomatoes, not to mention healthy dollops of mayo – quite yum.

Our day's drive to Curico, going directly up the ruta 5, should only have been 150 miles. Our diversion added 50 miles but kept us off the main road for a large chunk and we had glorious unspoilt views of the Andes in the distance.

Eventually we had to rejoin the 5 and no sooner had we done so than we were pulled over by a very attractive police lady with deep chocolate lipstick. She wanted to see H's driving licence. Despite having the top down it took her quite a little while to realize that it was not H who was driving. No mention was made of the volante on the right hand side not being legal and having seen my permit she cheerily waved us on. Too late I wished I had asked her if I could take her photo!

The hotel Villa el Descanso was perhaps Protours least successful. It was on the service road of the ruta 5, rather like the Express Holiday Inn in Aosta, but the rooms were well insulated, food good, and there was an attractive garden at the back with pool.

TOTAL MILEAGE: 21,083.
1.5 litres of oil added. That's 2.5 for 4,000 miles. Starting to use just a little.

SOUTH AMERICA

DAY: 227
18/03/11

CURICO BANDSTAND Our distance today was only about 60 miles, so first we drove in to Curico and found in the centre the most delightful bandstand. This had now been converted into a café on the first floor with deep leather sofas and a perilous access up a winding staircase. 'Elf and safety would never allow it back home! Regrettably one of us felt the need for some lemon pie at 11:00. Tsk tsk.

We arrived at the start of the Vendimia or Vendage festival. A band was setting up next to us, with occasional grossly overamplified practice notes, and the square was swarming with stands for wine as well as most other types of produce. We were accosted by a Canadian girl on an exchange system, who was working for the City council and helping stray tourists. She told us that Curico produced the best wine in Chile, but she would say that!

Sadly Curico, like everywhere around had been badly affected by the Concepcion earthquake on 28th Feb 2010. This was the worst quake for 50 years in Chile, but was overshadowed by the Haiti disaster, and so not much reported overseas. It was officially rated at 8.8 on the Richter scale, but we were told by several people that the government deliberately derated it, and it was in fact 9.2. Insurance companies don't pay out above 9, as they are considered to be act of God, which would leave the government holding the baby. The main church near the square had been split in half, and the elegant Colonial style Club fronting the square, which our 2009 guidebook highlights, looked like a crumbling wedding cake. The city is hard at work restoring things, but it is terribly sad to see the damage to buildings that have survived other quakes over several centuries. Later we saw several villages where terraces of lovely old adobe houses had cracked or totally collapsed. Although the earthquake was centred on Concepcion, it devastated a huge area.

Leaving Curico we stopped for petrol and the pump attendant asked if I had had any problems with the police as my steering wheel was on the wrong side. Oh dear, it seems the nearer we get to the capital, the more people there are who know the rules. Hmmm; one is getting a little paranoid.

Our intended destination was the Plaza Hotel in Santa Cruz, where H and I stayed in 2005. Sadly it was full and so we made for a lovely B&B just outside S C called the Bellavista, although why I am not quite sure as there was no view. Oleana, the owner, was charming and they had an excellent pool.

For dinner we drove 4 miles up the road to El Candil, a very elegant restaurant. We were alarmed to find we were the only people there, but it was 20:30. By 22:00 the place had filled up and Peter said it was the best meal he had had in Chile.

TOTAL MILEAGE: 21,150
Filled up in Curico 21,089 58.6 litres

Photo courtesy of P. Hughes

Geoffrey & Hilary Herdman

DAY: 228
19/03/11

WINE TASTING The big cheese round here is Carlos Cardoen. Born in Santa Cruz, of Belgian extraction he was involved in both metallurgy and arms manufacture. He now owns the Plaza hotel and the Santa Cruz winery, not to mention the Galerias Hotel we have been booked into in Santiago.

All four of us pile into 10DPG and head for the winery. En route going the other way we pass a topless Ferrari, the first we have seen anywhere in Latin America. We are met by Robinson and introduced to Emilio, one of Carlos' eight sons. We ask Robinson how he got his name. His mother was a Defoe addict and Robinson's brother is called Friday!

We do the statutory wine tour. There is not much to see. 161 hectares of grapes, picked by hand. 35% used for own production, the rest sold on. At the wine tasting we all prefer the Malbec and diligently spit it out – it being 11 in the morning! This winery is unusual in that there is a cable car to the top of a small hill. We take it and find Mapucho and Easter Island relics and representations. Not to mention a couple of llamas. That evening is full moon and the nearest the moon has come to the earth for 20 years. There is to be a huge family party at the winery for one hundred and forty guests. No wonder the Plaza hotel is full.

Continues overleaf

SOUTH AMERICA

PM: H and I go into Santa Cruz to the excellent museum, set up by Snr Cardoen, which we had remembered from before. It was damaged by the earthquake but has been rebuilt and seems as good – if not better than ever. The hotel Plaza, having been built or restored only 10 years previously, withstood the quake but all the sprinklers erupted and the hotel had to be shut for seven months, whilst it dried out and destroyed furniture was replaced. The tren del vino – a steam train running along the Colchagua valley – is out of action and the Estancia El Huique, glorious in 2005, has been badly damaged. The roof and tower of the chapel destroyed. I wanted to go and see it but Robinson advised against as he said it was too sad.

In the evening H and I go for a geriatric walk on horses with Sebastiano, who could talk for Chile, but couldn't ride and talk at the same time, so progress was not fast. I regret we understood about one word in ten. In the morning en route to Santa Cruz we had tried to find the stables. A misunderstanding led to about 10 miles of dirt roads – albeit very pretty dirt roads!

We rode up a steep mountain side to overlook the valley in the pearly evening light, with the huge full moon rising as the sun was setting in a cloudless sky.

And finally dinner at the Bellavista, by the pool and guttering candle light, served by Oleana's parents.

TOTAL MILEAGE: 21,185

DAY: 229
20/03/11 SANTIAGO VIA PANAMA!

We say goodbye to Pete and Fran. It worked – their excellent company saved the marriage for another fortnight.

Here we are just outside Santa Cruz. Could have saved ourselves a bundle on shipping fees if we had known how close we were!

Santiago is only 115 miles up the road by the Panamerica, but the navigator was bored with dual carriageways and so we took the scenic route. We found we were on a ridge with dramatic views of Andes and, closer to, pastoral scenes, but guess what? the paved surface ran out and we had 15 miles of dirt. "Not what the map said" came a voice. (And she was right. ED.)

The approach to Santiago is much like any other civilized capital city. Ring roads, flyovers in bewildering confusion, with TomTom losing the plot at critical times. But we made it to Hotel Galerias right in the centre. Not one of the greatest hotels, because downtown Santiago is not one of the greatest downtowns, but with a wonderfully central location, swimming pool on the 6th floor with thatched bar, a good dining room and most important of all CHEAP!

We dine in – splendidly, having started with a Pisco Sour, of which more tomorrow.

TOTAL MILEAGE: 21,325

Geoffrey & Hilary Herdman

DAY: 230
21/03/11

MARGARITA vs PISCO SOUR The photo is of the Santiago central post office. Built in 1882 it is every bit as elegant on the inside. It is located on the Plaza de Armas, where in 1541 Pedro de Valdivia built his first fort. Having founded Santiago de la Nueva Extremadura on 12th February, six months later the fort and all buildings were razed by the Picunches. The town was doggedly rebuilt and the central part is still to the same basic plan as laid out by P de V.

The actual naming of the city took place at the foot of a small hill; Santa Lucia, next to our hotel, but despite its significance it remained just that, a small hill until 1872. Then an enlightened mayor used one hundred and fifty convicts to convert it into an exuberant, part gothic, part romantic fantasy, with hermit's chapel, waterfalls and neoclassical stairways.

But to matters more important:

In Central America one of us discovered the Margarita, although both became quite partial to it, and here we are now on Pisco Sours. Both drinks are based on citrus juice, but here the similarity stops.

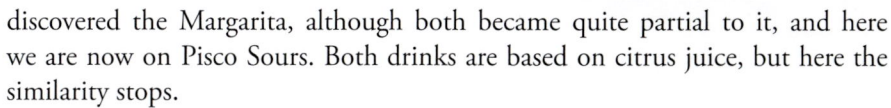

The Margarita is a Mexican cocktail made from Tequila, Triple Sec, and lime juice. The rim of the glass should be dipped in either sugar or salt. For our taste it should definitely be salt. Tequila is a distillate of the juice of the agave plant and Triple Sec is a variety of Curaçao made from bitter and sweet oranges. The classic proportions are Tequila 50%, Triple Sec 29% and fresh lime or lemon juice 21%. It can be frappéed with crushed ice, but to my taste is better on the rocks.

Pisco Sour is a Peruvian cocktail, although Chile also lays claim, with some justification, to its origins. It was invented in a bar in Iquique by Elliot Stubb, an Englishman, some time around the 1880s. Despite, or because of, Arturo Prat's sacrifice at the battle of Iquique, (see Day 225), the town having been Peruvian became Chilean in 1884. The drink itself is made from Pisco, lemon or lime juice, egg white, simple syrup and bitters, and to our taste is best served frappéed. Pisco is a colourless grape brandy developed by the Spanish settlers in the 16th C. The classic proportions are: Pisco 8 parts, lime juice 4 parts, simple syrup 3 parts, an egg white, and a dash of bitters.

Personally I prefer Margaritas. They are not so sweet as Piscos, and the salt lick is a salivating addition, but it is a close run thing.

SOUTH AMERICA

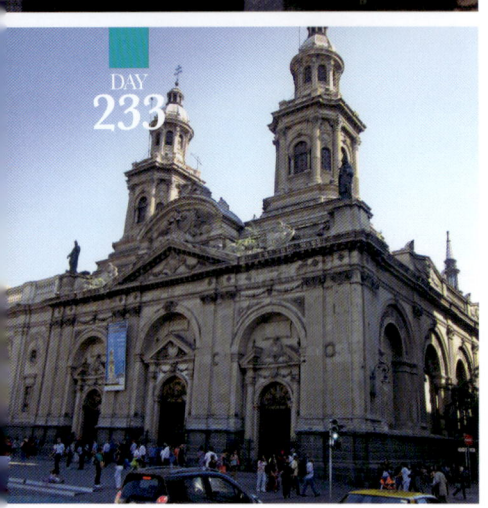

DAY: 231
22/03/11

MAPUCHO GUARDIANS OF THE DEAD

Sightseeing in Santiago. The pre-Columbian museum is thought to be the best in S America. Here we have guardians to watch over the souls of dead Mapucho.

DAY: 232
23/03/11

DINNER WITH KEITH & KATHY

A reflection of Santiago cathedral!

Having imposed ourselves on Kathy and Keith in Boston and having had dinner with them in Victoria, we have crossed paths in Santiago and join them for dinner at Acqui Esta Coco and meet their travelling companions Richard and Marilyn.

DAY: 233
24/03/11   LUNCH WITH JAL

This is the actual cathedral, as opposed to yesterday's reflection.

Lunch with José Antonio, who tells us everyone calls him JAL from his initials, and indeed his company is called JAL Fisheries. He drives us in a top of the range Subaru, amazingly quiet and with very clever 4 wheel drive.

I tell him about the police saying right hand drive is not legal, but he tells us that you can import on a temporary basis and it is quite legal. He says that many of the cars at the British Embassy are right hand drive.

We talk of fake watches. He is wearing a very elegant Patek Philippe, which cost him $100 in Shanghai and he shows us his Rolex which cost the same. Having had my Rolex stolen I am rather keen on the idea of a fake. He is going to give us the address in Shanghai!

After lunch I walk home. It turns out to be a 2 hour walk, mostly along the river, through sculpture gardens and parks. Santiago is growing on us.

Geoffrey & Hilary Herdman

In the evening we dine again with the 2 ks and their friends. I take the metro, which runs on rubber wheels and is like any other metro at rush hour but quieter.

DAY: 234
25/03/11 VALPARAISO AND BUREAUCRACY

On a glorious sunny day we drove the 75 miles to Valparaiso, and on a glorious sunny day we fell in love with Valparaiso. It is a mini San Francisco, built on even steeper hills, and like San Francisco suffered a devastating earthquake in 1906.

We are staying in the bright yellow Acontraluz, recently converted from a large family home. Our room has a balcony with the most wonderful views over the whole of Valparaiso. This is better than La Boca. The houses are of fantastic colours, are clad in corrugated iron, and give the impression of tumbling down the hills.

We walk round Paseo Atkinson, and have drinks in the "Brighton" next to it.

However we are at sixes and sevens. Our Australian shipping agent has told us we need a carnet to enter Australia. Mrs H has read all the forms and reckons we should be able to apply for a temporary import permit without a carnet. Far too late we send in the application and are advised that it takes fifteen working days even to consider our application.

We have also discovered that shipping will take a minimum of six weeks, as the container is transhipped in Hong Kong. If the car arrives in Australia without the permit it can be trashed!! H has spoken to Robert in Vehicle imports and he assures her – sort of – that the permit is just a matter of time. We think that we should perhaps get on with the shipping as we have time on our side in which to sort out the paperwork. However as soon I tell our agent Jorge that we want to go ahead he goes all silent. So here we are in Valparaiso – loving it but in limbo.

TOTAL MILEAGE: 21,402

SOUTH AMERICA

DAY: 235
26/03/11 **VALPARAISO AND SLEEPING DOGS** Just one of the hills TomTom thought we should attempt in trying to find our hotel! Cobbled, impossibly steep, and with a ridge at the top, not to mention the flowers. However this one block long section is the only part of Calle Templeman which is not drivable. The rest is just as steep, and cobbled. We are staying in Cerro Allegre, originally Mount Pleasant, but now Chileanized.

We spend the day sight seeing. There are dogs everywhere, either barking or sleeping. The car chasers are I suppose long since departed. Regrettably the pavements are NOT clean. None of the dogs have collars. They just lounge around in public places in groups of five or six, apparently dead to the world. There have been moves to have the canine population reduced but the Canine League is very strong here and wouldn't hear of it.

DAY: 236
27/03/11 **AN ORGAN RECITAL** One of the 40 lb cannons recovered from the wreck of the Esmeralda, Arturo Prat's ship sunk at the battle of Iquique in 1879. Arturo you needed better technology!

St Paul's Anglican church is advertising a service at midday followed by an organ recital at 12:30. We show up at 2 minutes to 12:00 to find the church locked. Around 12:10 someone unchains the front gate to a beautifully maintained garden. We are alone in the church. It was built by the English community in 1858. The Rough Guide tells us that in 1903 Queen Victoria donated the organ. It goes to show you can't always rely on the Rough Guide. [Although generally it has been wonderful. ED.] She died in 1901. The truth is that it was bought by the English community in 1903 in memory of Q V, whose dates are displayed in gold on the pipe case. Strangely they already had a perfectly good organ, which they gave to the Lutheran church next door and which is still playing to this day.

The 1906 earthquake caused no damage to the church – it had been designed by a railway engineer – but caused extensive damage to the new organ which was repaired forthwith.

By 12:40 the church had a congregation/audience of about forty. A few announcements and 1 Corinthians 13:11 "When I was a child…" all in Spanish and the service was over. The organist of the day was Sr José Saavedra, who acquitted himself adequately through Bach to an English composer, Andrew Carter. We had never heard of the latter but his "Gloria from Missa Brevis" was excellent.

In the afternoon by train to Viña del Mar, just up the coast from V and now the playground of rich Chilenos, not to mention Argentinians, complete with gothic follies built at the beginning of the 20th C by nitrate magnates. We walked along the wonderful beach, but are very glad we are staying in Valparaiso.

DAY: 237
28/03/11   ASCENSOR One of the thirteen remaining Ascensors. Built in the late 19th C to climb the precipitous hills and still running mostly with the original gear. The cost of a 2 minute ride is CP 300, (40p) the same as a 20 minute train ride to Viña, but absolutely worth it. They take off with an alarming judder and rattle along their scenic ways.

In the afternoon in true seaside fashion we take a boat trip round the bay and port. I am not sure what the waterline bulbous protrusion at the front of modern ships is called but they were all adorned with basking sea lions.

SOUTH AMERICA

DAY: 238
29/03/11 **JOSÉ AND VERONICA** Our hosts at the Acontraluz hotel are José and Veronica. José is a mining engineer. He and Veronica have lived in half the hotel for years, but recently bought the house next door and converted the two into a quite gorgeous hotel, adding a floor in the process, which is where we are staying. The hotel has been open for less than 2 years. Although he probably speaks far better English than I do Spanish, José patiently puts up with me massacring his mother tongue and all conversations are in Castellano as they call Spanish. They are both kindness itself and nothing is too much trouble.

As we have ended up staying five nights José, as a most generous present, has offered us a free guided tour of Valparaiso. Oliver, a Chilean/German but speaking perfect English, takes us on a 3 hour tour. We start in the Croatian house, now the City Art Gallery, built in the early 20th C for yet another mining magnate, who lived there in solitary splendour until his death 20 years later. The style can best be described as eclectic/arts and crafts with Matisse dancers adorning the exterior.

We continued with three astonishing banking halls, (clearly these banks could never fail), a replica of a Venetian Palazzo, now in serious decay, and a garage where we find pre-war Chevrolets and Fords in immaculate condition. He left us at La Sebastiana, the poet Neruda's house – see photo. Neruda won the Nobel Prize for literature in 1971. He designed the house himself. It has spectacular views, one bedroom, but large rooms for parties and is certainly quirky and enchanting inside. There is a sense of colour and fun to the house, and its contents, which reflects both the personalities of the owner and of the city.

DAY: 239
30/03/11 **NORTH TO LA SERENA** The crumbling Palazzo – see yesterday. The municipality has been trying to buy it, but doesn't have the money. Meanwhile there are a couple of offices and a small art gallery inside, but

Geoffrey & Hilary Herdman

the building is in a sad state of neglect, although we did find someone dusting.

It is going to be a week or so before we ship so we are heading up to La Serena, about 270 miles North. It is on the coast and the gateway to the Elqui valley, home of Pisco brandy.

The fog has rolled in and it is top up stuff, as it is really quite cold. But first we need to have various documents notarized for the shipping, and so are not on the road until gone midday. Does anything ever change?

North of Viña del Mar we pick up dual carriageway and then the ruta 5 for a rapid and uneventful, albeit very expensive drive. Tolls on the 5 add up to about £18 for the 200 miles. Although a "motorway" we pass cyclists, pedestrians and street vendors with tatty shacks selling farm produce. The road runs partly along the coast, where it was still misty, grey and cold, and partly inland, where the countryside is arid and bleak. Eventually we round a corner and there is Coquimbo, a port city just South of La Serena, with a huge cross dominating the town. Soon afterwards we arrive at the Hotel del Cid run by Scottish John and his elegant Chilean wife.

The hotel is in the centre of town and an amazing topsy turvy conglomeration of buildings, as they have added on bit by bit. The latest addition was a yard which they bought with the express intention of turning into a car park. However, having bought it, "Conservation" would not allow them to make an entrance in the wall, so they constructed all the paraphanalia inside the walls and one weekend a hole was created and electrically operated gates put in place. A very Greek way of doing things. Anyway 10DPG was securely parked.

Filled up in Valparaiso 65 litres 21,403 miles
TOTAL MILEAGE: 21,673

DAY: 240
31/03/11   PISCO COUNTRY
We have a date for shipping. It has been hard work getting there, but 10DPG goes into the container on 8th April, ship departs on 12th, and takes forty three days to Melbourne including being transhipped in Hong Kong. Now all we need is the permit to be able to import!

The Elqui valley is reported to be beautiful and we set off in heavy cloud and cold weather, with roof up and thick sweaters. Fifteen miles inland the cloud lifts. 10 miles further on it is turning into one of the hottest days we have had. As we are climbing 10DPG is running distinctly warmly.

The Elqui valley is renowned for two things. Pisco and observatories. Once inland they have three hundred sunny days a year and pollution free skies. The coastal cloud is actually a blessing to the observatories as it contains the town night glow.

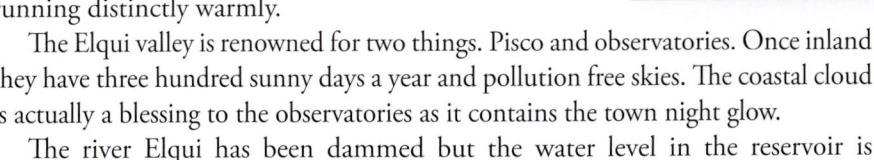

The river Elqui has been dammed but the water level in the reservoir is extremely low. Needless to say we pass vineyard after vineyard, mostly with Muscatel grapes. Vendimia or harvesting has started. It is all by hand.

In scorching weather we drive to Pisco Elqui, where the local brand is Mistral Pisco, named after another of Chile's Nobel poets, Gabriella Mistral, who comes from just down the road. In the village we have a fairly disgusting set menu lunch, but with delicious freshly squoze strawberry juice, and then make the statutory tour of the distillery. Although we are nearly 1,200 metres up we are surrounded by vineyards. The three hundred days of sun ensures a very high sugar content – ideal for distillation.

We drive back to La Serena. The cloud had lifted but it was still pretty cold. We arrived just in time to take a tour of an observatory, which meant going back up the valley by bus. We have a hugely enthusiastic guide, whose knowledge of astronomy seems unlimited and all in English. We started off in a James Bond like observatory, with a computer controlled "dial a star" telescope and domed roof which swung round in sympathy. Through this we saw what appears as one star to the naked eye in Orion's Belt, but turned out to be four, surrounded by a huge galactic cloud. Outside, through a not very large telescope, we saw Saturn and its rings brilliantly. We also saw parts of the Milky Way only visible in the Southern Hemisphere, including the Serpent and the Llama, as named by the Incas.

Filled up in La Serena 21,673 miles 52.3 litres
TOTAL MILEAGE: 21,797

DAY: 241
01/04/11   TIME FOR AN OIL CHANGE

Pictured – how they do an oil change in Chile. Well actually the original alembics at the Mistral distillery!

Mileage now 21,797, mileage at last oil change in Salta 17,056. Definitely time for a change. I drive round the block a few times, am stuck in traffic, and the oil warms nicely. There is a Shell garage and after a short wait a nice old boy has two cars over the pit and is changing both sets of oil simultaneously.

"Rojo" he says when he sees what comes out of 10DPG! He also checks the level in the diff. and adds a minute amount. £40 later and I am on my way.

John has recommended a restaurant 20 miles inland at El Molle, called Los Hornitos del Molle. Once again as we drive inland, the gloom – that is the perpetual sea mist hanging over La Serena – lifts and the temperature rises from 15°C to 25°C. We have a great lunch surrounded by a swimming pool and attractive Cabañas. Mrs Herdman has one of her many very good ideas and we book one of them for a few nights.

Geoffrey & Hilary Herdman

In the evening we drive to the sea, a couple of miles from La Serena. The fog has lifted and we take a geriatric walk along the beach, wondering at the endless blocks of high rise apartments, probably only used in January and February.

TOTAL MILEAGE: 21,848
Changed oil and filter 21,797

DAY: 242
02/04/11   MOVING HOUSE   This is almost like being on holiday. Having collected some money from the Banco Estado – all the others charge a commission – we drive back to Los Hornitos, where we have a splendid cabaña with two bedrooms. As we need to repack the car the spare bedroom is quickly filled with the entire contents of 10DPG. Looking at it, it is a wonder that it will all fit in. A 405 Drophead is THE most capacious car.

And then we slacked and lounged by the pool reading, tsk tsk, but not before cleaning a very grubby and deserving car.

The photo (see below) is of the local wine country complete with des res.

TOTAL MILEAGE: 21,868
Filled up at 21,851 miles 37 litres

DAY: 243
03/04/11   BODY MAINTENANCE   Herdman teamwork. Whilst I polished the paint and the chrome (5 hours) Mrs H fed the leather. We could almost hear the top of the dashboard soaking up the hide food, and had to apply two coatings. The steering wheel, which has a very thin leather cover felt completely different and much nicer to handle once it had been treated.

The hotel brought over a vacuum cleaner and by the end of it all 10DPG was looking pretty good. See the photo above and compare with Day 239!

When we go to Australia the first requirement is a sanitation inspection and theoretically the cleaner the better. However in New Zealand sanitation seemed totally random and a car straight from the paint shop was charged for a vacuum and steam clean, while one, not so pristine, got away scot free. We even found the vacuum they had used in the boot of a 406.

SOUTH AMERICA

DAY: 244
04/04/11   **OVALLE** Today can best be described as going for a walk in the car, through Pisco country to Ovalle, the home of both Capel Pisco and a Lapis Lazuli mine. The photo is of Ovalle main square. All over Chile they have a curious parking arrangement. As soon as you park a warden comes up and places a ticket on your car but needs no money. On leaving, they have eyes in the backs of their heads and are there like rats up a drain pipe for the fee. This turned out to be about £1.50 for just over an hour. Expensive by Chilean standards.

We were neither of us quite sure why we had gone, but Mrs H managed to find a hairdresser and I walked to the disused railway station, now a museum and rather fine.

At 150 miles, our walk in the car turned out to be rather a long one!
TOTAL MILEAGE: 22,018

DAY: 245
05/04/11   **THE IMPORT PERMIT** Our shipping agent contacted us and said we needed to be in Santiago on the morrow as she needed the originals of our notarized documents. We still hadn't heard anything from vimports@infrastructure.org.au about our application, which they had assured us would take fifteen working days. In the evening Mrs H rang them. "Oh yes" they said, "that was all approved and the original permit sent to your home address some days ago." Mrs H is quite brilliant; not only can she read a form, but she can both understand and fill it in correctly. (On her good days. ED.) All three things are quite beyond me. Anyway it seems we are allowed in without the dreaded and expensive carnet.

Earlier in the day we took 10DPG for another little walk up the ruta 41. This is the road which goes from La Serena on the coast to Argentina over the Paso del Agua Negra, 4,780 metres high. No-one can tell us how far the road is paved and we are not about to find out but drive 60 miles or so to 1,700 metres. The road

Geoffrey & Hilary Herdman

is superb, with the scenery changing from high vineyards to bleak but dramatic mountains. We are told by everyone that it is staggeringly beautiful at the top. Next year's plan is to come this way into Argentina with a Hilux.

On the way home we walk through strange patterned vineyards. (See photo.) The pickers are all just going home.

Over dinner we talk to Juan Carlos, one of the owners of Los Hornitos. He tells us that a grape picker will earn about 10,000 Pesos a day, whilst a mine worker, depending on skill, from 20,000. That is £13 and £26 respectively. Often the grape pickers will go back to the mines once Vendimia is over.

TOTAL MILEAGE: 22,144

DAY: 246
06/04/11 SOUTH TO SANTIAGO

We have to present our original documents to Atlas International, just North of Santiago and 260 miles down the road, at 16:00. We use the ruta 5 – dual carriageway all the way. The dual carriageway runs from Puerto Montt in the South to La Serena, about 1,500 ks. We have used pretty well most of it. From preference we would have driven cross country, but time doesn't allow.

We arrive at Atlas on the dot of 16:00 and are met by very charming Veronica and Elvira. They tell me the car will be loaded tomorrow at this very spot and I need to be back by 10.00 sharp.

We drive the final 10 miles into Santiago and find the Aubrey Boutique Hotel – see photo. This has recently – twenty months ago – been opened by an Australian called Mark, who has lived in London for 18 years and his partner William, also from London with a Goldman Sachs background. William tells us he tries to

SOUTH AMERICA

keep Mark in check, but Mark confides the whole thing has cost rather more than they had bargained for. We thought money well spent!

TOTAL MILEAGE: 22,471

Filled up outside La Serena 22,161 52 litres, and before entering Santiago another 20 litres at 22,389

We had imagined we would be driving to Valparaiso tomorrow for loading, otherwise we wouldn't have bothered.

For the record petrol costs about 800 Pesos or £1 per litre in Chile, and about 4.80 Pesos or about 75p in Argentina. It is about the only thing which is cheaper in Argentina.

DAY: 247
07/04/11   BACK IN THE BOX

On a glorious sunny day we drive the 10 miles back up to Atlas Movers' offices and consign 10DPG to Australia.

We can say it now.

10DPG has covered 19 miles short of 22,500 in North, Central, and South America. We have driven on atrocious potholed roads, on dirt roads sending up clouds of dust, climbed to over 10,000 ft several times, and what has gone wrong? A starter motor in July, rebuilt for $50. A starter solenoid in October, replaced for $50. A puncture at the same time as the starter motor cost $20, and a bent wheel trim and lost hubcap over the worst of all the potholes in Honduras. What a car.

It is going to take until the end of May to sail to Adelaide – via Panama!

Mrs H and I are now quite exhausted and need a holiday!

In the afternoon after a 4 mile walk, to her joy Mrs H finds the only branch of Ferragamo in Chile, with exactly the shoes she was looking for.

In the evening JAL picks us up from the hotel. He tells us he has tried often to get into the restaurant here but it is always full. Actually Mark has just closed it, as there has been a major falling out with the concessionaire. Mark will re-open but run it himself.

JAL drives us to his gorgeous house, 1,600 metres up in the foothills, presents H with a lovely scarf – see photo – and then having done a hard day's work sets to and cooks us dinner. We decide to buy an apartment in Buenos Aires – jointly!

TOTAL MILEAGE: 22,481

Carless Days

DAYS: 248-314
08/04/11 - 13/06/11

ARGENTINA AND ISLAND HOPPING TO AUSTRALIA

Having finally launched 10 DPG on what proved to be a much more leisurely voyage than we had expected, albeit on an enviable route, we decided to go back to Argentina, (driven across the Andes in a white van, a comedown from 10DPG!) and then fly to Australia via Easter Island, Tahiti, the Cook Islands and New Zealand.

Highlights:

- Staying at Colomé, the highest vineyard in Argentina, in a beautiful valley reached on awful roads (hired wheels) through dramatically coloured rocky highlands, with the surprise of a gallery built for the owner's collection of works by James Turrell.

Geoffrey & Hilary Herdman

Carless Days

- The Tren a las Nubes, climbing to over 4,000 m, the line winding and looping through astounding scenery, with a supply of coca leaves to chew to help with the altitude, and a versatile train crew, at the breathlessly high end of the line by the Chilean border, producing instruments to play the National Anthem, with all the Argentinians joining in.

- The spectacular Iguazu falls.

- Ballet at the vast, beautifully restored Theatre Colon; always shut or on strike on previous attempts.

- England vs Argentina polo match, held on the immaculate lawns at Palermo; unsurprisingly the home team won a fast and exciting match.

- The mysterious and impressive statues on tiny, remote Easter Island.

- Fakarava; a ravishingly perfect long low atoll of white sand in brilliant blue seas.

- The Cook Islands, with traditionally built ladies in wonderful straw boaters garlanded with flowers, and acquisition of a useful Cook Island driving licence for G, needed for scooter hire but valid worldwide for a year!
- New Zealand, where we enjoyed meeting dear Di Robinson again, and her parents; also the kind Smythemans, and visiting Claude Lewenz on beautiful Waiheke island in perfect sunshine.

IN SYDNEY, we joined a friendly meeting of the lively NSW BOCA.

Highlights:

- Concert & ballet at the Opera House.
- The Botanic Garden.

AS 10DPG SHOWED NO SIGN OF TERMINATING ITS CRUISE FOR SOME TIME, we flew to Perth.

Highlights:

- Maritime Shipwreck Museum in Fremantle.
- Wonderful dinner at the Leeuwin's Estate in Margaret River.
- Walking through the tree canopy of huge Tingle trees.

NEXT STOP DARWIN, where we hired a car to drive to the Kakadu National Park for two nights in the extraordinary Crocodile Holiday Inn.

Geoffrey & Hilary Herdman

Carless Days

Highlights:

- The glorious Dry season; warm but not humid, with a gentle breeze.
- Enormous estuarine crocodiles leaping clear of the water, when tempted (very touristy) by lumps of meat dangled from the boat.
- Rock paintings, and light at sunset seen from the huge ochre coloured cliffs of Ubirr.
- Yellow water evening cruise through the flood plain; cutting through floating masses of brilliantly green grass; waterlilies and birds everywhere.

ADELAIDE AT LAST, via the shockingly extravagant, but very enjoyable, Ghan train; three days and two nights, but with a couple of stops at Margaret and Alice Springs.

Highlights:

- Flying Doctor Museum, and chance to try the pedal wireless that gave a mantle of safety to almost unimaginably isolated people.

- The journey by train itself, bringing home the sheer isolation of the outback, the difficult terrain and the huge distances involved.

IN ADELAIDE, kind Ozy took us in, and made us incredibly welcome for far too long; a shocking abuse of his generous hospitality.

We were installed in the ground floor of his huge house, which features an unusual garage, two stories high and linked to the main house by a glass wall, giving panoramic views from the dining room of his impressive car collection. Access is via a precipitous slope, tackled by the owner con brio, followed by a car lift to the upper floor. The garage is beautifully floored, and a parquetry inlay on the lift platform features, of course, the word: "Bristol"!

As the car was obviously still several weeks away from being released for further travel, we took the chance of visiting the area.

Highlights included:

- Kangaroo Island.

- The Barossa and Clare wine valleys, and of course, their produce, especially the Clare Valley Paulett red, good enough to involve two visits!

Geoffrey & Hilary Herdman

Carless Days

ROUND THE WORLD WITH 10DPG

N

NORTHERN TERRITORY

QUEENSLAND

- Cairns
- Townsville
- Rockhampton
- Gladstone
- Carnarvon Gorge
- Bundaberg

AUSTRALIA

- Brisbane

SOUTH AUSTRALIA

NEW SOUTH WALES

- Bowral
- Canberra
- Adelaide

VICTORIA

- Melbourne
- Port Fairy

map is not drawn to scale, for illustrative purposes only

CHAPTER 4
Australia

DAY: 315
14/06/11   ARRIVAL OF THE CHRYSALIS IN ADELAIDE

After almost ten weeks from Santiago today our chrysalis arrived in our agent's yard.

It has been through the Panama Canal both North and South, having transhipped in Colon and sat on the docks there for a week. Not to mention sitting in the docks in Valparaiso for ten days due to a "muddle" with customs. Although, having stayed in a glorious hotel overlooking the dockyard, it was a wonder to us that anything ever found its way in and out at all.

From Panama the new transport visited Tahiti, Fiji, Nouvelle Caledonie, and Sydney, before the poor car was transhipped yet again in Melbourne – once again sitting in the docks for a week.

The final ship arrived in Adelaide last Saturday (11th June), but Monday was a bank holiday, for the Queen's birthday, and the long awaited phone call came for us to be at the yard at 12:30 tomorrow.

It will be noted that the sign above says "Fumigation Area"! We are in quarantine.

DAY: 316
15/06/11   THE BUTTERFLY EMERGES We arrive at the appointed hour (12:30) and friendly staff are to hand to open the container and release 10DPG. We may only move the car within the yard until Quarantine come tomorrow.

The car is pushed out of the container and unlike Buenos Aires, where all the leather and especially the steering wheel were covered in mildew, the car has travelled remarkably well. We had cleaned it thoroughly only a couple of days before loading it in Chile and there is a little surface dust but otherwise all seems well.

Having reconnected the battery we attempt to start. After much catching on one cylinder it eventually coughs into life under its own battery and I am allowed

Geoffrey & Hilary Herdman

to drive round the yard – a big happy grin. "Like a kid with a new toy" says the yardman to H, but it was a very happy moment after a long wait.

DAY: 317
16/06/11   THE SANITARY INSPECTOR
By the time we made it to the agents with Ozi, Emma, the Sanitary Inspector, had prescribed a steam clean. As much of Chile is probably still stuck to the underside of the wheel arches this did not come as a surprise. However, she was happy for us to take all the contents from the car first. Luckily, a low loader was just passing by en route to the cleaners, so by 10:30 the car was at "steam cleaning", but in a queue. They hope to have it ready by Monday – with any luck. Ozi then took us to Marque Restoration, to meet Gerard, the owner, and Peter, who restored Ozi's 405 DH, and is to service 10DPG. Both very knowledgeable, calm and patient men.

DAY: 318
17/06/11   ANOTHER 405 DH
There are only two 405 Dropheads in Australia; 10DPG and Ozi's, although the former is a temporary visitor – we hope.

After a total restoration Ozi's car was finally back on the road in early 2011 and he is about to join a five week rally with BOCA. The car goes by train to Perth, and having explored W Australia is to be driven back across the Nullarbor desert. The trip from Perth to Adelaide alone is about 1,700 miles.

We decide to give 445 (his registration) a shake down. The previous evening we have had drinks with 411 owner Robert Fenwick Elliott, who suggested we visit Parachilna in the Flinders some 350 miles North of Adelaide. Sadly the hotel is full so we opt for Blinman and the excellent North Blinman Hotel established in the mid 1860s, and the same distance.

Ozi and I take it in turns to drive and we all take it in turns to sit in the back with hood both up and down. It is surprisingly comfortable. I don't think I have

AUSTRALIA

ever been in the back of 10DPG!

His Solexes have been replaced with Webers and the car is doing about thirty to the gallon. Impressive stuff. Geoff Dowdle, whom we will remeet next weekend is the guru of the Weber. Must talk to him!

In the evening we meet the Salt Bush Bikers, who are a very cheerful crowd.

DAY: 321
20/06/11   ON THE ROAD   We arrive at Sanitation at 08:30. The poor car, having looked pristine out of the box, now looks bedraggled. There is water everywhere. I remove the distributor cap and dry the innards, but there is not a squeak of life from the engine. An industrial battery pack is produced – still nothing. A very helpful mechanic arrives and we find water in each of the sockets on the distributor cap. These are dried out. There is a faint flicker but nothing more – so we resort to extremis; a jolly good squirt of ether. 10DPG coughs into life and dies. More ether, more life, and eventually we are up and running, albeit raggedly. Something has happened to the trafficator mechanism. It is all mechanically connected but the clockwork is not functioning. Very, very irritating. It was perfect in Chile and sadly I didn't check when it came out of the box. Maybe sanitation have rotated the switch a few times to try and open the bonnet. We will never know.

We drive to "Roads Department" for an inspection. As we are to be only two to three months in Australia this is only to ensure that I have the correct permits and the chassis and engine numbers comply therewith. Bizarrely the inspector also checks my brake lights, but that's it mechanically. We now only need a permanent permit to allow us on the road.

Sadly the UK tax disc has irrevocably run out. Were it not so we would have been able to travel on UK plates. Alas we need to reregister in S Australia, which guess what? involves paying a stamp duty – non refundable. Of course having owned the car for 12 years and driven 125K miles the car is worth a fraction of what I paid for it so stamp duty is manageable.

Geoffrey & Hilary Herdman

And finally to Marque Restorations, who have rebuilt Ozi's 405DH, for a thorough service.

The photo is the rear wheel arch after Sanitation's spray job. See tomorrow.
TOTAL MILEAGE: 22,496

DAY: 322
21/06/11   THE 405 TOBOGGAN   Gerard wants me to see the underside of the car as there is something unusual. We peer earnestly and see that welded to the bottom of the chassis are two long runners of about 2½ inch square box section, tapered at the front. He tells me that there was no trace of them on Ozi's car, nor in the workshop manual. They have long gouge marks where we slid the poor car off the ridge in Chile (see Day 224). Had it not been for them, quite serious damage would have occurred to various underneath extremities.

I contacted Richard Peacock, the previous owner and restorer of 10DPG, who told me that Dr Wright, his predecessor, had in the 1970s asked BCL to make the additions as additional strengthening to the chassis. Thank you, thank you Dr Wright.

We also note that Sanitation have cleaned under the wheel arches, where the inspectors are going to check, but the rest of the underside is still engrimed with the soil of S America. $300 not well spent, but with the amount of damage they have done perhaps it is as well Sanitation didn't clean any further.

DAY: 326
25/06/11   CHANGE OF IDENTITY   Finally we collect S434AMC (formerly and futurely known as 10DPG) from servicing etc. and now adorned with a South Australian registration.

Whilst with Gerard, once the wheels had been taken off, we saw that the wheel arches had been stripped to undercoat of sealant by a combination of driving over gravel roads and sanitation power spray. All loose paint has been removed and an epoxy coating applied with a special topcoat. We have had a very thorough

AUSTRALIA

service, wheel bearings have been renewed and we have even found amongst Ozi's treasure trove a replacement trafficator mechanism.

During the last three weeks we have been renting a Toyota Corolla, a quite excellent car, in which we have managed to accumulate 1,500 miles. In convoy we return it to the airport, but have forgotten to refill it. Thrifty Cars tell us it will cost $2.80 per litre – exactly twice the going rate, so we beat a hasty retreat and put in $56 worth of petrol, which would otherwise have been $112 – outrageous.

10DPG running slightly raggedly and also quite hot. We suspect timing might not be correct. Gerard says they "never touched it" but the manual timing adjuster is now locked tight so something has happened. Tomorrow we are having a BOC of S Australia lunch to which Gerard is coming and promises to bring a strobe.

In the evening we have drinks in a local hostelry with Robert Fenwick Elliott.

TOTAL MILEAGE: 22,516
60 litres added at 22,500

DAY: 327
26/06/11 BOCA SOUTH AUSTRALIA To the Currant Shed in McLaren Flat for a splendid Sunday lunch through ridiculously pretty countryside. The assembled company were:

Ozi Osman 405 DH
Zerin Osman 404
Geoffrey & Hilary Herdman 405 DH
Peter & Jo Forrester 405
John and Pam Hollway 401
Paul & Jo Vivienne 400
Tony & Olive Bishop (400 & 401 under restoration)
Warren & Pam Leslie (400 under restoration)
Ian & Christine Webber (405 in the paintshop)
Gerard & Julie Miller (restorer extraordinaire)
Robert Fenwick Elliott (411S3 left at home)

Since the major service 10DPG has not been running well and after lunch Gerard, ably assisted by Peter Forrester, with Geoff Dowdle on the end of a phone adjusted

Geoffrey & Hilary Herdman

timing and mixture, revving the poor engine to 6,000 rpm briefly on occasion!

Whereas yesterday the car ran very hot in traffic and could only make it up Blyth St, where Ozi lives, in first, it seemed much better as a result, ran cooler and took the home hill in 2nd with aplomb. There is still quite a bit of travel on the brakes though and tickover is very ragged.

TOTAL MILEAGE: 22,606

DAY: 328
27/06/11

ADELAIDE TO PORT FAIRY The two "Australian" 405 DHs together with Ozi's immaculate 404. I have tried driving the latter but just as I can't fit in an AC Ace – knees round ears – nor can I fit comfortably in a 404. Never have been able to – head hits the roof.

At last we are properly en route, but are very sad to be leaving Ozi and his wonderful hospitality, enhanced by having Zerin, his daughter, with us for the last few days.

Everyone has told us that for Melbourne we should take the coastal route. Part of this is actually called the Great Ocean Road, and like the Blue Ridge Parkway in the States was devised as a way of providing employment. It doesn't officially become the G O R until Warrnambool, just after Port Fairy.

Exiting Adelaide is simplicity itself and soon we leave the main Melbourne road for the Princes Highway, which runs along the coast.

An uneventful but pretty drive. Port Fairy is gorgeous and was I believe the focal point for the BOCA 2011 rally. Our motel, the Victoria Lodge, comes complete with double garage. This is convenient as the driver's wing mirror has worked loose, necessitating removal of the door panel.

We are astonished to find the restaurant of our choice is full on a Monday night and cannot feed us until 20:30, which actually suits very well. Once there we sit in front of a blazing fire and talk to an Australian judge, who is also a director of the Melbourne race course.

Wimbledon starts at 23:00 local time, so a late night glued to the box.

TOTAL MILEAGE: 22,976
45 litres at 22,663

AUSTRALIA

DAY: 329
28/06/11   KOALAS AND MELBOURNE

Our motel does not even run to cornflakes let alone Weetbix, the sublime Australian version of Weetabix, so we breakfast out very satisfactorily on fluffy omelettes filled with all sorts of baddies – but very delicious.

Port Fairy is gorgeous, but it is time to leave and we are soon on the famous Great Ocean Road, which involves numerous stops to "Ooh" and "Aah" at "London Bridge", which has fallen down, the "Twelve Apostles", spectacular rocks, and the Cape Otway lighthouse. Access is by 13 ks of surfaced road, but as we come round one bend we are surrounded by cattle. We make the statutory visit to the lighthouse, which is very elegant but replaced by a modern and much smaller affair of very low power; 64,000 watts against 1,000,000 for the original. On our way back to the main road we see a small crowd gazing into the trees and there we find Koalas.

TomTom takes us precisely to the Royal Automobile Club of Victoria in the CBD (Central Business District) of Melbourne, and we are accommodated in great comfort.

More late night tennis.

TOTAL MILEAGE: 23,233
56 litres at 22,991

DAY: 330
29/06/11   THE AMAZING ROBERT McDERMOTT

Geoff Dowdle had suggested that I visit Robert McDermott to try and fix spongy brakes and ragged tickover. What an Aladdin's Cave. He has a huge warehouse at Footscray completely stuffed with Rolls-Royces and Bentleys of every sort and kind. I counted over fifty including a 1910 Ghost. Robert told me he has in his own collection over one hundred cars including fifteen Ghosts.

He also has interesting Bristols including the only 400 fitted as original with an 85BS engine, the same as an FNS, built for W H Lowe, the Ferrari Concessionaire in Australia. And a 403 fitted with Borani wire wheels as original, which must be unique?

After much bleeding the brake problem was diagnosed as either master cylinder or servo. On examination the master cylinder was shot and the plunger severely corroded so a new cylinder was fitted and the plunger machined to as new.

The misfiring was harder to fix as the poor carburettors are getting fairly worn and could do with a total rebuild, but he certainly made improvements. Whilst the master cylinder was being refitted he had to deliver a Silver Cloud 3 and invited me along for the ride. In his capable hands the thing certainly went and stopped impressively.

Geoffrey & Hilary Herdman

We had planned to meet Colin Young, Vice President of BOCA, for drinks in the evening but sadly works to 10DPG precluded and we had to cancel.

H meanwhile had a leisurely day walking in Melbourne, a very attractive city which is easy to explore on foot. The Ian Potter Centre at the National Art Gallery of Victoria had 19th C paintings with views of the growing city, plus a burning eyed, helmeted Ned Kelly on horseback, by Nolan, and three Russell Drysdales that she wanted to take home. The huge botanical gardens were marvellous, with the National Camellia collection beautifully displayed, and a nostalgic avenue of English elms that sadly cannot be seen at home any more. Don't know whether the Dutch beetle is still lurking to destroy, if cuttings were sent back to England, or whether it has died of starvation, having annihilated its food source, so the landscape could be restored? The gardens are even more magnificent than those in Sydney, although the situation in Sydney is unrivalled. However, Melbourne as a city generally seems rather more formal; could not imagine here the signs urging visitors in Sydney to walk on the grass, nor the plaque near a wattle with a quote from Monty Python, something along the lines of:

'This is the symbol of our native land; it's called the wattle.

You can hold it in your hand, or stick it in a bottle.'

Finished the walk with a beautifully sung short evensong in the imposing Anglican Cathedral, leaving just time to get G's birthday present ready for Saturday.

Splendid telly watching Big Jo Tsonga beat Roger Federer, but it meant lights out at 01:30!

DAY: 331
30/06/11

CANBERRA BOUND Wagga Wagga 44 and Adelaide 993. I just had to have a photo with 10DPG and Wagga Wagga (see overleaf). We are of course pointing in the wrong direction, but artistic needs must. Interestingly by going via Melbourne we have covered just over 1,000 miles from Adelaide.

We set out from Melbourne at 10:30, predictably late with a 6½ hours and

AUSTRALIA

DAY 331

420 miles drive. Weather glorious if a little chilly. For flogging up the motorway we do find it more comfortable with the hood up – especially as it is about 13°C.

Brakes are working much better although the pedal now needs quite a hard push. It used to be very soft, but maybe that is because of new seals!

For nearly all the way we are on dual carriageway – the Hume Highway which runs from Adelaide to Sydney. However once into NSW there are three or four patches of single carriageway but at each of them work is in progress. Once out of Melbourne the traffic clears and although there are some heavy trucks we are never held up. There are constant warnings about speed cameras, the limit is 110 k mostly, and we see a policeman with radar gun and even a helicopter cruising the roadway. Is this a good use of public funds?

And so to Canberra. An entirely uneventful trip through some very attractive countryside. It certainly beats the M1.

We phone Ozi, who has set out from Adelaide by the direct route in his 402 and find that he has encountered rain and had to put the hood up, but also says there are 3 inch gaps around the hood so it is only marginally drier up than down!

TOTAL MILEAGE: 23,652
56 litres at 23,262 and 44 litres at 23,525

DAY 332

DAY: 332
01/07/11

CANBERRA TO BOWRAL The photo is of the British embassy in Canberra. They must have had the same architect as for the Czech embassy in London – or come to that most of the other buildings in Canberra. It can't be much fun working there!

On 1st January 1901 the six independent States formed the Federation of Australia. Prior to that they were autonomous. They each minted their own money, charged taxes to pass from one State to another and even had their own railway gauges. It wasn't until the 1970s that you could travel from Perth to Sydney without changing train five times.

Sibling rivalries between Sydney and Melbourne dictated that the new parliament should be in neutral territory and thus was born ACT or Australian Capital Territory, rather like DC in the United States. It is an area less than half the size of Greater London and was carved out of New South Wales. The capital

Geoffrey & Hilary Herdman

of course is Canberra which in the indigenous language means "Meeting Place".

The first parliament building in Canberra was not actually opened until 1927 – until then Melbourne was the seat of the Federal Government. By the 1980s it was too small and so the present Parliament House was built, opened by the Queen in 1988, at a cost of AUS$1.1 billion – the most expensive building in the S hemisphere at the time.

H and I walked the barren Commonwealth Avenue to the parliament and longed for the glory of a Hausmann to create elegant shops and cafés. Parliament itself was engrossing and we took the very well informed guided tour. Even the receptionist gave us 10 minutes on the Australian Constitution vs the UK version! Pride of display was a Magna Carta dating from 1297, when it was reissued by Edward 1. It had been bought from Bruton School in 1952 for £12,500.

And then it was time for the 100 miles to Bowral, just South of Sydney. We had booked into what turned out to be a very strange accommodation. There were no signs at all and it transpired that it was a condominium development. Unsold condos were being managed by Accor as the Grand Mercure Motel.

Ozi was already in residence, having driven single handedly from Adelaide in his 402 in two days. A distance of 1,300 ks. What a great effort! Just across the road was a very new and superb restaurant called La Biota, which we throughly recommend. The owner is prominently on display in the open plan kitchen – always a good sign!

TOTAL MILEAGE: 23,755

DAY: 333
02/07/11 WHAT LIES IN THE EYE OF THE BEHOLDER

You may be forgiven for thinking you are seeing a plagiaristic version of a well known number plate. What you are actually seeing is registration capital I, capital O, capital O, MPH on Hugh Knox's Britannia.

From our motel we drove, perhaps rather foolishly with the hood down, along the splendidly named Bong Bong St to our rendezvous with the BOCA of NSW. Due to our Southern Australian registration we were accused of not having brought 10DPG!

One of the great pleasures in life is driving on open roads with other Bristols. There was very little other traffic and we were thus able to "get a move on" albeit a very cold one. We swooped, we climbed, we twisted, we were enveloped in cloud and froze, we came back into the sunlight and nearly thawed. We drove through Kangaroo Valley, over Camberwarra Mountain, along the

Shoalhaven river to Greenwell Point for a picnic lunch. Most fortunately there was a quite excellent fish and chippery to hand and we were able to purchase a seafood platter and a dozen local oysters.

In the afternoon we headed for Kiama and an enormous converted school for overnight accommodation. Dinner was at the Back Deck restaurant nearby, run by a very mouthy Edinburgh lass. Somehow word got out and my brownie and ice cream came with a candle and a round of "Happy Birthday". I replied that I couldn't imagine a better way of spending one's birthday. It came from the heart.

Participants were:

Geoff & Darin Dowdle	400	BRI400 (Saturday only)
David Flynn & Richard	400	NZZ411
Greg & Beverley Mead	400	34624H
Ozi Osman	402	UML600
Des Lane	403	XX470
Bob & Glenda Leffler	403	30129H
Vic & Patty Smiley	403	VS403
Geoffrey & Hilary Herdman	405DH	S434AMC (aka10DPG)
John & Val Cooper	406	30927H
Hugh & Maureen Knox	BRIT	IOOMPH
Russell Beers & Colleen	MERC	MW1722
Sandy Hellmrich	Cadillac	
Trevor & Di Inglis	Porsche	
John May	Citroen C5	
Russ & Margaret Olsson	Mazda	MXX053
John Pagan & Gina	Mazda	

TOTAL MILEAGE: 23,849

DAY 334

Geoffrey & Hilary Herdman

DAY: 334
03/07/11 PRESENTATION A meeting at the "blow Hole" at Kiama at the civilized hour of 09:30 for 10:00, followed by a couple of spectacular climbs through gorgeous countryside, ending at the Illawarra Fly, which turned out to be a tree-top walk along freely suspended walkways waving alarmingly in the gentle breeze. Notices claimed they were safe in winds up to 200 kph but I would not like to have been there in something a quarter as much.

Lunch was taken at Illawarra in the company of nine Bristols. We were very touched when Bob Leffler made Hilary and me a presentation of a limited edition print entitled "The Bristol Sixes 1947 - 1960" with the inscription: "Presented to Geoffrey & Hilary Herdman by the Bristol Owners Club of Australia Inc 3rd July 2011."

Post lunch we headed up to Whale Beach, a very smart seaside resort, to stay with Ronnie and Susie in their amazing new house. Due to a slight technical hitch the old one had collapsed about 3 years ago whilst major building works were in process!

En route to Whale Beach we found ourselves on a fee paying motorway with no cash booths. One of us thought that as we would be leaving Australia in six weeks or so it didn't really matter. The other thought of all the final demands piling up on poor Ozi's door, where the car is registered, and found we were able to pay over the phone.

TOTAL MILEAGE: 24,006
Filled up in Kiama 23,850 miles 56 litres

DAY: 335
04/07/11 THE BEGINNING OF PROBLEMS! R&R at Whale Beach today with a splendid lunch at Palm Beach. Sadly the excitement of our visit was too much for Ronald, who took to his bed.

Alarming correspondence from Geoff Dowdle, who had had a blow by blow account from Robert McDermott of works done, including the replacement of a missing one way valve in the brake master cylinder. Geoff thought this should not have been there on a car with disk brakes and certainly they have been behaving inconsistently since. Second opinion in England confirmed his thoughts and he very kindly agreed to remove the offending article tomorrow.

Fortunately Ronald had recovered sufficiently by the evening to a) drive back to Vaucluse (an hour and a bit away) and b) come out to dinner at The Pier in Rose Bay, where we ate sumptuously if in some degree of isolation – it being a Monday night.

TOTAL MILEAGE: 24,037

AUSTRALIA

DAY: 336
05/07/11 — **BRAKES TROUBLE THE BLEEDING WITH**

The above may be permed into any appropriate combination. Two make sense and either will do! A drive out to West Pennant Hills, where Geoff set to work on removing the offending non return valve, replaced the master cylinder and we set about bleeding, and bleeding, and bleeding. But whatever we did the pedal travelled a long way and felt very insecure. Geoff was tied up tomorrow – as were we and he kindly offered to recommence battle on Thursday.

We returned spongily to Vaucluse and dollied up for the evening's entertainments. A suit no less – only the second time in a year!

H meanwhile had a wonderful morning with Susie, who is one of a group of thirty sponsoring a new production of La Boheme at the Opera House, and so invited to a conductor's rehearsal at the opera house studios. We sat behind the conductor, listening to a rehearsal of the second scene in Act One. To my surprise, it seemed a work in progress for a production due to open in a week, but we subsequently found it had already been performed in Melbourne, although with a different conductor and some minor cast changes, so the staging is already well known. It was fascinating to hear the conductor's comments, and as these were sometimes critical, an audience would not generally have been permitted, unlike the final dress rehearsals.

An early and very good dinner at the opera house with a recovering Ronald, and Susie, and their friends Peter and Liz St George, followed by a gorgeous John Cox production of Capriccio. He is surely one of the greatest operatic directors. Both Cosi and Marriage at Garsington were utterly sublime and every nuance tonight was perfect – even the curtain call was arranged as a set piece. The Countess was sung by the most attractive Cheryl Barker, who acted as well as she sang and is going to do Salomé next year. I feel a return visit to Sydney coming on! The orchestra was the same as at the morning's rehearsal, but had scrubbed up well!

TOTAL MILEAGE: 24,090

DAY: 337
06/07/11 — **THE OZ ZAGATO** A trip out to Castle Crag on the North side of the Harbour to pay our respects to Sean and Antoinette McSharry, and his beautifully restored 406 Zagato. His is the first of them and was the Motor Show car. He kindly took us for a drive with H sitting comfortably in the back.

Then a wonderful fish roulade prepared by Antoinette with views over the harbour. Location, location or what?

On our return to Vaucluse we were whisked back to the opera house for a behind the scenes tour followed by 1½ hours of the musical director's rehearsal for Bohème. Some of the scenery from Capriccio was still under the stage, mingled with La Boheme; the effort involved in taking down one performance ready for the next day's rehearsal, followed by a third production defies belief, carried out with silence and precision in an extraordinarily cramped space. We realised how cleverly the Capriccio sets had been put together.

Geoffrey & Hilary Herdman

Dinner at Susie's golf club with the charming Edelmans; he a solicitor and a former rower at Oxford, she also a solicitor but now a Local Councillor.

TOTAL MILEAGE: 24,116
Filled up at 24,111 56 litres

DAY: 338
07/07/11 BACK TO GEOFF

An interesting fitting in the Zagato boot. Not sure if it comes refrigerated as well!

A return to the ever patient Geoff Dowdle. On arrival we were alarmed to find the level in the brake reservoir was substantially down. He found a leak where the banjo joins onto the rear brake cylinder and it transpired the mating face of the cylinder was corrugated. More bleeding, and then more bleeding.

By way of a test drive we visited Ivan Glasby the son of the Rhodesia importer for Bristols. They didn't sell very well, but Ivan's father bought a 404 for his mother. That car is now owned by John Cheffins and has air conditioning fitted!

H & I came across one of the Rhodesian 401s in Mauritius, where it had been imported as a basket case. Clency Leal, the local BMW agent, set his repair shop the task of a total restoration and when we saw it in 1989 it was immaculate.

Sadly just as I was leaving Geoff that evening I found my brake foot descending gently to the floor. The Saintly Geoff lent me his C5 and wonderfully offered to return to the fray tomorrow.

H meanwhile was visiting the Turkish Consulate, to enquire about import regulations for 10DPG. The Consul was out when she first got to the large, slightly dilapidated house in a very salubrious suburb, but expected back shortly. When she returned, she found all the staff out in the garden drinking coffee in the sunshine, as they found it too cold in the house; rather endearing! The friendly advice was no problems expected, and she left with a carrier bag full of tourist leaflets; we wish we could spend three months there!

TOTAL MILEAGE: 24,173

AUSTRALIA

DAY: 339
08/07/11   A NEW 400 CAB IN THE MAKING   Sun in the wrong position, sorry about that, but Geoff with his 400 Cabriolet in the making.

Having tried everything else we loosened the back plate of the servo – or booster as we call them over here – and found moisture. Out came the booster and it was full of brake fluid.

Hilary had come out for the day and the three of us set out for the local brake shop. They could either send the booster away for repair, but it would take two weeks and cost $800, or supply us with a brand new one in about an hour for $500. Guess which option we took!

Having had lunch in a local pub in Parramatta we collected the new booster, with various seals and fittings and returned home. Interestingly, whereas the old one needed a large vacuum tank the new one, although much smaller, would work very well on its own. Poor Geoff, by the time he had finished it was about 19:30, but happily we were able to take him and Darin out to dinner to the "Excellent Chinese Restaurant" and it was. Mud Crab in Black Bean sauce – a very messy affair followed by Parrot Fish, which had been presented to us still wriggling some 15 minutes previously.

And so back to Vaucluse with wonderfully firm brakes. Geoff had always made it very clear that he doesn't do brakes, but he made a superb job of poor 10DPG and I fear we tried Bristol Owner Camaraderie beyond the limit. As he pointed out for 125,000 miles the brakes hadn't done too badly!

TOTAL MILEAGE: 24,198

Geoffrey & Hilary Herdman

DAY: 340
09/07/11 GLOUCESTER SHIRE

At last we finally set off for points North, but we have mislaid the faithful camera. Brain racking determines it can only be at Geoff Dowdle's. Bless him he was waiting outside the house with it as we drove up. A huge relief to him that we weren't driving straight into his garage.

On Geoff's recommendation we were driving to Brisbane by the inland route rather than via the Coastal Expressway. We drove through Newcastle before entering Gloucester Shire. Stroud was infinitely more attractive than that disaster of urban planning – its namesake, and we stopped for lunch in Gloucester town. As we coffee'd a Mk II Jaguar 3.4 cruised by, and parked over the road was an MG TC. The owner suggested we go up Thunderbolt Way, which we were planning on anyway, but he warned us of steep hills.

Thunderbolt was a 19th C highwayman and the hills were dramatic, climbing to 4,500 ft, before coming to Armidale, still 1,000 metres up. The previous night it had been -4°C and we covered the car and removed the windscreen washer bottle!

Restaurants either closed at 20:00 or were full, but we managed to find a BYOB Thai, where we had a quite excellent dinner.

TOTAL MILEAGE: 24,508 (just over 2,000 miles in Australia)
Filled up at 24,268 33 litres

DAY: 341
10/07/11 NEW ENGLAND HIGHWAY

The overnight temperature turned out to have been a heady +1°, rather than the -4° of the previous night. Breakfast was an expensive option at the Motel so we wandered downtown and fed equally expensively at a caff. Armidale is rather a pretty place full of period buildings with first floor verandahs and filigree wrought iron railings.

Our route should actually be called the New Britain Highway. We passed by: Black Mountain, Llangothlin (sic), Ben Lomond, Glencoe, Stonehenge, and Warwick to name but a few. We climbed from 995 metres at Armidale to 1,415 at one point and stayed high for much of the day. Lunch was taken in the Municipal Arts Centre in Tenterfield, a most prepossessing set of buildings.

And so to Carindale, Brisbane where we were to stay with dear friends Tom and Bronwen. They are ideally located; close to the motorway for ease of access and far enough away not to hear it. We had told them we would arrive at 17:00 and at 17:00 we pulled up. We were delighted to find that our visit just overlapped with a visit from Canada by Laura, whom we had last seen in Barrie; a very convivial evening!

TOTAL MILEAGE: 24,808
24,524 40 litres (not full)

AUSTRALIA

DAY: 342

11/07/11   BOCA QUEENSLAND Chris Stafford had kindly arranged a BOCA get together at Le Relais Brassan at Flaxton. H was otherwise engaged so in glorious weather, having cleaned the car and discovered a loose radiator grille, I set out for points North. On leaving the motorway the road started climbing and then I was on a quite amazing ridge with views down to the far away South Pacific Ocean.

Having stopped for petrol I was a few minutes late, but was given the warmest of welcomes, followed by a photography session. A tiny bit of John's 403 can just be discerned off stage left, ditto Robert's 405 centre stage right. Kevin's 405 is clearly visible and parts of Chris' 407.

Le Patron greeted me volubly in French and fed us splendidly. He boasted an eclectic collection of French cars in their own conservatory. I am told that round the back there is also a Porsche and a Ferrari.

Not only did my hosts kindly pay for my lunch but also presented me with a very fine book of the BOCA Noosa rally in 2009. One was very touched!

Geoffrey & Hilary Herdman

Those attending the lunch were:
Chris & Peggie Stafford	407
Robert & Marilyn Van Wegen	405
Kevin & Susan Bowe	405
Geoffrey Herdman	405DH
John & Annabel Fraser	403
Peter & Sheila Mason	Prospective owners!

En route home they had suggested that I avoid the motorway and drive via Mt Mee, which turned out to be an excellent piece of advice. Rural Queensland driving is pretty damn good! I also ventured through the centre of Brisbane. It is at times like this that the increasingly sensitive TomTom throws a wobbly and downtown navigation becomes fraught!

TOTAL MILEAGE: 24,948
54 litres at 24,832

DAY: 343
12/07/11

THE FIRST 25,000 MILES Today at Bronwen's suggestion we are heading for Carnarvon Gorge, nearly 500 miles inland. But first the grille needed attending to. A visit to Peter, a friend of Tom's, and in no time we had the bonnet off and a couple of self tapping screws in place.

Bronwen had found us accommodation at the splendidly named Chinchilla, but it was after lunch before we set out for the 200 or so mile journey. She apologized for the Motel but said it was the only bed available. At a price of $80 we were somewhat alarmed!

Our road, the A2 is one of the main routes inland. In the opposite direction were innumerable Road Trains. Going our way everyone goes at the maximum speed, sometimes 100 ks and sometimes 110, so there is no call for overtaking, and often we had the road to ourselves – or appeared to. The photo shows the sort of thing, with Eucalyptus lining our way.

We stopped for fuel at Toowoomba and found coincidentally that 10DPG had covered exactly 127,000 miles since April 2001 when we first took delivery at the BOC AGM.

En route we also clocked up our first 25,000 miles since leaving Miami almost exactly a year ago.

The Chinchilla Motel can best be described as simple, but it did have telly and after a rather liquid dinner at the "Commercial Inn" Mrs H set to to watch the Tour de France live for 3 hours. (Really sad; ED.)

TOTAL MILEAGE: 25,186
45 litres at 25,072

AUSTRALIA

DAY: 344
13/07/11

'X' MARKS THE SPOT The manager of the Motel tells me that we are very lucky to have secured a bed. This is coal and gas country, and crawling with miners, engineers etc. A nearby coal fired power station, 3 years old – yes they are still building coal fired, despite the enormous amounts of gas available – is having its first shut down next week and the whole surrounding countryside will be stiff with maintenance men. Oh and by the way the Motel is up for sale for a trifling $3,000,000. Not sure how many cabins there are but maybe thirty and judging by ours can only have cost $2 - 3,000 to build. The price seems a little imaginative.

When checking the oil at cold it was looking – "well used". The last change was at La Serena in Chile. We stopped for lunch in Roma and asked a couple of garages if they could do a quick change. For a 10 minute job they both had the greatest delight in telling me that they couldn't do anything for ten days and three weeks respectively.

Our destination could reasonably fairly be said to be in the middle of Queensland, see 'X' opposite, without internet or even phone coverage – shock horror. From Chinchilla we travelled due West, but in Roma the road swung round to the North. Then just as the sun was lowering we headed West for the last 40 ks. The second half was on gravel, but 10DPG has been there and done that many times before. The sun however was a nuisance, but we managed to use a camper van as our gnomon.

Just as we arrived at the Carnarvon Gorge Wilderness Retreat I heard a strange tinkling from the offside wheel. Inspection revealed the loss of the 2 litre badge. Its lugs and spring clips floating around inside the hubcap. As this was the badge on the replacement hubcap,

Geoffrey & Hilary Herdman

fitted in B A – not very impressive manufacturing.

We are staying in glorified tents. I have always threatened Mrs H with the T word. These however come with canvas walls and roofs but on top of the roof there is a corrugated iron covering. We even have a bath and most essentially a gas heater.

TOTAL MILEAGE: 25,454
20.4 litres at 25,187 and 30.5 at 25,361
1 litre of oil in Chinchilla 25,186

DAY: 345
14/07/11   FIRST ANNIVERSARY; CARNARVON GORGE

Logically one would expect this to be Day 366, but when we returned to Europe in September 2010 for "Bristols to Bristol" for three weeks we stopped counting the days.

In glorious weather we set out on a fruitless "hunt the 2 litre badge" drive, and thence to the Information Centre at the end of the road. Having parked the car we found ourselves surrounded by peacefully grazing Roos.

The main part of the Gorge entailed a 9.3 ks walk – each way! – to Cathedral Cave, criss crossing the river bed over less and less obvious stepping stones. We managed to keep our feet dry going, but sadly not on the return, although the water was not cold. The Cave itself was adorned with aboriginal paintings. Some carbon dated to over 3,000 years and looking remarkably fresh. Numerous silhouettes of hands and everyday objects in a red ochre based paint, but also drawings of massed boomerangs. (See photo.)

Not having taken any recent exercise the return was a bit of a struggle. Back in our hut there was almost a fight for the first relaxing bath!

TOTAL MILEAGE: 25,460

DAY: 346
15/07/11   BACK TO THE GORGE
Awoke, not stiff exactly but aching slightly, however there was more to be seen. The weather was looking gloomy but we were told the Gorge looked best in the rain! Our destination today being Mickey's Creek, followed by the Moss Garden, a total of 11 ks rather than yesterday's 20.

During the afternoon a fine drizzle turned to a light rain. Having done the Moss Garden Mrs H was advised that the Amphitheatre, an additional 2.2 ks,

AUSTRALIA

was worth a visit, but her wimpy husband pleaded exhaustion and returned to the car. Needless to say it was reported as being the star attraction. (It was actually quite claustrophobic to squeeze through the rock entrance, almost a tunnel, but magnificent, and as there was no-one else there, an opportunity to declaim a little Shakespeare. ED.)

By the time we had returned to base the rain had set in solidly and we put the cover over an already wet car. It would at least stop any more water from getting in!

TOTAL MILEAGE: 25,464

DAY: 347
16/07/11

CACTOBLASTIS CACTORUM During the night it rained incessantly and hard – onto our corrugated iron roof – noisy! The corollary was that the 18 ks of unmade road were turned into very slippery mud. Small hills were interesting! but we made it and en route back to Chinchilla we stopped in Miles at the excellent Historic Village.

Our main interest, although there was much more to see in this excellent museum, was the story of how the Prickly Pear was overcome.

When Australia was first settled in 1788 the cochineal beetle was introduced to dye the army tunics. The cochineal lives on the prickly pear and that too was introduced from Brazil. By the turn of the 19th / 20th C prickly pear had grown completely out of control and had devastated huge tracts of farm land in NSW and Queensland.

In an inspired Australian piece of entomological research the above named moth was found to be the perfect antidote. Living and reproducing massively amongst the pears, and dying out as the pears were eaten and eradicated. Within 12 years of its introduction in 1925 it had conquered the menace, thus far without any counter effects.

And so onwards to our hosts for the night, friends of Tom and Bronwen, the wonderful Beasleys just outside Chinchilla. Incidentally the name comes not from the animal but as a corruption of an indigenous word for a type of tree.

Shortly after we arrived their daughter Susan came for a two week stay. We had been quartered in her bedroom so she nobly took to the family caravan!

That evening we all repaired to the Commercial Inn for dinner.

TOTAL MILEAGE: 25,727
40.3 litres in Injune at 25,557

Geoffrey & Hilary Herdman

DAY: 348
17/07/11

THE WONDERFUL BEASLEYS Our hosts Glen, Susan, and Barbara Beasley with from left Joe and Sam in attendance. (Joe is the proud father of no fewer than seven delightful four week old puppies, which it is hoped will have inherited their father's great skill as a cattle dog, with the brains of their mother Misty, who was on maternal feeding duties and so not available for the photo call.) On a telephone introduction the Beasleys kindly took us in for a couple of nights, insisting one wasn't enough, as they wanted to show us the farm.

Their son, Dr Brian Beasley, having given up on a career as a lecturer in English literature, due mainly to the internal politics at his university, was running a very successful workshop on the farm. This was of acute interest as it is now 4,000 miles since our last oil change in Chile. Whilst up on the hoist Brian also noticed that the front bearings needed tightening and did the business.

During the afternoon Glen took us "drive about" on the farm. His land is the type called Melon Hole Brigalow. The melon hole is a reference to the large dips that cover the land with a non porous undersoil so the water doesn't drain and the Brigalow to a useless type of native tree. Farming is a constant battle against extreme climate; 10 years of drought followed by the recent worst floods in living memory. It is also a matter of not flogging the land to death, and after three generations they have found the ideal stocking level to be one cow per 10 acres. For his 3,000 acres that's 300 cows. It is also a matter of finding the right type of grass. The most successful to date has been a S African seed called Rhodes, which always seems to have green shoots around its base. They have many hectares of grassland now, the result of years of hard work in clearing the scrub, by chainhauling from two dozers, and then continuing to clear the persistent regrowth, reseeding as necessary. The result is a beautiful pastoral landscape, the grassland scattered with groups of shelter trees.

BUT his land is on coal and gas and Glen recognizes that it is a given that within 2 years he will have gas rigs. There are currently two hundred in the area, but they are projected to increase to six thousand over the next 4 years. Here's the rub, the payoff is miserly as the farmers do not own their own mineral rights and the mining companies have automatic rights of access. However there is now an increasing grass roots reaction to the march of the miners.

That evening we had a romantic dinner sitting round a camp fire, including a delicious casserole from Bronwen, which we had delivered frozen, en route to the Gorge.

TOTAL MILEAGE: 25,751
Oil change at 25,735

AUSTRALIA

DAY: 349
18/07/11 — **COAL FIRED POWER STATION** See all the smoke? The power station is actually going at full welly. On day 344 I fulminated against coal fired, but having seen the reality it is hard to complain or see the difference between this and gas fired.

This is Kogan Creek power station, and it is air cooled. The large horizontal building in front has 7,800 sq metres of cooling surface and forty eight huge fans. The coal comes from a mine some 5 miles away by conveyor belt. There are reserves of 400 million tons in this one mine and the power station uses 2.8 million a year!

And so back to Bronwen and Tom. Shortly after our arrival H went walk about with Beatrice, the family labrador. Two hours later we had to send out a search party, but she and canine friend returned of their own accord, wagging their respective tails, having had a navigational misunderstanding. Dumb dog!!

TOTAL MILEAGE: 25,969
50.5 litres in Dalby 25,827 miles

DAY: 350
19/07/11

ADMIN IN BRISBANE A day of catching up on paperwork whilst H went sight seeing with Bron in Brisbane, travelling up river on the ferry for a most enjoyable walkabout in this very attractive city. And no there aren't any wild baboons in Australia, but this is such a nice picture that I couldn't resist it. South Africa 2003.

Geoffrey & Hilary Herdman

DAY: 351
20/07/11

NORTH TO HERVEY BAY In convoy with Bron and Tom in their Disco, we set off for Hervey Bay and Fraser Island, driving via Flaxton, as I wanted H to see the views. Sadly Le Relais is shut on Wednesdays so we had a rather bracing picnic. This is a novelty for the Herdmen but Bronwen rustles up mean provender. The view from our mountain top is not done justice by the photo. I put it down to the cheap camera – nothing to do with the photographer.

After lunch we played musical cars and I drove the Disco whilst Bronwen and Hilary went off in 10DPG. The replacement trafficator mechanism has irrevocably packed up, but at least the switch still works. It is just that it is no longer self cancelling. Apart from the tell tale green light there is no indication that one has left one's trafficator going.

At one stage I must have been following for over a mile with hand on horn trying to attract their attention, but you know how it is. They thought a police car was trying to pick them up!

TOTAL MILEAGE: 26,182
52.5 litres at 26,129

DAY: 352
21/07/11 **FRASER ISLAND** 10DPG was abandoned in secure parking on the mainland, complete with cover as we took the ferry for the 45 minute sail over to the island.

Bronwen and Tom had taken a rather classy three bedroom chalet, managed by Accor.

The island itself runs for about 75 miles up the coast of Queensland, is 15 miles wide at its widest and is considered to be the largest sand island in the world. Despite being pure sand, 113 cubic kilometres thereof, it rises to 800 ft at its highest and each of the walking trails involved some steep climbs as we were to find out!

The island is a 4 x 4 paradise. Tom was keen to show us the sights and we set off in the recently serviced Disco on VERY bumpy roads. Within the first 5 ks we had three warning lights, for ABS, traction control and hill descent control – electrics – electrics, but using low ratio we bounced our way around this very beautiful island, stopping here and there.

As 10DPG does not feature we will resume on Monday.

DAY: 356
25/07/11 **HEADING NORTH** Our goal is Townsville where we have become Gold members for this year's Chamber Music Festival. Twenty concerts in 8 days!

Bron has prebooked our accommodation in nice easy stages. Today we are headed for Bundaberg, via Childers. The hotel above is in downtown Childers. Absolutely typical of rural hotels in Australia with fine cast iron lace work and verandah.

The Pokie or one armed bandit is ubiquitous. Every hotel, pub and club advertises Pokies, including this one. Australians have the highest per capita gaming losses in the world. I think it is around $1,200 for every man woman and child.

TomTom swore he knew where the Rose Comfort Inn was in Bundaberg, but

Geoffrey & Hilary Herdman

took us to entirely the wrong part of town. On arrival at the correct destination 10DPG was starting to run very raggedly especially at tickover with much backfiring and missing.

Phone calls suggested that it was almost certainly electrical and time to start changing things sequentially.

TOTAL MILEAGE: 26,262

DAY: 357
26/07/11   1770 We are heading up the coast to Rockhampton but Bronwen suggests a visit to 1770. This involves an out and back diversion, but was absolutely worth it.

1770 is the name of a small village of fifty six permanent residents. No prizes for guessing when it was discovered or by whom! It is now an idyllic seaside resort.

As we had been too late for breakfast in the motel – Us – shurely shome mishtake – we found a splendid hostelry on the water's edge serving BLATs, which turned out to be enormous bacon, lettuce, avocado, and tomato rolls. These followed by a geriatric potter along the glorious beach. See photo of mangroves opposite.

Before setting out I had changed the distributor cap. No change to the bad running. One thing ticked off – several still to go. Oh dear!

TOTAL MILEAGE: 26,489
45 litres 26,346

DAY: 358
27/07/11   COAL AND SUGAR COUNTRY The whole of Queensland seems to be covered in sugar and coal. Sugar is on the surface and the coal not far below. Since Bundaberg we have been driving through sugar plantations, most with their own railways, running alongside and frequently criss crossing our road.

The railways are 2 ft gauge and there are about 4,000 ks in Queensland transporting 36 million tonnes of cane. The season is from June to December and the cane must be at the crusher within about 18 hours of being cut.

The coal is mostly open cast, and of the highest quality for iron smelting. Queensland is the largest coal producing state, in the largest coal producing country in the world. In 2009 production was close to 200 million tonnes, 85% for export. There are currently huge rows over the degree of Chinese ownership and farmland being bought up by Chinese interests to be destroyed for its excavation. Also, the pathetic amount of compensartion offered to the farmers for access; about 74c/ $1,000 profit, according to a local paper.

We drive to Mackay and take a taxi to the marina. Our taxi driver worked in the coal fields for 8 years as a truck driver. They now work 12 hour shifts and earn approximately Aus$150K per year. That's £100K. Each truck can carry 350 tonnes and basically the driver does a round trip of 15 ks over and over again.

The marina is full of expensive yachts and we are told many are the living

AUSTRALIA

quarters of the workers in the coal fields. Over in Western Australia the truck drivers' cleaners are flown into work on a fortnightly basis. It's a weird economy. Meat had gone up from $5 a kilo in 2000 to $16 now and bananas are being sold in Sydney at $15 a kilo. Australia is by far the most expensive place on our tour, worsened by the terrible exchange rate: £1 = $1.50 approx.

We eat wonderfully in George's Thai restaurant overlooking the marina.

TOTAL MILEAGE: 26,694
Filled up at 26,544 45 litres

DAY: 359
28/07/11 A LOT OF BANGING AROUND
We are heading to Townsville and the Australian Festival of Chamber Music. A bit of a kultur shock after somewhat of a desert.

Despite the change of distributor cap and rotor arm poor 10DPG is still missing badly. When we arrive at our splendid two bedroom apartment, which we are sharing with Tom & Bronwen, slow speed manoeuvring is fraught with bangs and backfires. As it is slightly worse when hot than cold there is a slight suggestion that it might be the coil. As I have a spare; a job for tomorrow. The poor car is also running hotter then normal; 95° as opposed to 90° - 92°.

It is Tom's birthday tomorrow, when we will be at the opening concert so we celebrate tonight splendidly on Bugs, which are a kind of crayfish, at the Pier. It transpires we were lucky, as the place is for sale and a subsequent visit, borne out by Tripadvisor reports, was dire.

TOTAL MILEAGE: 26,945
Filled up at 26,703 32 litres

DAY: 360
29/07/11 NO IMPROVEMENT
I am at the limit of my technical skills changing the coil. Fortunately management has a socket set. I resolve to buy one. A year ago on the Blue Ridge Parkway I would have been able to remove the starter rather than being towed in if only I had brought one with me…

The new coil makes no difference. There is a word which springs to mind – unprintable. One is mildly depressed, but the car will not be needed for a week or so, so we abandon it and resolve to enjoy the music.

Today is Tom's birthday, after yesterday's unbirthday, so we walked along the Strand for a delicious birthday brunch, with Buck's fizz. Here he is with Bronwen.

The Festival opens with Messiaen's Quartet for the End of Time, written whilst he was in a German prisoner of war camp in the winter of 1941. Haunting and very

Geoffrey & Hilary Herdman

beautiful. As we sat in warmth and comfort, we thought of the prisoners, some brought in on stretchers, who had listened in near freezing conditions to that first performance. We finish with the Four Last Songs. Perhaps a strange choice for the opening concert, but beautifully sung!

DAY: 366
04/08/11 LITERARY STUFF

Into the second year of our sojourn, excluding the trip back to Europe last September.

Apart from three concerts a day, we have been busy. Rather gratifyingly my first publication: Paxos and Antipaxos is selling out faster than I had imagined. A diligent reader has even written in to report a major typo. H & I have been reproofreading and picking up some more!

Additionally the RAC have asked me for an article about the trip of 800 - 1,000 words. The first attempt came to 2,500. Much easier to write than to excise!

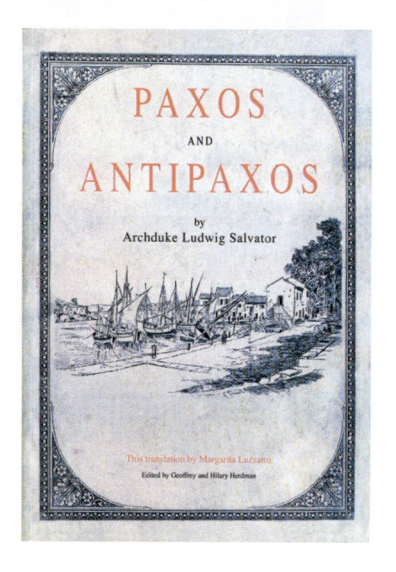

DAY: 367
05/08/11 WITH A LITTLE HELP FROM THE BOC

As we were running late and I had promised to show the car to one or two people we drove to the morning's concert. Just as we were about to drive into the garage on our return a car pulled up and a voice said; "Hello I am a member of the BOC and I have a 400." It was David Pearse from Canberra, although not in a Bristol. He was a member of both BOCA and the BOC. What good taste!

We reported our woes to him and despite now living in Canberra he had lived in Townsville for many years. He tells us of a garage who might be able to help. This is wonderful news. Townsville, the largest town in N Queensland with 175,000 souls, does not boast too many Bristol agents and all my attempts to find a substitute thus far have proved fruitless. A quick phone call and Scott says to bring the car straight away and he will drop everything.

Scott goes to work and finds a fine layer of sediment in the fuel filters and jets. He cannot find a new main filter so cleans it and needs to keep the car overnight to let it dry.

The photo is of a collection of didgeridoos. I always wondered what they looked like. I think you blow into them and they make a curious fog horn type sound.

TOTAL MILEAGE: 26,950

AUSTRALIA

DAY: 368
06/08/11 **PROBLEM SORTED** Townsville has the highest proportion of "old" buildings of anywhere in Australia.

Scott rings to say the car is now running perfectly. He has cleaned the air filters, last cleaned in Bariloche, and reset the tappets. At that point things were still a little rough so ultimately he has reset the timing. He is clearly pleased with himself. Charlie always thought it might be the timing!

We pick up the car and it is certainly massively better. Gone is all the banging around, but it is still missing slightly. I try retarding the ignition on the hand control and hey presto we have a sweetly running car again. Phew!

One of the advantages of "Gold" membership for the concerts is that we always sit in the same seats. Our next door neighbours are Doug and Joan, who have driven from near Sydney in their camper van to come to the Festival. Sydney is 2,100 ks to the South. Although Joan does have a car at home Doug does all the driving; sometimes 50 ks a day, sometimes 300. Doug and Joan are 92 and 88 respectively. What a lovely couple. H and I hope we are in half as good nick if we are spared that long!

Their grandsons are with them for the final concert and I take them all off to show them the car.

TOTAL MILEAGE: 26,955

DAY: 369
07/08/11 **LOGISTICS** Despite being "Concerted Out" we are also having withdrawal symptoms.

The original plan had been to drive to Cape York if possible. Some have said the road is sealed all the way, some have said not. All have said it is a pretty boring drive and the only real point of going is "Because it's there!"

We settle on Cairns for the most northerly point, BUT we have a logistical

Geoffrey & Hilary Herdman

problem. We would like to have the car in Turkey for early October and the shipping dates keep changing. Joanne, our agent sent us an e-mail on Friday, too late for us to reply to, saying she now needs the car for Friday 12th, rather than the following Tuesday. Brisbane is three to four days to the South and this would entail starting the return in the morning. We resolve to see if the service is in fact weekly and if so will delay shipping for a week.

So; tomorrow we will phone Joanne first thing and either take an extra week and do Cairns or head South. Today we will stay another day in our apartment. The view is not bad, sandy beach, lapping sea, palms and a coffee pot! The RAC article has to be cut down to size. I manage to reduce it to 1,200 words. The RAC still think it is too long and threaten to edit it further. I wonder if Shakespeare had the same problems?

DAY: 370
08/08/11 BANANA COUNTRY

A phone call to the agents confirms that ships sail on a weekly basis and are supposedly somewhat quicker than we had originally been told. If we deliver the car on the 19th August the ship will sail on the 23rd and SHOULD be in Mersin in S Turkey by the beginning of October – Somali pirates permitting. We will believe it when we see it but meanwhile resolve to head North for Cairns.

It is not a particularly interesting drive. Cairns is 220 miles N of Townsville and the road is seriously under repair from the floods last Summer. We stop for lunch by the seaside in Cardwell, much of which was destroyed by a cyclone earlier this year. We also stop for a photo opportunity in banana country.

Thanks to Scott's ministrations the car is going like a dream and running much cooler (90°C) despite the day being sufficiently hot that when we change drivers we decide to put the hood up to stop our poor brains from frazzling.

TOTAL MILEAGE: 27,170
Filled up outside Townsville 55.5 litres 26,960 miles

AUSTRALIA

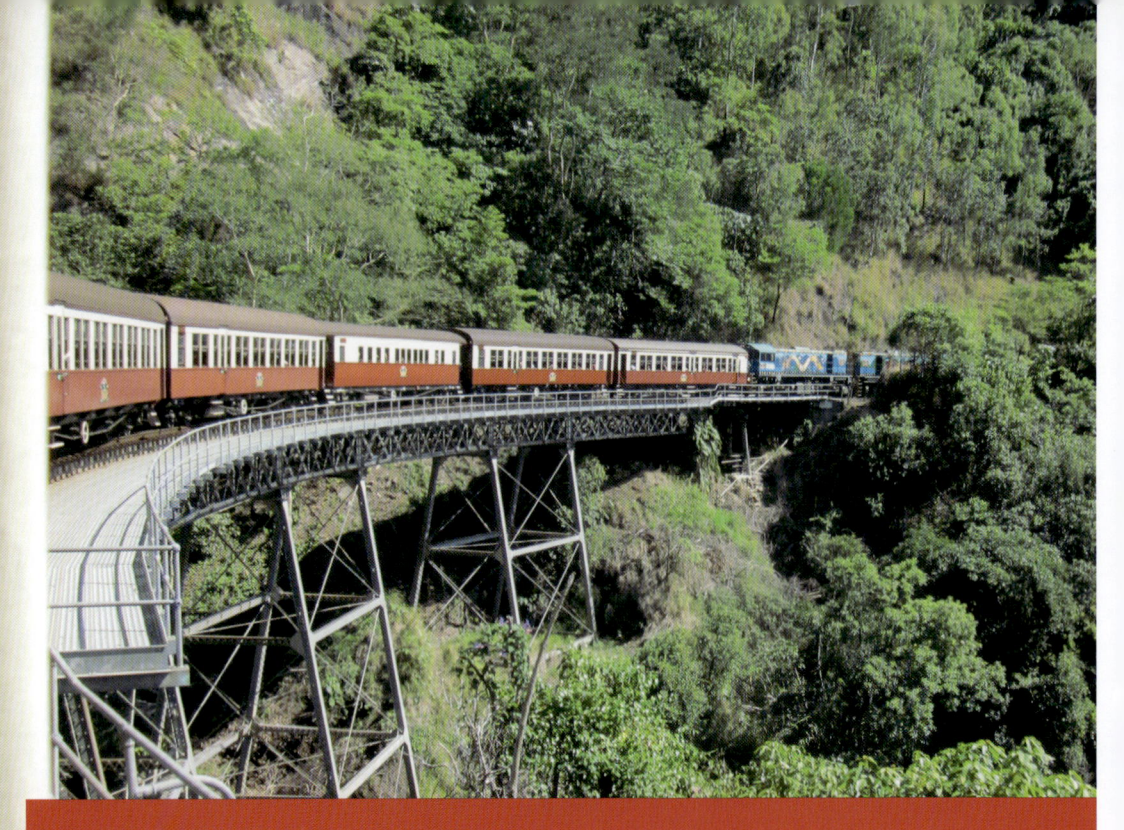

DAY: 371
09/08/11   5TH GREAT TRAIN JOURNEY From Cairns we take the train to Kuranda, built to service the gold mines in the 1880s, but soon becoming a tourist train, as it is today. We upgrade to Gold Class and are fed and watered very satisfactorily, and continuously for the rather slow, but very beautiful journey. Our carriage is 100 years old, but heavily modernized.

Our other four trains have been chronologically:
Mount Washington
The Old Patagonian Express
The train to the Clouds from Salta to 4,200 metres
The Ghan from Darwin to Adelaide

One of us is not as wild about train journeys as the other, but neither of us would have missed any of them.

On arrival at Kuranda we are in a tourist maelstrom, but escape to a butterfly sanctuary, where we are surrounded by 1,500 of them, fluttering like anything and very beautiful.

Then it's time for the trip back. This time we travel by two cable cars which soar over the forest and cover 7.5 ks. Whilst waiting for the return bus we are riveted by a water skiing lake, where they have a continuous loop of fast moving wire. Hook on and away you go – or not – as the case may be.

Geoffrey & Hilary Herdman

DAY: 372
10/08/11 — IT'S TOUGH DOING A BLOG!

A true bucket and spade day. We take a motor catamaran out to Green Island on the edge of the Barrier Reef. We walk round the island in about half an hour. Despite all the day trippers they have done it rather well and there is a comfy looking hotel in the tropical forest, which must be bliss when the last tourist boat has left.

From Green Island we and a million Japanese, Koreans, Malays and Indonesians take another boat to the Barrier Reef proper, where we park alongside a floating pontoon. Lunch is served – should have been caviar and Krug at the price, but its not bad and in the afternoon we try a semi submersible. The view is rather amazing. I have never been in one before and am completely hooked!

Having failed to get the correct optical face mask, I opted out of the snorkelling, but understand from H it was thrilling, with beautiful coloured coral, masses of fish, and no shoals of other tourists once a few metres away. A bonus on the return trip was a pod of humpback whales spouting just like the ones in the charts in the museum in Nantucket.

One of the species to be found on the island

DAY: 373
11/08/11 — CARDWELL BEACH HEADING SOUTH

Our Australian visas are due to run out on 17th August and we won't be leaving until 26th or thereabouts. Fortunately there is a dept of Immigration in Cairns. We visit and are told that we can either leave the country and come back, or renew our visas for $260 each! For the former the nearest place we can go to is Port Moresby in PNG and guess what? flights costs $280 return. As we start filling in application forms the helpful girl tells us there is a new tariff and if we apply on line it is only $110. Hard to believe really.

What with one thing and another it is nearly midday by the time we are finally on the road. Mrs H also opts for the pretty route via Silkwood. The road is narrower, but misses many of the road works on the main road. We also pass signs for the splendidly named Murdering Point Winery, home of exotic tropical wines! Sugar cane is all round us, as are cane trains and refineries, belching steam and smoke from burning the waste cane.

We have a frugal lunch back in Cardwell, where the road meets the sea. Our goal is a return to Townsville and this time we stay at the Comfort Inn. The prop. has a 1964 Daimler saloon with 2.5 V8 engine. He says it is impossible to just drive off in it as the engine needs a lot of warming up!

Mrs H applies on line for our visa extensions and finds to her dismay that it still costs $260 online. What a surprise! I wouldn't have bothered but she has visions of being detained as we try to leave the country.

TOTAL MILEAGE: 27,393
Filled up in Cairns 41 litres 27,175

AUSTRALIA

DAY: 374
12/08/11   I TAKE NO PRISONERS
Despite having taken some photos of some curious Moreton fig trees on the sea front, and visited Scott and Les to demonstrate the car is still running and express our thanks, we are still away from Townsville by 10:00.

We are heading for the Eungella National Park for a couple of nights, where one has the best chance of seeing Duck Billed Platypuses.

Until we turn off, somewhere N of Mackay, this means pounding down the A1, or Bruce highway, in common with some interesting drivers. The above photo is of a fully laden, articulated car transporter just before he overtook us. His next overtake must have scared him a bit. He only just made it back in time and was quite circumspect for at least the next 10 minutes.

We arrive at the Broken River Mountain Resort, after a splendid climb to 2,400 ft and almost immediately go on a platypus hunt. To our great joy we see bits of at least three. Very strange animals!

TOTAL MILEAGE: 27,651 (added 1.25 litres of oil)
Filled up in Ayr 45.5 litres 27,452

DAY: 375
13/08/11   DUCK BILLED PLATYPUS
One of the two accepted plurals for duck billed platypus is duck billed platypus. The other is platypuses. I rather prefer the former. Anyway poor Mrs H stayed out watching them far too long last night and by the time she returned to our chalet was frozen. I had been wrestling with wet wood and a guttering fire, without much success. Even the hair dryer trick seemed to just blow ashes all over the place rather than jollying things up. Today she had a stinker of a cold. Worse – one was almost kept awake at night.

Despite this, after breakfast we were dumped off 5 miles up stream and left to

Geoffrey & Hilary Herdman

walk back along the banks of the Broken River on the Crediton Trail. This had been carved out at the water's edge a century ago by loggers, and now – especially for we non sufferers – made for a superb walk.

During the afternoon 10DPG was given a good cleaning, always a good opportunity to find loose things e.g. a rear overrider and bomb bay door catch!

Once again in the evening we sallied forth in search of platypus and were astonished to find a wedding party by the river in photographic mode. The bride in full white fig must have been frozen. We were rewarded with a positive plethora of D B P. The photo is the best I could do, as rather tryingly they can dive extremely quickly. However there aren't many places in the world where you can see them in the wild, so we were rather pleased to have any sort of photo. This one was perhaps 8 inches long, whereas we had been told they could grow to 20.

DAY: 376
14/08/11 SOUTH TO GLADSTONE

Poor thing the lurghi had struck with a vengeance, so I drove whilst she mostly slept. Since Scott cleaned things up the economy has improved dramatically and we seem to be nearer 27 mpg than the 22 we had been doing before his ministrations. Memo to self – if economy drops off clean air filters!

TomTom took us on the Mackay bypass, which involved very pretty but in some cases unsealed roads. Sadly once back on the A1 it was a rather boring 5 hour run down to Gladstone.

People had warned us that Gladstone was not the ideal place for a stop. It is an ever enlarging industrial port for shipping coal and gas outwards. But tomorrow we are going to Heron Island and need to depart from Gladstone. If we had to stop here the suggestion was Rydges, which turned out to be expensive and dire.

On entering town H noticed an advert for a concert that evening by the Australian Chamber Orchestra. At reception we asked where the ACO concert was. The receptionist gave us a look of dumb stupidity and had not the first idea. Shortly afterwards the ACO checked in. It took her half an hour to check-in sixteen of them and then some found their rooms already occupied.

Having cleaned the car yesterday we had our first rain for some time and the poor thing was once again filthy on arrival.

After dinner H took to her bed whilst I went to the excellent concert, at the end of which I tried to buy Thomas Gould, the leader, a drink but Gladstone had long since shut up shop. It was 22:00!

TOTAL MILEAGE: 27,985
Filled up at 27,744   49.4 litres

AUSTRALIA

DAY: 377
15/08/11
HERON ISLAND 10DPG is parked in "secure" parking in the Marina as we take a 34 metre catamaran. This is longer than the Endeavour (32 metre), Captain Cook's ship when he "discovered" Australia. Thirstier too. For the 140 k round trip the catamaran uses 1,500 litres of diesel!

It is though a whole lot quicker; we cover the journey in under 2 hours. The island itself is a sand on coral paradise of just 40 acres, yet it has three separate communities: Tourist Resort, Queensland University Research Station, and National Parks, all living in separate compounds, hidden amongst the mangroves and Pisonias. Despite, or because of, its remoteness the island has all mod cons. Desalination, sewage treatment and power. It is also home to 70,000 Noddies. We counted them! Of course living amongst them the smell of guano is ever present but not offensively so.

During the afternoon, as we are walking along the beach, we are amazed to come across our second wedding party in three days. This time the marriage is actually being conducted on the water's edge. Bride and groom have flown in from Harvard, where the groom is a research physicist, and the bride a vet, with their respective families.

We wine and dine splendidly, and although provided with earplugs against the dawn chorus sleep like logs without. Mrs H's cold is buch better.

DAY: 378
16/08/11
WONDERS OF THE REEF Mrs H much better and wriggling sexily into a wet suit takes herself off snorkelling. I had tried to buy an optical face mask in Cairns, but they didn't have anything extreme enough for my eyes!

PM: we take the very instructive reef walk. The above is one of five different types of sea cucumber found locally. They are apparently very high in protein and considered a delicacy in parts of the world. They can, in extremis, be eaten raw. They clean up the coral as they live on bacterial algae found in the sand.

Geoffrey & Hilary Herdman

DAY: 379
17/08/11　　**FAREWELL TO HERON ISLAND** South to Bundaberg, where H had found a B&B just outside town on the road to Bargara. An excellent dinner in Kacy's.

On the drive South we overtook a caravan being towed by a Silver Shadow. I hope he was a member of the Australian Rolls Royce Caravan Owners Club!

TOTAL MILEAGE: 28,108
Filled up at 28,002 miles 46.4 litres

AUSTRALIA

DAY: 380
18/08/11 TROUBLES WITH OIL FILTERS

As we are now back in Brisbane, and our shipping point, the above shows our route in Australia. To put it in perspective Cairns is 1,720 ks north of Brisbane.

Tomorrow 10DPG goes in the box bound for Turkey and it occurred to me that although not yet due for an oil change it would be an awful lot easier to do it in Australia than the wilds of Bulgaria. Thus it was that at about 16:30 we turned up to a very helpful garage. The last filter from the UK was already in use, but Gerard from Adelaide had sold me a supply of the Australian equivalent. We filled the car with fresh oil, started the engine and once we had oil pressure, topped up and retightened the filter. As I was about to move off the ramp I noticed that we no longer had any pressure. It is always a delicate question as to how long you run the engine to see if the gauge will come to life, but as it should have been instant, we decided to revert to the old tried and tested Mahle.

There has been much correspondence on the forum on exactly this topic and one way valves. The thing I don't understand is that on first starting the engine we did have pressure, but subsequently none. Anyway I was assured that although not ideal to reuse a filter, they should be good for many more miles than mine had covered. There was of course no alternative anyway!

TOTAL MILEAGE: 28,342

Petrol added 12.75 litres at 28,278 we needed to be fairly empty for the container

DAY: 381
19/08/11

METAMORPHOSIS AND ADIEU Today is shipping day. We have to be at the docks by 11:00. By 07:30 I am up and cleaning, and then changing the number plates back to 10DPG.

Unbelievably by 10:45 all is done and the car repacked; many, many books, maps, a printer, and three suitcases.

We are not sure if we have ventured onto toll roads en route to the docks, but being back on UK plates one of us is rather less worried than the other. The car is expertly packed in the container and they even put down bags of silica to absorb moisture, but they do handle a car a day on average.

We have had a wonderful time in Australia. We didn't get to Tasmania, nor Cape York. We were sad about the former, but none too sad about the latter.

We have still driven 5,869 miles. We have spent far more on maintenance than in the whole of the rest of the trip, but have a feeling that to a large degree this was caused by making good some rather careless workmanship. We have been very lucky with the weather, which for the winter has been fantastic.

We have also met incredible kindness from members of BOCA; especially from Geoff Dowdle, and dear Ozi who put up with us for three weeks.

One day I would still very much like to do a circumnavigation. There are those close to me who are not quite so sure. As we say: "We will see!"

TOTAL MILEAGE: 28,350

AUSTRALIA

Carless Days

DAYS: 382-428
20/08/11 - 05/10/11 CROSSING ASIA AND TURKEY

Back in Brisbane from Cairns, for a few more days with the long suffering, endlessly hospitable Tom and Bronwen, and dear Beatrice, their yellow labrador, who loved going for walks with us; it was mutual! We then flew to Turkey, via Bali, Bangkok, Laos, Bhutan and Nepal.

Highlights:

- A day's walk in the beautiful Lamington National Park, in Queensland, last visited 17 years ago, and as lovely as we had remembered it.

In Bali:

- The exceptionally charming Pavilions hotel where we stayed. Green, green paddy fields.
- Barong dancing, especially the Tiger.
- Geoffrey bravely eating a durrian; it smells revolting and apparently tasted even worse!

In Laos:

- Luang Prabang, with city houses from the French colonial era.
- Bathing the elephants.

▌ The Mekong river, where we took a trip upstream in a beautifully constructed longboat.

In Bhutan:

▌ Prayer flags seen fluttering in long lines on the hillsides and over the river gorges, when we drove in a 4 WD, over dreadful roads, along lovely valleys and through beautiful mountainous country.

▌ The Tiger's Nest, reached by a heart pounding, lung bursting climb, culminating in seven hundred uneven steps to its seemingly impossible perch, clinging to the sheer cliff face.

▌ En route to Nepal, wonderful views of Everest.

In Kathmandhu, not a highlight, but a vivid memory, of an earthquake. Two shocks, the walls of our old wooden hotel bulging and shaking. It was the edge of the huge earthquake centred in Sikkim; the hotel was undamaged, but sadly people were killed in the town, when the British Embassy garden wall collapsed into the street.

Geoffrey & Hilary Herdman

Carless Days

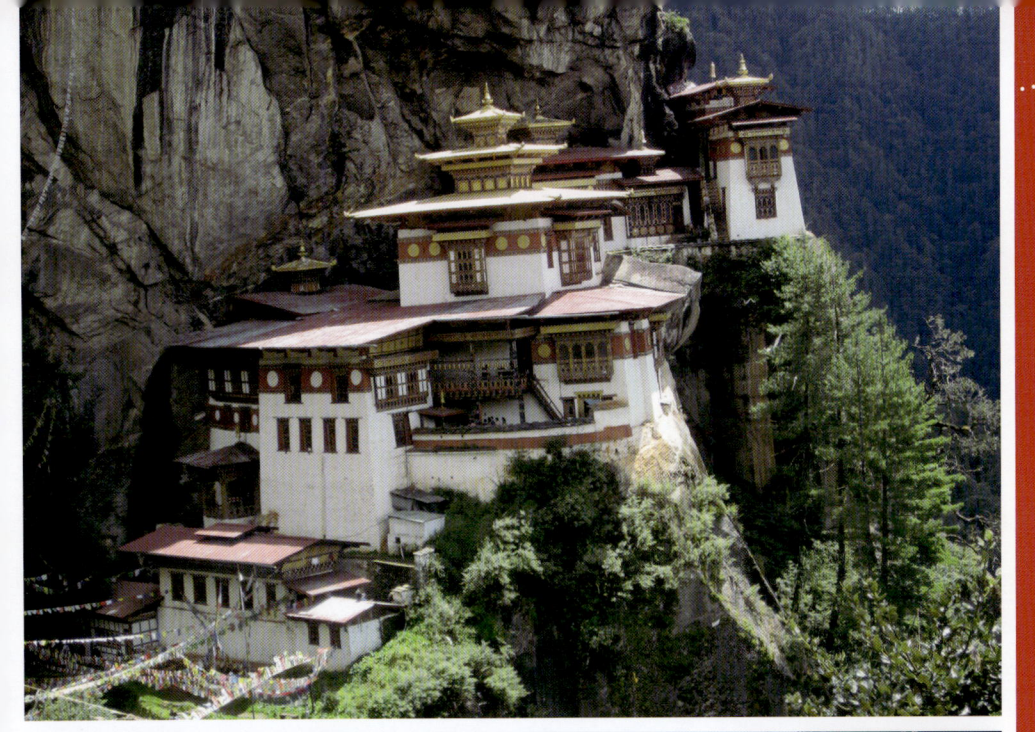

We then flew to Istanbul, returning to Europe almost exactly a year since we left London for Halifax. We had a most enjoyable couple of days there, before returning in hired wheels to the Asian side of the bridge, to retrieve 10 DPG in Adana, on the South East coast. At least the delay gave us time to explore the fascinating South East of Turkey, and enjoy the cuisine!

ROUND THE WORLD WITH 10DPG

CHAPTER 5
Asia and Europe

DAY: 429
06/10/11   **INTO ASIA**   After a journey of six weeks, being transhipped in Singapore and Gioia Tauro (where's that? – South Italy opposite Sicily), and dodging Somali pirates, 10DPG has finally arrived in Mersin, Southern Turkey. Although Minor it still qualifies as Asia and thus the car has now visited all major continents, except Antarctica.

Whilst 10DPG has been travelling we have:

Crossed both the Euphrates and the Tigris and the great and fertile plain of Mesopotamia; climbed to the Tigers Nest monastery in Bhutan; drunk Laotian "whiskey" on the banks of the Mekong; and witnessed funeral pyres by the banks of the river in Kathmandu. The last was perhaps the most unforgettable and the least likely to be repeated!

DAY: 436
13/10/11   **PORT TROUBLES** After five days' waiting our agents had advised that we can collect the car today. Their representative, Serdar, who speaks excellent English arrives at 08:00 and together we drive to Mersin in our rentacar, about 50 miles away.

Arrival at the port was chaotic. It is Singapore owned and supposedly the largest container port in the Mediterranean. Immediately inside the main gate a goods train sat for half an hour. Soon all cars were hooting and one of the drivers stood on a rostrum conducting them. However eventually we found the correct container, which had already been unsealed, and 10DPG appeared to have travelled well. As the battery was disconnected we pushed the car out and then tried starting. I had bought some "Ezy Start" in Australia and with Serdar squirting ether into the K&Ks eventually the engine caught.

We still had to arrange insurance and a Turkish driving permit, not to mention an exit permit from the port. This last proved tricky as there is only one man who can issue these and he was back in Adana, where we were staying. We had to wait until 16:30 for him to turn up. Having arrived at the port at 09:15 it was about 17:45 by the time we were clear. Whilst waiting 10DPG attracted a large group of admirers. It was like S America all over again.

Serdar patiently waited whilst I returned the faithful rentacar to the airport. We had covered over 5,300 ks in it, averaging 55 mpg. It was a Turkish built Renault Fluence – very comfortable!

Finally I drove Serdar back to his office and arrived back at the Adana Hilton at about 20:00. A long day but we have 10DPG back on the road, and the weather is gorgeous.

TOTAL MILEAGE: 28,421
Filled up at 28,369 58 expensive litres

Geoffrey & Hilary Herdman

The 6 minarets of the mosque of Adana, the second largest in Turkey

DAY: 437
14/10/11 ON THE ROAD PROPER
Slightly behind schedule today we set out for the journey home. The immediate plan is to drive round the South Western coast of Turkey, before taking a ferry to Gallipoli and Europe.

Today's destination was Antalya, about 350 miles away. TomTom (aka Simon) wanted us to go inland via Konya and suggested it would take 6 hours. We reprogrammed him for the coastal route and were surprised to find that although shorter the suggested time was now 9 hours – clearly Simon having a bad day.

Having met Serdar at 07:30 to pay outstanding amounts we were en route by 09:15 in glorious weather and topless. To Mersin, a road I was beginning to know quite well, we were on motorway, and then dual carriageway, and then single carriageway, and then road under construction. The scenery was wonderful but the going was as Simon had suggested – very slow. Our ETA was 19:15 and eventually we abandoned Antalya for Side, some 50 miles nearer.

All the way we had hooting cars and Turks giving us the thumbs up! Plus of course cars drawing alongside for a photo, just as we were about to overtake a truck!

The approach to Side is spectacular. You drive through the arch of a Roman amphitheatre and are surrounded by Roman remains. Sadly these give way to the most appalling stretch of shopping hell. Finally the road runs out, but when we tell the police we are going to the Beach House hotel he lowers the car barrier

ASIA AND EUROPE

and we drive through a pedestrian shopping precinct with all the world saying "Beautiful car – come to my place for dinner!".

The Beach House is run by Tasmanian Penni and her Turkish husband, Ali. Penni has lived here for 32 years and has remained surprisingly sane. If you come back to her hotel 3 years running you have a plaque with your name attached to your bedroom door. Most doors had several plaques. During the course of a short walk in the twilight to more spectacular Roman remains we were set on by at least five restauranteurs, and eventually had a rather unsatisfactory and expensive meal from a morose Kurd. At least it was by the water's edge, but we thought any more than a couple of days in this tourist trap would send you mad.

TOTAL MILEAGE: 28,727
Filled up at 28,521 29 litres

DAY: 438
15/10/11

ASPENDOS AND A SURPRISE All our married life H has mentioned Aspendos, which is the best preserved Roman theatre in Anatolia (the Asian part of Turkey). Comparisons with the theatre at Orange sprang to mind, and as at Orange, opera and ballet are performed here in the Summer. There were many tourists, one of whom sang an anthem, not even on the stage i.e. well away from the acoustic centre, but it could be heard all over the auditorium, which is still complete, and can hold 7,000. As the ancient town had a population of no more than 20,000 they must have been an artistic lot.

While H was foraging for orange juice I volunteered to make the hotel reservation near Gocek. On Tuesday it is her birthday and three couples, unbeknown to her, are arriving to help celebrate. The plan had been to have the party on Chios, a Greek island very close to Cesmé. I had booked the ferry tickets and most efficiently the ferry company had phoned yesterday to advise that due to a Greek customs strike the ferry would not be running tomorrow. We had planned to "bump into" Pete and Fran on the ferry, but it looked as if that wasn't going to be possible, so I arranged to stay in the same hotel as they.

Many years ago we had sailed into Gocek harbour, when it was completely undeveloped. Now there were good hotels by the water's edge and H was

Geoffrey & Hilary Herdman

expecting to stay in one of these. However P & F were flying in to Dalaman and had booked a hotel a little further on.

Once we had driven through the sprawl of Antalya, Turkey's fourth largest city, the scenery became spectacular, now climbing, now swooping with the sea on our left. This is what 405 Drophead motoring is all about! Weather gorgeous, 26°C in October, and all was well with the world.

And then we drove straight past Gocek and the questions started.

And then we found the hotel and the questions became even more marked.

At about 22:00 a taxi drew up. I had warned P & F to be as quiet as mice as we were sitting outside. As he approached Peter put his hands over Hilary's eyes and said 'Guess who'. Bless her she had had no idea.

TOTAL MILEAGE: 28,980
Filled up at 28,756 46 litres.

DAY: 439
16/10/11   CESMÉ AND ANOTHER SURPRISE   A taxi arrived at 09:00 and off we set in convoy for a rentacar for P & F from the airport. Weather sadly grey and cold, so top up. We had heard from Loukia that the strike was cancelled and we would be able to sail to Chios.

A rather uninspiring drive, of which the last third was on motorways. Fortunate really as Izmir, the seconf largest town in Turkey looked a real dump, much best seen from the motorway. We did at least manage some excellent baclava and coffee en route in a small friendly café, which had to send forth in one direction for turkish coffee and in another for the baclava, but shook hands with all of us profusely on our leaving.

We arrived in a rather bleak and cold Cesmé at about 15:30. They had told us to check-in at 17:00, but for now all gates were very shut. A further phone call established that the ferry was definitely going and so we phoned Peter Armstrong and joined him and Vivienne for drinks.

ASIA AND EUROPE

Perhaps a little later than we should have we remade our way back to the port. There we found that our Turkish ferry had been cancelled and we were now on a much smaller Greek ferry. As we had not arrived at the appointed one hour before, we could no longer take 10DPG and we had to be very quick anyway as we had to clear emigration before departure. There was also the question of how we would return as no-one knew the strike situation for sure. Question – should we even go? As there were more surprises on Chios there was only one answer and soon we were bouncing around in a very rough sea, with sea water crashing over the four cars at the back. I was mightily thankful we had abandoned 10DPG on Turkish soil.

On arrival at Chios, and having been examined by customs, there waiting for us were Theo and Loukia, again, bless her, taking Hilary completely by surprise. A very joyful reunion. We then rented a small car, Theo had his Spitfire, and made our way to the elegant Perleas mansion. This followed by an excellent and very cheap dinner in a local restaurant, which made Paxos look expensive and Australia exorbitant, but most other places in the world we have been to do that!

The photo (previous page) is of Peter and Theo in Theo's Spitfire.

TOTAL MILEAGE: 29,231
Filled up at 28,996 46 litres

DAY: 440
17/10/11

DISASTER AND A THIRD SURPRISE Despite being, at its closest, only 2 miles from the Turkish mainland, Chios is Greek. Like the rest of Greece it was a part of the Ottoman Empire from the 16th to the early 20th C. Due to its very valuable mastic – (see Day 442) and shipping, it was one of the wealthiest parts of the Empire. For this reason the local populace were unmoved by the Greek War of Independence in 1822, until a small army of freedom fighters arrived from Samos and fomented revolution. The Turkish garrison was besieged in the town fortress. In retaliation a force of 40,000 arrived from Turkey.

It is estimated that in the ensuing massacre 5/6ths of the 120,000 population were slaughtered, enslaved or expelled. The family of a Herefordshire Bristol owner were amongst those who were affected.

Unable to face the horrors of Turkish enslavement a whole village at Nea Mona jumped to its death. Having visited the precipice it would at least have been quick!

Finally in 1912, after the First Balkan War, Chios became a part of a free Greece. It has never regained its former glory or wealth, and the current population is about half that of 1822.

Faced with continuing uncertainties as to how they were going to get off the island Peter, accompanied by Theo, left us in the middle of dinner to "check the possibility of flights."

Sitting at the next table was someone bearing, from the rear view, a remarkable likeness to another Bristollian, so very shortly after Peter and Theo's return, when someone looking very like Janet Hathaway came into the restaurant H at first thought it was another amazing coincidence until she was closely followed by Robert!

DAY: 441
18/10/11 ONE'S BIRTHDAY One's birthday being celebrated with a flaming dessert, accompanied by the Hathaways, Hughes, and Papathanasiadises on Chios.

Our wonderful tour guide, Loukia, had taken us on a trip to the Southern part of the island and especially to Mesta, an almost perfectly preserved Byzantine village. During the Genovese "ownership" of the island from 1261 to 1566, when the Ottomans took over, the island was under constant threat of attack from pirates. As a consequence all villages were built as fortresses.

If one may interject (one may, ED.) it was a wonderful day, and I am so grateful to Peter, Loukia and Geoffrey for all their secret arrangements, and to everyone who made such an effort to get to an unexpectedly difficult destination!

DAY: 442
19/10/11 MASTIC Mastic gum comes only from Chios. It is used for flavouring, especially in Arabia and Turkey, for healing purposes, and in perfumes. During the heyday of the Ottoman empire it was literally worth its weight in gold. Theft of mastic was punishable by execution. Nowadays, rather more prosaically it is sold for about €80 per kilo, but is incredibly labour intensive.

ASIA AND EUROPE

DAY 443

The ground under each tree is swept clear and chalk powder laid in a circle. Shallow incisions are made in the trees and sap oozes over a period of time and forms a gum. Some stays on the tree, some falls into the chalk. On average a tree will yield 200 grams of mastic. Chios produces 150 tonnes a year. That's an awful lot of trees. The tiniest pieces are gathered up, and finally the fallen leaves are swept up and taken into the village where old ladies sieve them for tiny scraps of mastic, and remove any trace of dirt. What will they do when the old ladies have died?

Loukia had commandeered Vassilis, a graphics designer from Athens who had returned to the home of his forefathers and now has five hundred trees. He took us to a grove and showed us the primitive routines. Speed he said was of the essence! The demonstration was followed by an al fresco picnic with some "interesting" local wine and a speciality of dried figs stuffed with almonds.

Later we drove to Pirgi to see the ladies sitting on their doorsteps sieving away. They must have the patience of saints.

DAY: 443
20/10/11   STRIKING GREEKS George Papandreou (he was born and educated in the USA so his Christian name really is George) must have the least enviable job in the world. He is being forced by the IMF to institute some sort of accountability amongst his countrymen. Today there is a vote in parliament, to reduce pensions, increase taxes, and curtail some of the industrial closed shop practices. To an outsider these are probably extremely sensible and long overdue measures, but rather naturally the 4,000,000 Greek workers are to say the least unhappy. Theo says he is only redressing the ills of his father, Andreas, who gave the workers far too much. But for two days some of the biggest strikes ever seen in Athens have been raging.

In far off Chios we are stranded. Customs are among the strikers and rumour has it that they will extend the strike for another 48 hours. An extra couple of days is actually bliss as the weather, which was very cold at the beginning of the

Geoffrey & Hilary Herdman

week, has perked up no end, and H has even swum! but longer than two days would be frustrating.

We drive to the West of the island climbing on wonderful hairpinned roads to over 2,000 ft. The scenery is spectacular. We round one hairpin and are surrounded by two to three hundred goats, all with jangling bells. Five dogs and four goatherds are in attendance, one leading a horse, and then we are through them all. We visit a hot water spring, on the edge of the shore, with miraculous healing powers, and climb the castle of Vossilos, before returning to Chios town. Behind it is the Genovese fortress, and within its walls are cafés, hammams, houses and even a mosque, now converted to a church. Just as we are going home the rentacar agent, who knows far more than the shipping agents, comes running after us to say that the strike is over and we can catch the 08:30 boat tomorrow morning – Phew!

DAY: 444
21/10/11   EPHESUS   In perfect weather and a flat calm sea we sailed back to Cesmé. 10DPG having been abandoned by the roadside was waiting patiently, needless to say with doors and boot unlocked! We even had a promise of a refund of the usurious €120 ferry fee for the car. It's only 7 miles each way!

In convoy with Peter and Fran we drove South again to Ephesus (Efes in modern Turkish – like the national beer!) and were amazed. Despite being out of season there must have been thousands of tourists there and the weather was a perfect temperature for sight seeing. In the middle of August it cannot be much fun! The photo is of the library of Celsus, built as a memorial by his son, as both a tomb and a library, holding over 12,000 scrolls, sadly burnt in the fire that followed the devastating earthquake of 262AD. You don't get too many sons like that nowadays!

The approach to Ephesus, like the approach to most other Turkish monuments was lined with the usual rag tag and bobtail of street vendors. However one proclaimed to be selling "Genuine Fake Watches" and had literally hundreds of

ASIA AND EUROPE

them of different "brands". The expensive ones are made in Italy and the cheap ones in China. I regret to say that I now have an Italian "Patek Philippe". It gains a minute a day, something I am sure a non Patek Philippe agent can fix, but at least all the dials work.

We stay the night in nearby Kusadasi.

TOTAL MILEAGE: 29,334
Filled up with 40 litres at 29,235

DAY: 445
22/10/11   HEADING NORTH

Team photo in Kusadasi – hold your tummy in Geoffrey! We say goodbye to Peter and Fran as they head back to Dalaman and we towards Europe.

H has found an idyllic sounding hotel at Behramkale, opposite Lesbos. We divert from the main road to Çandarli for Turkish coffees and a swim for H. We also stop in Ayvalik for baklava and tea and for far too long wander through precipitous and narrow streets, with some fine Greek houses, many in sad need of repair. (In the population exchange, the Greeks were moved to Lesbos, just offshore, and the Turks from Lesbos moved to Ayvalik.) I am slightly reminded of Valparaiso. As a result of our dallying it is dark by the time we approach Berhamkale. The hotel is up a very steep and cobbled street, and not easy to find, [a forgiving understatement! ED.] but we are made extremely welcome on arrival. Lutfe, the owner, is Turkish but lived in the UK for 20 years as a director of the Tricycle Theatre. He really wanted to be an architect and his hobby is restoring buildings. It seems to have turned into more or less a full time occupation. Our hotel, Bebir Evi, was a ruin and is now enchanting. He has five more houses on the go round about, as well as doing all the cooking for us. He is ably assisted by Behan, who guided us in brilliantly.

TOTAL MILEAGE: 29,553 1 litre of oil added here.
Filled up at 29,478 47 litres

Geoffrey & Hilary Herdman

DAY: 446
23/10/11
BEHRAMKALE OR ASSOS
Assos is the ancient name for our village, although in those days it was a major town. Above us are the remains of a Hellenic temple to Athena, with four columns standing, and all round us are Roman buildings and walls.

Aristotle set up an academy here, and when the town was sacked by the Persians he fled to Macedonia, where he became tutor to Alexander the Great.

St Paul was here, to meet St Luke, and the photo is of the road along which he walked before sailing from the port for Lesbos, and from there his final journey to Rome. The ancient harbour is now ridiculously pretty, but also ridiculously expensive by Turkish standards. A modest lunch of small fishes, a couple of glasses of wine and a beer set us back £35. It would have been less than half that anywhere else.

The stone built hotels in the harbour are clearly converted warehouses. Lutfe tells us that they were used for storing acorns. The acorn had a multiplicity of uses. It was crushed for its oil, and the liquor which came with the oil was used for medicinal purposes. The residue of course was a valuable animal feed. He also told us that you never find bugs round the roots of an oak tree and when corpses were buried around them they became mummified, as nothing would destroy them.

DAY: 447
24/10/11
TROY AND THE DARDANELLES
Troy's fortune was made by the wind. The city is located on the Southern side of the Dardanelles and before ships learnt how to tack they would wait in the harbour for a favourable Southerly wind to take them up the Marmaris and Black Seas.

The site was rediscovered by Heinrich Schlieman in the 1870s. We climbed inside the horse, although I doubt if the original had windows! The site was in constant use from about 2,500BC to the Byzantine era, when Constantinople took over. Three thousand years of continual building and rebuilding make things a little confusing, with Schliemann's original huge trench cutting through the ground like a slice into a cake, but there is a very good boardwalk with explanatory signs. Homer extolled the beauty of the walls. Without mortar or the use of iron tools the blocks were so finely worked that it was difficult to see the joins.

From Troy across the Dardanelles to Europe. At its nearest Europe is only about a mile away from Asia. It is presumably here that Byron swum the Hellespont? Certainly Xerxes, and Alexander after him, crossed their armies by creating a line of boats between Çanakkale on the Asian side and Kilitbahir on the European. There are still impressive fortresses at either location, although of much more recent date.

As we drove round the Gallipoli peninsula we were overwhelmed by the memorials. Something like 46,000 allies died here, and twice as many Turks.

Whilst driving round the peninsula we were stopped by two police motorcycles – a first for Turkey, but it was only because they had seen us pass a little earlier and were interested in the car! 10DPG scores again. Needless to say they spoke excellent English.

TOTAL MILEAGE: 29,678

TURKISH REFLECTIONS We arrived in Istanbul on 20th September and between then and now (25/10/11) have driven some 5,000 miles through Turkey; 3,500 in a Renault Fluence – very economical – and 1,500 in 10DPG.

From Istanbul we drove the whole length of the South coast of the Black Sea to within 15 miles of Georgia, headed South and cut back through the middle, across the Great Anatolian Plain, through Erzurum, Sivas and Goreme, before heading South to see our shipping agents in Adana.

As 10DPG was still a week or so away we then headed East again for Antakia (Antioch), and continued to Mardin, not shown on the map but about 100 miles SE of Diyarbakir.

Finally we headed back to Adana and having collected 10DPG drove round

Geoffrey & Hilary Herdman

the SW of Turkey to Edirne on the Bulgarian and Greek borders.

For all of this we have been excellently guided, both for things to see and places to stay, by the Lonely Planet. In an earlier iteration I expressed our joint exasperation with the book. I am happy to report that familiarity has bred enormous respect and it has been our invaluable Bible.

To us Turkey appeared to be an absolutely wonderful country. The economy is booming and the people some of the friendliest we have ever met. It helped that when we had 10DPG on the road they were wildly enthusiastic!

In 2005 they divided their currency (the Turkish Lira) by 1,000,000. There are now about 2.8 Turkish Lire to the £ whereas there used to be 2,800,000! Since the measures taken in 2005 the economy seems to be not just stable but highly successful. Whenever we mentioned the EU they shrugged and said that they didn't need it. They could survive very well on their own. They also commented that they are, demographically, a young society, and see the EU as an elderly society, with attendant problems.

Their road building programme is astonishing and more or less every road we travelled on, if it wasn't already first class was being upgraded, or brand new roads were being created. This did lead to some interesting driving. In places, where in any other country the unmade road would not have been opened, we would bump over some pretty rough and ready surfaces, surrounded by road making equipment. Not for long though. At the rate they are going Turkey will have one of the great road systems in 3 - 4 years time. Even where roads weren't being built they were being maintained.

Turkish driving however does leave a little to be desired. In the words of the Lonely Planet; "The rules are that they drive on the right and give way to traffic coming in from the right. In reality they do neither and indicators are never used."

We can absolutely attest to all of this. We frequently found cars, to save them from having to go out of their way for a U-turn, approaching on the hard shoulder on the wrong side of a dual carriageway. They did at least usually have their hazard lights going – so that was all right!

In the far East of the country massive Hydro schemes are in progress, with consequent rehousing programmes, as whole valleys and communities are to be flooded. This gives rise to some quite spectacular road building with motorways being built high above the valleys and carved into the side of some impressive rock faces. Not too sure where the funding is all coming from, as they must be spending 10s if not 100s of billions on their various construction programmes. These include the enormous GAP programme, which should transform their agriculture through massive irrigation schemes.

Personally I like the sound of the muezzin, but like the bagpipes think it sounds better from afar. Originally of course the Imam would climb his minaret and sing the various "calls". Nowadays this is done by loudspeaker and in some cases to my ears rather overamplified! I think I prefer the former system! There is a large mosque building programme and no village – however small – was without one. I cannot remember the last time I saw a church being built at home.

ASIA AND EUROPE

The loos are interesting. In all hotels we had a western style bowl but all came equipped with a nozzle at the back of the rim. I tried one of these out of interest – once only – and nearly flooded the bathroom. Outside hotels the "hole in the ground" is ubiquitous.

There are some astonishing sites. We managed four out of the five most visited museums; Hagia Sofia and the Topkapi in Istanbul, the open air museum in Goreme (Capadocia), and Ephesus. We also managed to visit some much less accessible sites, including an 8th Century BC Hittite palace, a wonderful Mosaic museum in Gaziantep and the statues high on Mount Nemrut.

Being at the cross roads between Asia and Europe Turkey has had its fair share of warring tribes each leaving their imprint. Their current problem is with the Kurds, who comprise between 20 and 25% of their 80,000,000 population. Ataturk, when creating the modern Turkish state between 1923 and 1936, wanted a country for Turks only. Other citizens, such as those of Arab origin in the South East, have accepted this but some Kurds want their own state and have created a paramilitary arm – the PKK. As a result some Eastern parts are unwise or impossible to visit.

There was some bitterness about the EU response to the efforts they feel they have made over Cyprus, and human rights generally, although they acknowledged that there was not yet total freedom of the press. There was also considerable resentment of the Israeli inability to do more than 'express regret', when asked for a formal apology over the deaths on the humanitarian convoy in 2010.

In summary; it is a wonderful country, cheap by European standards, with the notable exception of petrol, and one where we had nothing but kindness and grace.

DAY 448

Geoffrey & Hilary Herdman

DAY: 448
25/10/11

GALLIPOLI & EDIRNE With the Ottoman empire in decline Winston Churchill's plan was simple; force the Dardanelles, knock out Constantinople and thus gain access to the Black Sea and Russia, without having to use icebound waterways. A naval bombardment in early 1915 failed with the loss of three battleships, so on 25th April 1915 allied troops landed around the Gallipoli Peninsula. Unfortunately the Anzac troops were swept by strong currents from a flat landing ground to what is anything but, and has become known as Anzac beach. They were met by troops under the able command of Mustafa Kemal, later to become Ataturk and the founder of modern Turkey.

Rather than a swift knockout the attack soon settled down into the stalemate of trench warfare and in December 1915 all allied troops were withdrawn. At least the withdrawal was successful with no loss of allied lives.

Erik, our genial Belgian host at Gallipoli Houses, is an expert on the campaign and had various relics. He recommended us to the excellent Ozey museum, where this ammunition cart is to be found (see photo opposite).

Our destination for today was Edirne (Adrianopolis, named after Hadrian). It has one of the great mosques of Turkey. Designed by Mirar Sinan (1490 - 1588; 98 years old in the 16th C – not bad going), who designed numerous other buildings around Turkey including the Suleiman Mosque in Istanbul. The Edirne mosque was his favourite, and is absolutely magnificent. The centre of town is dominated by three mosques and I suppose most of the businesses come under their patronage. The result was an alcohol free dinner!

Before dinner, H finally managed to have a Turkish bath, administered by a smiling but strapping lady, rather surprisingly attired in Maidenform bra and track suit trousers. It was in a beautifully restored 15th C hammam near the Sinan mosque; lots of marble and no other customers made it luxurious until the pummelling started! Anyway, she is now very clean.

TOTAL MILEAGE: 29,832
Filled up at 29,724 50.4 litres

DAY: 449
26/10/11

INTO BULGARIA Bulgaria is not a large country, somewhere between England and Scotland. Edirne is in the top left hand corner of Turkey about 10 miles from the border and our original plan was to drive across Bulgaria and into Romania. However on checking hotels in Giurgiu, just across the Danube from Ruse, we

ASIA AND EUROPE

quickly changed plans and settled for a night in Bulgaria.

At the Turkish border the customs officer, after a 15 second pause, looked up and said "Mr Herdman?" This without a previous word or request for passports. One was impressed – by Turkish technology of course!! We were soon through the Bulgarian frontier as well, but with fierce warnings that we needed a vignette to drive on the roads or face a 300 Lev fine (£100). We tried buying one, only to find they wouldn't accept credit cards, but were assured that 10 ks down the road we would find a Shell garage that would. This pattern repeated itself several times – and then we were stopped by the police. However it was only to be told that the road to Nova Zagora was in very bad condition and we should turn round and drive via Stara Zagora instead. No mention of the missing vignette. Shortly afterwards we found a cash machine and were thus able to be legal.

North of Stara Zagora there is an amazingly beautiful switchback of a road through a beech forest, leading to a not very high pass (about 1,100 metres). We were alarmed to find snow from 700 metres upwards, although clearly a week or so old. Snowy roads and 10DPG are not really meant for each other. However it is after all the end of October and we are planning to be in Eastern Europe for at least another week. Fortunately TomTom (who does weather forecasting among his many tricks) and Apple are at idem that we should have clear skies for the foreseeable future. Let's hope they are both right!

Our hotel, the Ana Palace in Ruse, had been built as a very rich man's private house in the late 19th C but has had a chequered history since. Just one such incident occurred in 1910 when it was lost in a game of poker. One gambler staked the Ana Palace, the other his wife!!

And here we are at one of the great waterways of the world, the Danube. We walked along its banks by twilight and saw a boatel gliding silently upstream. It looked rather enticing!

TOTAL MILEAGE: 30,060
To use up Turkish currency 21 litres at 29,835

DAY: 450
27/10/11   INTO ROMANIA Across the Danube and into Giurgiu, Rumania, with no fuss at either border. Eat your hearts out all Central American frontiers! (Is this why they are not yet Schengen?)

We had been warned that roads are either very busy or very bad. The warnings were right! TomTom is not really up to speed on Romania and we got lost before we had even really started – in Giurgiu. The real navigator is determined to avoid Bucharest. Our goal for the evening is Sibiu, which was the European Cultural capital in 2007 and has been adjudged by Forbes as Europe's eighth most idyllic place to live! Their favourite is Patmos. H & I may be biased but we think they have a letter or two wrong!

We drive through Alexandria and the quite extraordinary Bezescu, with astonishing modern 'gypsy palace' houses, featuring fantastically ornate shiny metal turrets and twirls. Sadly we have mislaid the camera after over 6,000 photos and so have lost our record of them. Then it's Rosiorii de Verde and up the 85A to Pitesti, (red on our map but a mass of potholes,) where the Romanian Renault (or Dacia) factory is located. From Pitesti to Sibiu we are at least on a main road, the 7 or E81, which from Ramnicu runs through the valley of the river Olt and becomes quite beautiful. It would be even more so if it weren't for the traffic!!

In Turkey we had met the occasional horse and cart; in Bulgaria a few more; but in Romania it seems that off the main roads they are still the standard means of transport. Wooden iron shod wheels have given way to car tyres, which must make for an infinitely more comfortable journey, and often we see husband and wife side by side chatting, with one or two well cared for and gaily caparisoned horses trotting peacefully along. Mind you, the main roads have their fair share too, as we were soon to find out, driving at night with no lights or even reflectors.

We are booked into the Sibiu Hilton, which means crossing from one side of the town to the other just as dusk is falling. TomTom takes us down what turns out to be a one way street, with an awful lot of flashing traffic coming the other way. It is also very narrow. What with constant traffic and the impossibility of a U-turn we soldier on to the end and turn left to the astonishment of traffic all around.

TOTAL MILEAGE: 30,310
Filled up in Giurgiu 30,068 41 litres

DAY: 451
28/10/11 SAXON ACCOMMODATION

A very chatty and helpful "client relations officer" at the Hilton told me at length about the sights of Sibiu, which clearly we weren't going to have time for today. However half a mile from the Hilton there is the largest open air museum in Romania. This is no hollow epithet. It was wonderful. Houses, wind and water mills, presses of every description, churches, and even an entrance to a gold mine, all in danger of destruction, had been brought here and re-erected. Aided and abetted by an excellent coffee in a period restaurant we spent a very happy 2 hours. It helped that the weather was stunning.

A word about the weather. We had seen snow by the roadside in Bulgaria and end October, early November is a risky time to be driving an old car in Eastern Europe. We can't remember when we last had rain. Our days are sunny, with little wind and temperatures of 15 - 18°C. Our nights are cold. -5°C for one is predicted! By lunch time we are motoring topless most days, although it certainly does get a little parky towards 17:00 in the afternoon! The forecast for the foreseeable future is for much the same. Hurray!

ASIA AND EUROPE

DAY 451

Photo courtesy of T. McDonald

We walked back through the forest to the Hilton and were soon on our way. Very sadly we mislaid the faithful Canon camera. In all our travels it is the first thing we have lost thus far!

Our destination is Malancrav near Sighisoara. Tom McDonald, 405 owner, who worked in Bucharest for a couple of years, is flying in from Moscow to show us the Saxon Villages. He has arranged, through the Mihai Eminescu Trust, to stay in one of their restored houses. Sadly the manor house is full and we are in an interesting village house. The photo is of the manor house with Tom and H.

Malancrav is about 10 miles off the main road and as we drive towards it many of the fields are smoking from burning stubble. There is no wind and the smoke lies along the valley with an acrid and pungent smell.

Village houses are built end-on to the road, with an enclosed courtyard. We find ours with a little help. Our beds are like a chest of drawers. Hilary sleeps on top of the chest, very high up, under strict instructions not to get up in the night, as she will only be able to get down by stepping on my face. I sleep in one of the drawers, which has fortunately been pulled out! We have a vast porcelain stove in the room which is giving out prodigious heat, but most unfortunately the smoke from the fields, and a forest fire, has penetrated the room and proves very difficult to ventilate away.

Tom arrives in a very sporty BMW 335, which he still keeps in Bucharest and we have a wonderful dinner in the kitchen, of venison and rabbit goulash, which has been cooked over an open fire outside. It is washed down with quantities of rosé, made by our guardienne.

After dinner Andrea, the hard working Tourism officer for the Trust, joins us to tell us about the Trust and where we should go.

TOTAL MILEAGE: 30,373
Filled up in Medias 47 litres 30,348

One of the towers at Viscri photographed from another

Photo courtesy of T. McDonald

DAY: 452
29/10/11   SAXON VILLAGES AND CHURCHES

For centuries Transylvania was a part of Hungary. In 1142 King Geza invited German citizens to move to Transylvania to help fortify the country. They stayed for eight centuries, merchants and farmers, speaking German and reaching a maximum population of 750,000 in 1930. They lived in their own villages and built fortified churches for times of siege. Each church had strongrooms in which the villagers would keep supplies of emergency food, marked with their household sign.

    1930 was the peak. After the war Stalin rounded up huge numbers in retaliation for their siding with the Germans and sent them to 7 years slave labour in Siberia. Very few returned. With the fall of the Iron Curtain, Germany invited any German speaking people living abroad to return, which created a huge exodus. There are now only a handful of Saxons left in Romania, but their villages and churches live on. Incidentally they didn't even originally come from Saxony, but from the Rhineland and Luxembourg regions.

    Today we travelled in Tom's BMW. First port of call was the fortified church of Crij, which was closed, as a movie team were in residence. Then Sighisoara, which is superb. The old town is built on a hill, with the new in the plain below. There is a plaque on the house in the main square, where Vlad the Impaler was born in 1431. The various guilds (shades of Meistersinger) were charged with building individual towers in the surrounding walls.

    Our final visit was to Viscri, where Prince Charles has a farmstead. We were told that Camilla doesn't do Romania! The church was locked but a call to Andrea, and the wonderful mother of the director of the Trust came and let us in. As she arrived so did about twenty other tourists. Apparently Germany is now helping to support some of the Saxon churches. Our keeper of the keys, speaking in slow, clear French, told us that Viscri has a current population of three hundred and fifty gypsies, sixty Romanians and only fifteen Saxons, so this

ASIA AND EUROPE

Photo courtesy of T. McDonald

beautiful church is not much used. (The gypsies are not Lutheran.) Long may it stand though. From the interior of the church, we were able to climb high up into the tower, with wonderful views of the walls and fortifications, and the surrounding autumn countryside.

DAY: 453
30/10/11 BIERTAN, RICHIS, AND BACK TO SIBIU

Malancrav, where we are staying, has the largest remaining Saxon population of any of the Transylvanian villages. The church is used regularly and communication with our guardienne is by rudimentary German (H not me).

Most of the village water still comes from wells (photo courtesy Tom McDonald) and we wake to the happy sound of cattle wending their way along the village street. The acrid smoke has more or less dispersed from our room and my only complaint is that I am a little too long for my drawer (bed)!

Although occupied, Andrea has told us we can visit the Manor House. It has been beautifully restored. The weather is gorgeous. From the library there are views over beech forests and the village. Tom would like a house in Romania and we ask Andrea if it is for sale, but sadly not. We all fall in love with it and vow to return.

Everyone has told us to visit Biertan. Tom is making his way back to Bucharest at lunchtime so we travel in convoy. It has been -5°C overnight and 10DPG's engine only just turns over, but starts. As the battery seems in good shape either a connection needs tightening or the starter is wearing.

Biertan has a large square and the wonderful Andrea invites us into another Trust house for coffee. As with most other churches Biertan seems to be closed, even though we have paid 6 Lei to go in. We can at least climb the mediaeval covered stairs, and maybe we didn't try the handle hard enough as Andrea is very surprised that we couldn't get in. She then drives us in her van to Richis, where we find the last Saxon couple. He is 78 and the church caretaker. In piping German, ably translated by Andrea, he tells us of the history. The village used to

Geoffrey & Hilary Herdman

be famous for its wine and as it was once on the main road from North to South was extremely wealthy. The last wine made here was only 2 years ago.

The church is bitterly cold inside but he is a mine of information and shows us stone carvings of "green men". These have attracted worldwide interest from green men experts. The Trust is to make a video of the caretaker this winter to record his knowledge for posterity.

We return to Biertan and wave goodbye to Tom, and then have an excellent lunch in a beautifully restored restaurant on the village square. Andrea has told us that to get back to Sibiu we can go back through Richis and the road is now good. The road is very pretty but not good to start with. And then to our surprise we hit an excellent surface and beat TomTom's estimated arrival time by an hour for a journey of 50 miles.

Rather than the Hilton we stay in the Imparatul Romanilor on the edge of the main (and pedestrian) Square. A christening party is under way, which involves very loud music till midnight, although the hotel is well insulated for sound, unlike Nicaragua! Outside we are slightly surprised to see a Maybach parked.

TOTAL MILEAGE: 30,442

DAY: 454
31/10/11 SIGHTSEEING IN SIBIU

A non driving day wandering round this beautiful town. Bizarrely the Small Square and many roofs were covered in artificial snow as they were shooting a commercial for Orange. Must have been some budget!

We love the eyebrow windows in the roofs of the old houses.

PLF IN REVERSE Starting at the age of 18 Patrick Leigh Fermor walked, and occasionally rode by boat, horse and car, from Rotterdam to Istanbul.

In "A Time of Gifts", published when he was 61, he tells of the journey from Rotterdam to Esztergom in Hungary. Although place names have changed and at times he is a little vague about dates it is reasonably easy to work out more or less on a day by day basis where he was.

"Between the Woods and the Water" was published 9 years later and places and dates are a little vaguer. In Romania he went off on a three day toot by car. For the next few days we intend to follow that route, including Brasov, which he had intended to visit, but which was cut short by an untimely phone call to his companion from her husband!

DAY: 455
01/11/11   TO CLUJ-NAPOCA

First task this morning is to find a replacement camera. Next door to the hotel is a small but helpful photographic shop, where we buy the last or only Nikon in lurid purple.

Sibiu to Cluj, capital of Transylvania, is only about 100 miles. We stop en route in Alba Iulia. The old town is magnificent, built on a hill top, and enclosed in a massive star shaped 18th C fortress. Inside there is still an active army barracks, university and two cathedrals, one Catholic and the other Orthodox. The Catholic cathedral is 13th C with a 17th C bell tower, but is sadly shut. The Orthodox cathedral was built in just over a year for the coronation of King Ferdinand and Queen Marie in October 1922. There are great earthworks being undertaken and we are astonished to see Roman walls and slabs with inscriptions in excellent condition, seemingly being unearthed by JCB. In the cloisters of the Orthodox cathedral many more of these inscriptions and statues are on display.

In Cluj we stay at the excellent Plaza hotel. H goes for a walk round the attractive centre of the town. The museum is in a building where Liszt gave two recitals; it was still part of Hungary then, not a foreign tour! As it is All Saints Day, the museum is shut, but the huge Gothic cathedral was of course open, and the caretaker of the house where Matthew Corvinus was born kindly allowed her to look into the courtyard and hall. The building is now an art college.

Meanwhile I try the spa. Sadly the masseuse is fully booked for the day so I try the sauna, which I have to share with a very attractive Italian with a towel problem! and that was before she had a shower. I may never be the same again!!

TOTAL MILEAGE: 30,555

Geoffrey & Hilary Herdman

DAY: 456
02/11/11

ROMANIAN POLICE It has been -4°C overnight and is still very cold. The starter manages half a turn, but it is enough and 10DPG bursts into life.

We stop in Targu Mures for some coffee and have just got underway when we are pulled over by a policeman. Other than being helpfully told in Bulgaria that the road was closed, this is the first time we have actually been stopped since Chile. He wanted to see the car registration. I hand over the V5. He wants my driving licence. I hand over my driving licence. He wants my identity. I hand over my passport. He wants to see my insurance. This is a bit of a problem. We do of course have insurance but having recently arranged it in England it is all in the computer. I tell him it is in the computer. He wants to see the computer. I tell him I need internet and at this stage he gives up and hands back the other papers. We have no idea why he stopped us, probably bored, but with a serious sense of humour failure! We were very glad they don't have the Iron Guard any more.

Rather than the direct route from Sighisoara to Brasov we had to follow in the master's steps as far as Fagaras.

With the exception of the church, Agnita turned out to be rather a dump, not helped by the main road being a building site. However just down the road Merghindeal is gorgeous and we thought very suitable for a house for Tom!

From Fagaras to Brasov we drove on one of the best roads in Romania, apart from the short section of motorway round Cluj. Although not quite following in the master's footsteps, Brasov in evening light looks stunning. We stayed in the charming Bela Muzica, which is not clearly marked and meant a couple of U-turns in a very busy High Street, not to mention parking on a blind bend to unload. The Romanians seem very forgiving, but maybe it is the 10DPG effect!

TOTAL MILEAGE: 30,764
Filled up in Targu Mures 54 litres 30,637

ASIA AND EUROPE

DAY: 457
03/11/11
TEMPERATURE PROBLEMS
A very cold night. We visit the Black Church, reputedly the largest gothic church between Vienna and Istanbul and in wonderful condition. The walls are lined with 17th C Ottoman prayer rugs as these were an acceptable form of decoration in Lutheran churches. Rather more chilling are the four bullet holes in one of the columns where police fired on people hiding in the church in 1989.

Out of town there is thick fog. There is not a breath of wind and a combination of burning off the fields and the cold air have made visibility trying at times. However, by the time we had climbed up to Bran, the mist had cleared, and we had blue sky and vivid autumn colours. We visit Bran Castle, returned to the royal family and restored since the overthrow of Ceausescu, before setting off for what Top Gear apparently calls the greatest drive in the world, the Transfagarasan Highway. I notice that we appear to have little or no water temperature. The heater appears to be working and the radiator is hot so rather than the thermostat it must be the temperature gauge. This was fitted by BCL in 1972 and was actually the incorrect gauge for a 405 so hopefully after 40 years it can be rectified.

We drive a part of the Top Gear highway, which twists and turns dramatically as it climbs and, even better, the autumn colours in the afternoon sun are sensational. (See photo.)

And so back to the Imperatul Romanilor in Sibiu. There is a concert this evening. We make our ways separately. One is told it is completely sold out, the other (arriving as the bell was ringing) manages to sneak in and freeload. Guess which way round that was!

TOTAL MILEAGE: 30,901

Geoffrey & Hilary Herdman

DAY: 458
04/11/11   **TOWARDS THE DANUBE** Our hero now made his way down to the Iron Gates, and crossed over by boat to Serbia, and there the story hangs tantalizingly in suspense. As we are doing him in reverse we do feel we should at least start from the Danube and have a rather uneventful drive down to Caransebes.

En route we stop at Sarmizegetusa, where there are some most impressive Roman remains, following Trajan's conquest, including an oval amphitheatre and forum with a wealth of detail. We also ask to see the museum and get the impression that we may be the first people this year to have done so, but it is rather good.

Our hotel, the Armando, costs €30 a night. The E70 comes past the front door, although a bypass is in very advanced stages of construction. Fortunately we are staying at the back. The room shakes a bit as 40 tonners pound past and bump over a large pothole just outside, but is very comfortable and for €30.....

In the bar we meet Phil from Yorkshire, who has lived in Caransebes for 4 years helping improve quality control at a brake lining factory. He is about to move on to either China or S Africa and rather thinks he prefers China if offered, if he can't find another job in Romania.

We eat in the hotel as Phil has said it is the best/only place to eat anyway. It comes as quite a shock nowadays to find people are allowed to smoke in restaurants.

The photo is of Bran castle from yesterday.

TOTAL MILEAGE: 31,029
Filled up in Sibiu 30,902 50 litres. Gas/Petrol stations are all self service in Romania.

DAY: 459
05/11/11   THE BLUE DANUBE AND SERBIA

One very grubby car beside the Danube. That's Serbia on the other side.

    We have driven down the E70, which goes to Bucarest and from which you can branch off and cross the Danube to Belgrade. It seems as if we have driven with most of the trucks in Europe. I had just overtaken one of them when I was confronted with a large plastic sign in the middle of the road. Fortunately I had just passed him and was able to do a rather alarming swerve. Shades of Argentina 2006!

    We head for Orsova and then turn right to drive along the Danube, losing all other traffic in the process. In 1972 the Danube was dammed 10 ks downstream from Orsova, raising the water level by 33 metres. It was a joint effort between Romania and the former Yugoslavia and each has a 1G power station on their respective sides. It has however sunk large parts of old Orsova, not to mention a very beautiful island, and the cliffside road built by Trajan.

    Our riverside road deteriorates and so we return and have pancakes – outdoors. Note photo of car with hood down on 5th November! We drive past the dam, which also serves as a bridge across to Serbia and try to see the few remains of Trajan's bridge at Dobreta-Turnu Severin, or Severin as it is more familiarly called. There is a large scale model at the entrance to town but most of the roads are closed so we call it a day and return home via the old Spa of Baile Herculane.

    What with one thing and another – mainly not setting out until 11:30 – it is very dark by the time we get back to Caransebes. We can attest that horse drawn carts carry no lights or reflectors and are almost impossible to see until you are on them.

TOTAL MILEAGE: 31,219

Geoffrey & Hilary Herdman

DAY: 460
06/11/11

SLEEPING ROUGH From Budapest our hero left the Danube and followed the Tisa and the Maros, the latter becoming the Mures in Romania. We determined to stay by the riverside for the night. According to the Rough Guide in Savarsin there is a 19th C royal residence, which has now been returned to the royal family and converted into "The comfortable Hotel Castel Royal". Ominously phone calls went unanswered!

Yet another glorious day so 10DPG had a long overdue clean and rather belatedly we set off for Hunedoara and its magnificent castle. This has been very much restored since PLF was here, but is beautifully done and has commanding views over the countryside – including a communist era steel works, which is fortunately now being dismantled.

Just East of Deva we joined the E68, which follows the Mures and came to Savarsin. With difficulty, in a not very large town, we found the Royal Residence which was firmly shut and certainly NOT a "comfortable hotel!"

Often of a night PLF aged 18/19 slept rough, under a haystack or even with gypsies in the open. Mrs H determined that we too would sleep rough. At this stage there wasn't much choice, and thus we came to Lipova and the Pensiunea or Pension Faleza. Again we had difficulty locating same but a very helpful local jumped in his car and guided us there. In fact a perfectly adequate double room cost £16 breakfast included and the dinner was quite excellent for £20, including a bottle of wine and tip; schnitzel of a tenderness and deliciousness that we haven't known for some time!

The photo is of a "gypsy palace" at Hunedoara. There were about a dozen, each outdoing the others in vulgarity.

TOTAL MILEAGE: 31,372
Filled up at 31,230 57.5 litres

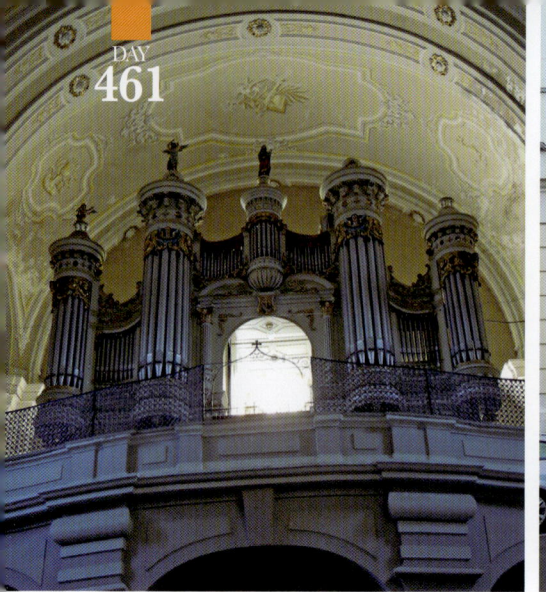

DAY: 461
07/11/11
FAREWELL TO ROMANIA

We walk to the Maria Radna Monastery, where PLF stayed the night and played skittles with the monks. (See photo of the organ loft). Yet again the weather is gorgeous and we are once again motoring top down. Our plan had been to cross the frontier at Turnu, but there is a huge traffic jam, which seems stationary so we turn round and head for Varsand and the crossing to Gyula. At the Romanian side we are asked for the car papers. although not the insurance. Unlike Targu Mures this would not now have been a problem as we have been able to print out the necessary. At the Hungarian side there was no-one and we drove straight through.

We are both very sad to leave Romania. Transylvania was spectacular and we loved the countryside with its horses and carts and wells and way of life which is perhaps 100 years behind other parts of Europe.

Driving into Gyula it is as if someone has flicked a light switch and we have joined the 21st (or at least the late 20th) century. Mind we still counted four Trabants (marginally but not much better than a horse and cart, and far less companionable!)

We avoid motorways and driving via the unpronounceable Torokszentmiklos, and Szolnok we arrive in Budapest. The clocks have changed between Romania and Hungary and it is dark by 16:30. We stay at the excellent Gellert, which I think we last visited in 1999 and have a dinner of goose liver and venison at Rezkakas, which we also last visited in 1999, washed down with liberal quantities of Tokay.

TOTAL MILEAGE: 31,580
Filled up at Varsand on the border to use up Lei.
31,431 miles 33 litres

Geoffrey & Hilary Herdman

DAY: 462
08/11/11 A LITTLE KNOWN OPERA

The Budapest Guide tells us that the Hungarian State Opera House is a must see. We then find that they are doing Anna Karenina there this evening. Neither of us has ever actually heard of the opera but that doesn't count for much.

In glorious weather we walk by the banks of the Danube to the Box Office to buy some very reasonably priced tickets and then get way laid by a branch of Max Mara, for someone who has been quite starved of retail therapy. As we amble back we pass the British Embassy, which has a couple of Jaguars outside (one sporting HE's standard) and flanking the main entrance two large electronic signs giving the countdown to the London Olympics and Para Olympics.

Nonplussed by our ignorance H Googles Anna Karenina to find it is a ballet devised as long ago as 2005 to an assembly of pieces by Tchaikovsky and some rather strange electronic music. Anyhow the performance is excellent and the opera house absolutely stunning.

DAY: 463
09/11/11 IN THE MASTER'S FOOTSTEPS TO VIENNA

The plan had been to follow the loop of the Danube via Visegrad to Esztergom, but there was a misunderstanding with TomTom, who doesn't do loops if there is a straight road instead. Rather crossly we found ourselves at Esztergom and the border with Slovakia, having missed our objective. Back we went, this time by the edge of the Danube and came to Visegrad. The castle appeared some distance off at the top of a steep hill. We started climbing, but having mounted one ridge the castle seemed as far away as ever. At this stage one of us wimped out but the other determined to carry on at least a little way.

An hour later she returned, with the postcard, very pleased. Needless to say at the top there was a fairly full car park, but such a glow of virtue to have struggled up the hill!

We returned to Esztergom and crossed the bridge and into Slovakia. There were no barriers or guards. It was just a simple matter of crossing a river and driving from one country to another. (The photo is of the basilica)

Our route through Slovakia, following PLF, took us through; Pribeta, Bajc, Nove-Zamky, Bratislava and to Vienna. Pretty depressing it was too. Vast featureless prairie with the

ASIA AND EUROPE

occasional drab village or grimy urban sprawl in between. One wonders what it must have been like in 1934. Maybe the villages were prettier then?

As it was getting dark we joined the motorway just before Bratislava and arrived at the Hotel Bristol – where else? at 17:30. The hotel is bang next door to the opera house and people were sitting outside watching the (sold out) live performance of Siegfried on a huge screen. We found that the Emerson Quartet were playing Mozart, Bartok and Dvorak at the sublime Musikverein, and so wended our way there having made the statutory visit to Cafe Sacher.

TOTAL MILEAGE: 31,786
Filled up in Esztergom 31,630 miles 35.6 litres

DAY: 464
10/11/11 PROPER ACCOMMODATION Sightseeing in Vienna, not to mention a fun performance of Die Fledermaus at the Volksoper followed by an excellent dinner in the Sacher Hotel.

Not only was it proper accommodation but VERY comfy too!

DAY: 465
11/11/11 ROMANTIKSTRASSE Many photo opportunities at the Hotel Bristol for the doormen! and as a point of principle we had to put the top down, although it was VERY cold! We managed for an hour or so under clear blue skies.

Heading West from Vienna we follow PLF's route through Klosterneuburg, Melk, Mauthausen and Linz. The riverside road, running along the Danube is absolutely gorgeous and called the above.

First stop was Stein where PLF had coffee in the Square by the statue of St John Nepomuk. The orangey building is the café. Seventy seven years and nine months later we too had coffee there. Just along the road is Durnstein, where Richard I was imprisoned by Duke Leopold V of Austria, following an insult

Geoffrey & Hilary Herdman

during the 3rd Crusade. Leopold handed him over to Emperor Henry VI, who released him in February 1194 on payment of 65,000 pounds of silver, equivalent to twice the GDP of England at that time!

Our original plan had been to drive to Salzburg. By motorway it is only 3 hours from Vienna, but we of course were not on the motorway, so thought we would stop in Linz. However the outskirts looked fairly depressing and Tripadvisor didn't come up with anything very exciting so we pressed on and found the delightful Gasthof Zweimuller in Greiskirchen. The cost of B&B is exactly the same as the cost of breakfast alone at the Hotel Bristol!

I asked our host, Alois, where I could get the oil changed on a Saturday. He said all the garages would be shut but his friend Fritz, who would be coming to dinner, could help. By the time we went downstairs the restaurant was absolutely packed and later Fritz, his friend Wolfgang, Wolfgang's two daughters and Alois all joined us for drinks until rather too late. Fritz has three Austin Healey 3000s and an XK140, all restored by him and has all the requisite facilities. Alois is going to guide us there in the morning.

TOTAL MILEAGE: 31,961
Filled up 31,929 49 litres

DAY: 466
12/11/11   AN AUSTRIAN SAINT   Alois, owner of the Zweimuller, very kindly guided us to Fritz' house, where we arrived on the dot of 10:30. We pushed Fritz' latest project, a total restoration of a Healey 3000 expected to be completed this winter, out of his immaculate garage, to make room for 10DPG. Alois had warned me that Fritz would let me use his facilities but I would have to do everything.

In fact Fritz did everything, ably assisted by Alois. He even had Castrol Classic 20/50. As soon as the car was up on the ramp and the oil draining he started greasing nipples, and noticing that one was broken on the pedal box, replaced it.

ASIA AND EUROPE

The nearside bomb bay door catch has been out of alignment for some time and was waiting for the return home for attention. Fritz had it off and straightened, again assisted by Alois. He checked the brake fluid and was all set to tighten the fan belt, but we had already imposed on his good nature for too long. The photo (on the previous page) is of Fritz on the right and Alois on the left in front of the Healey restoration.

Since the last oil change in Brisbane 10DPG has struggled to maintain 60PSI at 3,000 rpm, but I think it might have been 15/40. With the Castrol all was back to normal. An hour and a bit after arriving we were on the road. What wonderful hospitality. Thank you both very much, Fritz and Alois.

A lovely sunny day but the temperature is only 3°C so we had the hood up as we resumed "The Route" through Riedau and Frankenburg, before making a slight diversion along the West shore of the Attersee.

Shortly after 16:00 we were in Salzburg opposite Mozart's house at …The Hotel Bristol!

TOTAL MILEAGE: 32,061
Changed oil at 31,971 miles

DAY: 467
13/11/11

INTO GERMANY A climb to Salzburg Castle, passing the famous Carillon at the appointed hour of 11:00, but today's rendition was disappointingly "Eidelweiss". I am sure it can have had nothing to do with "The Sound of Music" being on at the nearby Landstheatre!

Back on The Route by around 12:30. Apart from a small sign saying Germany with the EU symbol there was nothing at the frontier. Hurrah for Schengen. Our destination tonight is Munich. The route: Teisendorf, Traunstein, Rottau, Sollhuben, Rosenheim and the Hotel Platzl, complete with underground parking.

Although dusk was falling we walked to the English Garden, which we thought a cross between Richmond Park and Stourhead. It was designed in 1789 by Benjamin Thompson, and is one of the largest urban gardens in the world, complete with a ten Ionic columned circular temple. However the roof is cone, rather than dome shaped, and somehow not quite so satisfactory.

The brother of our hotel's owner has a brewery, so copious quantities of good Munich beer helped to wash down an excellent dinner

TOTAL MILEAGE: 32,151

Geoffrey & Hilary Herdman

DAY: 468
14/11/11

A DEVIATION! Between Munich and Ulm the only stopping place noted by PLF is Augsburg, so we made a bolt for freedom to visit Neuschwanstein.

Very cold this morning and when we left Munich we were in fog, but fortunately by the time we reached Hohenschwangau it had lifted and turned into a glorious if cold day. With the windows shut, despite all the various draughts, the heater works very well and 10DPG, in outside temperatures hovering on or below 0ºC, is very cosy. We have been unbelievably lucky with the weather and have had no rain for weeks, with none forecast until we get back home. With these temperatures it would more likely be snow! Not good news.

The castle was built between 1869 and 1886 by King Ludwig II of Bavaria in homage to his hero Richard Wagner and inspired by his ideas of a gothic ideal. Due to the excessive costs of his extravagant building projects, in 1886 the Bavarian government formally deposed him and two days later he was found drowned, aged 40, in circumstances which have never been explained. The Bavarian state took over ownership of the castle the next day and turned it into a hugely successful tourist venue with over 1,000,000 visitors a year. All of Ludwig's amazing decorations are still in perfect condition. He was deposed on the grounds of madness, although he was never formally examined. Mad he may have been but he certainly created one of the great follies of the world. We wondered how he would have got on with Randolph Hearst. Hearst Castle and Neuschwanstein have much in common.

TOTAL MILEAGE: 32,310
Filled up at 32,191 53.6 litres

ASIA AND EUROPE

DAY: 469
15/11/11 — **BRUCHSAL AND HEIDELBERG** Today's route was Goppingen, Stuttgart, Bruchsal and Heidelberg, but not before a visit to the cathedral in Ulm, where the fantastic spire soared into the morning mist, and the remarkable figures in the choirstalls survive, as described by PLF.

Stuttgart is astonishing. First we passed Mercedes Benz City, followed shortly by Porsche Town, and hardly surprisingly a little later the Bosch works. All of them huge but immaculate.

PLF stayed the night as a guest of the Burgomeister in Bruchsal Castle. Not a bad life being a Burgomeister! Sadly four weeks before the end of the war Bruchsal and the castle were more or less flattened, but the recreation is superb. See above. All the rooms are decorated to the same standard. We were highly entertained by the museum of musical automata, pianolas, wurlitzers, elaborate orchestras driven by paper rolls and frankly making the most appalling but very entertaining noise, which the knowledgable and enthusiastic curators were happy to play.

In Heidelberg PLF visited the Red Ox, a student pub, which by 1933 was in the third generation of ownership. Although not a hotel they took pity on him, and put him up for the night. We made our way there and were greeted with an institutional smell of cabbage! Apart from the prices not much can have changed since the Spengel family acquired it in 1839, and certainly not since PLF was there in 1934. Over a glass of wine, we talked to charming Philipp Spengel, sixth generation and current owner and asked how Heidelberg had avoided being bombed. He replied that the Americans had earmarked it for a major post war headquarters and rather wanted it intact!

An excellent dinner of mussels, steak and perhaps a little too much wine at the Nepomuk by the Old Bridge.

TOTAL MILEAGE: 32,440

Geoffrey & Hilary Herdman

DAY: 470
16/11/11 THE ELIZABETH GATE

Pictured: details from the Elizabeth Gate, Heidelberg castle, built by the Elector Palatine Frederick V in 1615 for his wife Elizabeth Stuart. She was sister to Charles I, and it is through her that the British royal family descends to the present day. After the death of Queen Anne, Elizabeth's grandson became George 1.

Although there is a funicular up to the Castle, PLF climbed the three hundred or so steps to pay his respects to the gate, as did we.

I have distant memories, probably from E type days, nearly 40 years ago, of driving through Mannheim and being beset by trams, with them coming in all directions as I wondered which way to go. Nothing has changed and once again we were attacked by trams.

We stopped in Worms for coffee and a visit to the cathedral and in the afternoon crossed the Rhine by ferry, seemingly narrowly avoiding a huge bitumen laden barge. The flow of river traffic is quite astonishing, often with two cars parked at the back of the living quarters for Herr and Frau Bargeman to go shopping.

From Bingen to Koblenz the drive by the banks of the Rhine was absolutely beautiful, and we lingered as we drove. The Michelin map shows the roads on either side, one yellow and one red, as both being edged in green, and thus officially pretty. It is bang on.

The original plan had been to drive to Koln or Cologne, but a) there was a trade fair and not a room to be had, b) it would have been very late – after 19:00 by the time we arrived (it gets dark around 17:00 so not much fun driving for 2 hours in the dark), and c) by settling for Koblenz we had one of our cheapest evenings for a long time. And the dinner was excellent!

TOTAL MILEAGE: 32,563
Filled up in Worms 32,474 55.7 litres

DAY: 471
17/11/11 THE GREAT CATHEDRAL OF KOLN

The forecast for the overnight temperature was for -5°C, so we put the cover over 10DPG as it was parked in the open. I had also managed to point down-hillish, in case of starting reluctance, although it would have meant a perilous road crossing. In the event the temperature can have been nothing like -5°C and starting was a doddle.

ASIA AND EUROPE

As will be deduced from the above we paid our respects to the largest gothic church in N Europe and Germany's most visited building with 20,000 visitors a day. Miraculously, despite receiving hits from some seventy bombs, it survived the Second World War intact and repairs were completed by 1956. It certainly takes one's breath away, both externally and internally, with flying buttresses and soaring columns creating one of the highest imaginable ceilings. The weather was glorious, and sun streaming through the stained glass windows filled the immense space with coloured light.

From Koln to Krefeld, only in reverse of course, PLF hitched on a barge. From our rather small scale map we were in a sea of autobahns and so gave up the struggle of trying to keep to the river's edge. However from Krefeld to Tiel in Holland we tried as much as possible to keep to the "Route", which involved driving along the ridge of a dyke by dusk with the river on our left. He describes walking along the same dyke, and this little bit at least must have changed very little since his day and was very rural and gorgeous.

Finally, thanks to Tripadvisor to whom we are heavily indebted, we came to the mad folly of Villa Augustus in Dordrecht. As a hotel it was only opened in 2007. We are sleeping high up in the 1886 water tower, with wonderful views over the gardens and the water, and have dinner of excellent goose and premier cru Mercurey in the pumping station, surprisingly built in 1942. The gardens have been formally laid out, complete with parterre box hedges, which are astonishingly mature for hedges no more than 8 years old.

TOTAL MILEAGE: 32,774

DAY: 472
18/11/11   GUESTS OF OUR EUROPEAN SECRETARY

Teb had very kindly invited us to stay and as it was no great distance away we diverted via Aachen. H wanted to pay her respects to the tomb of Charlemagne. Having parked, two separate worried Germans came running after us and pointed out that we had parked in a disabled bay and would surely be clamped or worse. With the by now usual mid street U-turn we reparked.

The market square was filled with Christmas stalls and wanting to buy some champagne we were astonished to find a shop selling pipes and a huge variety of tobaccos and cigars, but both the Germans and Austrians still smoke in restaurants.

Sadly Herma was away in the Congo, and so Teb and his daughter Anna and we repaired to the excellent restaurant next door. Before setting out Teb presented us with five chocolate letters making up 10DPG.

We asked Teb what news of Simon and Ingrid Dammer. He told us they were on the BOC South East Section trip to Antwerp. A slight diversion tomorrow and an early start, accompanied by Teb, were clearly called for.

TOTAL MILEAGE: 32,916
Filled up at 32,794 54 litres

ASIA AND EUROPE

DAY: 473
19/11/11   A CHANCE MEETING AND THE END

Vincent very kindly offered to take Anna to hockey practice in Teb's place and the two set off on a pedal bike with Anna waving her stick precariously from the back, whilst we set out for Antwerp.

As our TomTom was more up to date than Teb's we led. Within the first 2 miles, to Teb's astonishment, we had carved up some oncoming traffic at a rather awkward intersection before driving up a bicycle lane entering the motorway. When we next stopped I said to him that he must wonder how we had made it round the world – to which he replied; "He didn't like to mention it … but!" Teb thought he would ring Ingrid and tell her he was coming but in the event couldn't get through. And so it was that as two 405s bounced their way over the cobbles, there standing outside their hotel were Mark and Liz, Simon and Ingrid, just taking the air and completely unaware of our impending arrival. It was a very jolly reunion.

And then sadly it was a routine, although foggy, drive across Belgium and France, via the Chunnel to Sussex.

It has been the most fantastic adventure and Hilary and I rather look at each other and think What Now?

If you have been following any of the story we would both like to thank you very much – and the bad news is that the book will be out some time in 2013.

The Star of the show is of course 10DPG, which went on display in the rotunda of the RAC from 2nd - 8th January 2012.

Thank you and good bye.

TOTAL MILEAGE: 33,196
Filled up at 33,014 53 litres

Geoffrey & Hilary Herdman

ROUND THE WORLD WITH 10DPG

FACTS & FIGURES

DAY	DATE	LOCATION Overnight	MILES	PETROL US Gallons or Litres *	Cumulative Imperial	MPG Average	Spot
1	14/07/10	Miami					
2	15/07/10	Miami					
3	16/07/10	Miami	20				
4	17/07/10	Key West	188				
5	18/07/10	Key West	188				
6	19/07/10	Naples	320 430	14.00 US	11.67	27.43	27.43
7	20/07/10	Sarasota	556				
8	21/07/10	Orlando	723	10.30 US Not full	20.25		
9	22/07/10	Orlando	755				
10	23/07/10	Orlando	775				
11	24/07/10	St Augustine	955	12.50 US Not full	30.67		
12	25/07/10	Savannah	1,103 1,165	13.50 US	41.92	26.31	25.88
13	26/07/10	Savannah	1,165				
14	27/07/10	Charleston	1,335				
15	28/07/10	Charleston	1,335				
16	29/07/10	Charleston	1,375				
17	30/07/10	Asheville	1,416 1,635	14.85 US	54.29	26.08	25.29
18	31/07/10	Asheville	1,754 1,840	15.80 US	67.46	26.00	25.67
19	01/08/10	Asheville	1,848				
20	02/08/10	Blowing Rock	1,963	1 Ltr of oil			
21	03/08/10	Boone	1,970	Starter problems			

Geoffrey & Hilary Herdman

DAY	DATE	LOCATION Overnight	MILES	PETROL US Gallons or Litres *	Cumulative Imperial	MPG Average	Spot
22	04/08/10	Boone	2,043	15.70 US	80.54	25.37	22.09
23	05/08/10	Roanoke	2,223				
24	06/08/10	Nellysford	2,354 2,385	15.00 US	93.04	25.30	24.88
25	07/08/10	Nellysford	2,482				
26	08/08/10	Chambersburg	2,698	15.23 US 1 litre, one shot	105.73	25.52	27.10
27	09/08/10	New Haven	3,003 3,045	14.23 US	117.59	25.54	25.72
28	10/08/10	New Haven	3,045				
29	11/08/10	Mystic	3,098				
30	12/08/10	Hyannis	3,220				
31	13/08/10	Nantucket	3,220				
32	14/08/10	Hyannis	3,220				
33	15/08/10	Truro	3,320				
34	16/08/10	Milton	3,335 3,420	16.64 US First service	131.46	25.37	23.94
35	17/08/10	Milton	3,420				
36	18/08/10	Marble Head	3,460				
37	19/08/10	Marble Head	3,470				
38	20/08/10	Marble Head	3,490				
39	21/08/10	Lenox	3,635 3,715	15.25 US	144.16	25.21	23.61
40	22/08/10	Lenox	3,715				
41	23/08/10	Ashland	3,903				
42	24/08/10	Ashland	3,976 4,053	16.10 US	157.58	25.23	25.42

* As marked : US or Ltrs

FACTS & FIGURES

DAY	DATE	LOCATION Overnight	MILES	PETROL US Gallons or Litres *	PETROL Cumulative Imperial	MPG Average	MPG Spot
43	25/08/10	Kennebunkport	4,140				
44	26/08/10	Deer Isle	4,331	16.00 US	170.91	25.34	26.63
45	27/08/10	St Andrews	4,510				
46	28/08/10	St Andrews	4,510				
47	29/08/10	Digby	4,656	58.50 Ltrs	183.80	25.33	25.22
48	30/08/10	Halifax	4,834				
49	31/08/10	Air Canada	4,834				

Between 1st September and 21st September we were in Europe. As this was not part of Round The World, Day numbering ignores the European period. For the rest of the trip, whenever we were without 10DPG, as those days were part of the Trip we counted them in.

DAY	DATE	LOCATION	MILES	PETROL	Cumulative	Average	Spot
50	22/09/10	Halifax	4,834				
51	23/09/10	Fredericton	4,960 / 5,116	60.00 Ltrs	197.02	25.18	23.00
52	24/09/10	Tadoussac	5,246 / 5,406	52.00 Ltrs	208.47	25.16	24.97
53	25/09/10	Quebec	5,547 / 5,583	57.00 Ltrs	221.02	25.10	23.97
54	26/09/10	Quebec	5,583				
55	27/09/10	North Hatley	5,739				
56	28/09/10	Montreal	5,834				
57	29/09/10	Montreal	5,834				
58	30/09/10	Kanata	5,897 / 5,933	67.50 Ltrs	235.89	25.00	23.54
59	01/10/10	Barrie	6,204 / 6,212	63.00 Ltrs	249.77	24.84	22.12
60	02/10/10	Barrie	6,212				

Geoffrey & Hilary Herdman

DAY	DATE	LOCATION Overnight	MILES	PETROL US Gallons or Litres *	Cumulative Imperial	MPG Average	Spot
61	03/10/10	Penetanguishene	6,310				
62	04/10/10	Penetanguishene	6,335	The second service			
63	05/10/10		6,404	32.00 Ltrs	256.82	24.94	28.38
		Sault Ste Marie	6,702	53.50 Ltrs	268.60	24.95	25.29
64	06/10/10	Thunder Bay	6,897 7,130	32.50 Ltrs 45.00 Ltrs	275.76 285.67	25.01 24.96	27.24 23.51
65	07/10/10	Winnipeg	7,327 7,568	38.00 Ltrs	294.04	24.92	23.54
66	08/10/10	Regina	7,624 7,960	48.00 Ltrs 58.00 Ltrs	304.61 317.39	25.03 25.08	28.09 26.30
67	09/10/10	Brooks	8,247 8,346	56.00 Ltrs	329.72	25.01	23.27
68	10/10/10	Lake Louise	8,469 8,584	56.00 Ltrs	342.06	24.76	18.00
69	11/10/10	Kamloops	8,654 8,885	33.60 Ltrs 33.80 Ltrs Not full	349.46 356.91	24.76	25.00
70	12/10/10	Vancouver	9,155				
71	13/10/10	Vancouver	9,155				
72	14/10/10	Vancouver	9,155				
73	15/10/10	Salt Spring Island	9,206	23.00 Ltrs Not full	361.97		
74	16/10/10	Victoria	9,256				
75	17/10/10	Victoria	9,290				
76	18/10/10	Victoria	9,290				
77	19/10/10	Lake Quinault	9,291 9,440	16.00 US	375.30	24.76	24.65
78	20/10/10	Lake Quinault	9,470				

* As marked : US or Ltrs

FACTS & FIGURES

DAY	DATE	LOCATION (Overnight)	MILES	PETROL US Gallons or Litres *	PETROL Cumulative Imperial	MPG Average	MPG Spot
79	21/10/10	Seal Rock (Jim)	9,611 / 9,750	15.40 US	388.14	24.76	24.94
80	22/10/10	Port Orford	9,890				
81	23/10/10	Eureka	9,931 / 10,069	14.50 US	400.22	24.81	26.48
82	24/10/10	Little River	10,218				
83	25/10/10	San Francisco	10,270 / 10,420	17.00 US	414.39	24.78	23.93
84	26/10/10	San Francisco	10,420				
85	27/10/10	San Francisco	10,450				
86	28/10/10	San Francisco	10,480				
87	29/10/10	San Francisco	10,504	12.50 US	424.80	24.73	22.46
88	30/10/10	Monterey	10,624				
89	31/10/10	Monterey	10,624				
90	01/11/10	Monterey	10,624				
91	02/11/10	Monterey	10,624				
92	03/11/10	Monterey	10,690				
93	04/11/10	Cambria	10,795				
94	05/11/10	Venice	10,808 / 11,045	17.00 US	438.97	24.62	21.46
95	06/11/10	Venice	11,045				
96	07/11/10	Venice	11,065				
97	08/11/10	Venice	11,121 / 11,181	15.00 US	451.47	24.63	25.04
98	09/11/10	Venice	11,181				
99	10/11/10	San Diego	11,334				
100	11/11/10	San Diego	11,360	14.30 US	463.39	24.52	20.06

Round the World with 10DPG

284

Geoffrey & Hilary Herdman

DAY	DATE	LOCATION Overnight	MILES	PETROL US Gallons or Litres *	PETROL Cumulative Imperial	MPG Average	MPG Spot
101	12/11/10	San Quintin	11,565	38.00 Ltrs	471.76	24.51	24.49
102	13/11/10	Guerrero Negro	11,832 11,835	45.00 Ltrs	481.67	24.56	26.94
103	14/11/10	Loreto	12,099				
104	15/11/10	Loreto	12,099	49.60 Ltrs	492.59	24.56	24.44
105	16/11/10	La Paz	12,311				
106	17/11/10	La Paz	12,311				
107	18/11/10	Ferry to mainland	12,325	40.00 Ltrs	501.41	24.58	25.65
108	19/11/10	Guadalajara	12,620				
109	20/11/10	Guadalajara	12,620	59.60 Ltrs	514.53	24.53	22.47
110	21/11/10	Guanajuato	12,788				
111	22/11/10	Guanajuato	12,788	29.00 Ltrs	520.92	24.55	26.30
112	23/11/10	San Miguel	12,843				
113	24/11/10	Mexico City	13,009				
114	25/11/10	Mexico City	13,009				
115	26/11/10	Mexico City	13,009				
116	27/11/10	Mexico City	13,009				
117	28/11/10	Taxco	13,021 13,134	51.00 Ltrs	532.15	24.47	20.74
118	29/11/10	Puebla	13,280				
119	30/11/10	Puebla	13,280	56.00 Ltrs	544.49	24.39	21.00
120	01/12/10	Oaxaca	13,499				
121	02/12/10	Oaxaca	13,499	Oil change and exhaust brackets			
122	03/12/10	Oaxaca	13,499	48.40 Ltrs	555.15	24.32	20.54
123	04/12/10	Tehuantepec	13,659	31.00 Ltrs	561.98	24.31	23.43
124	05/12/10	Tapachula	13,920	41.90 Ltrs	571.21		

* As marked : US or Ltrs

FACTS & FIGURES

DAY	DATE	LOCATION Overnight	MILES	PETROL US Gallons or Litres *	PETROL Cumulative Imperial	MPG Average	MPG Spot
125	06/12/10	Posada de San Miguel	14,087				
126	07/12/10	Antigua Guatemala	14,169	15.00 US	583.71	24.27	23.47
127	08/12/10	Antigua Guatemala	14,169				
128	09/12/10	Esquipula	14,384	12.60 US	594.21	24.21	20.48
129	10/12/10	San Miguel	14,507				
130	11/12/10	Leon	14,590 14,741	12.00 US	604.21	24.15	20.60
131	12/12/10	Liberia	14,820 14,930	13.50 US	615.46	24.08	20.44
132	13/12/10	Arenal Nayara	15,014				
133	14/12/10	Quepos	15,062 15,160	48.40 Ltrs	626.12	24.06	22.70
134	15/12/10	Corcovado	15,246				
135	16/12/10	Corcovado	15,246				
136	17/12/10	Corcovado	15,246				
137	18/12/10	Boquete	15,345 15,377	13.50 US	637.37	24.08	25.16
138	19/12/10	Panama City	15,674				
139	20/12/10	Panama City	15,680				

Car shipped to Buenos Aires

DAY	DATE	LOCATION	MILES	PETROL	Cumulative	Average	Spot
184	03/02/11	Buenos Aires	15,692	59.00 Ltrs	650.36	24.13	26.70
185	04/02/11	Cordoba	16,012 16,123	53.00 Ltrs + 1 Ltr Oil	662.04	24.19	27.41
186	05/02/11	Catamarca	16,397	21.00 Ltrs en route 46.00 Ltrs	666.66 676.80	24.23	26.09

Geoffrey & Hilary Herdman

DAY	DATE	LOCATION Overnight	MILES	PETROL US Gallons or Litres *	Cumulative Imperial	MPG Average	Spot
187	06/02/11	Estancia Las Carreras	16,551				
188	07/02/11	Salta	16,591 16,753	46.00 Ltrs	686.93	24.15	19.15
189	08/02/11	Salta	16,753				
190	09/02/11	Purmamarca	16,919 16,935	62.40 Ltrs	700.67	24.15	23.86
191	10/02/11	Salta	17,010				
192	11/02/11	Cafayate	17,056 17,182	Oil change 48.00 Ltrs	711.24	24.16	24.88
193	12/02/11	La Rioja	17,494	61.00 Ltrs	724.68	24.14	23.22
194	13/02/11	Mendoza	17,742 17,864	36.00 Ltrs Not full	732.61		
195	14/02/11	Mendoza	17,864				
196	15/02/11	Mendoza	17,864				
197	16/02/11	Cavas Wine Lodge	17,906				
198	17/02/11	San Rafael	18,036	65.50 Ltrs	747.04	24.14	24.24
199	18/02/11	Neuquen	18,402	27.40 Ltrs en route	753.07		
200	19/02/11	St Martin de los Andes	18,428 18,665	40.70 Ltrs	762.04	24.18	26.13
201	20/02/11	St Martin de los Andes	18,665	35.50 Ltrs	769.86		
202	21/02/11	Termas de Puyehue Chile	18,774				
203	22/02/11	Termas de Puyehue Chile	18,774				

* As marked : US or Ltrs

FACTS & FIGURES

DAY	DATE	LOCATION Overnight	MILES	PETROL US Gallons or Litres *	Cumulative Imperial	MPG Average	Spot
204	23/02/11	Peuma Hue nr Bariloche	18,910				
205	24/02/11	 Peuma Hue	18,944 18,974	42.00 Ltrs Not full	779.11		
206	25/02/11	Esquel	19,176	1 Litre oil			
207	26/02/11	Esquel	19,240	68.00 Ltrs	794.09	24.23	25.34
208	27/02/11	Futalaufquen	19,308				
209	28/02/11	 Peuma Hue	19,428 19,468	35.00 Ltrs (guess)	801.80	24.23	24.39
210	01/03/11	Calafate	19,480				
211	02/03/11	Calafate	19,480				
212	03/03/11	Calafate	19,480				
213	04/03/11	Calafate	19,480				
214	05/03/11	Calafate	19,492				
215	06/03/11	Peuma Hue	19,518				
216	07/03/11	Peuma Hue	19,575				
217	08/03/11	 Puerto Montt	19,644 19,818	54.70 Ltrs	813.84	24.14	17.93
218	09/03/11	 Castro, Chiloe	19,900 19,948	52.00 Ltrs No record!	825.30	24.11	22.35
219	10/03/11	Castro, Chiloe	20,035				
220	11/03/11	Puerto Varas	20,171	62.00 Ltrs	838.95	24.04	19.84
221	12/03/11	Puerto Varas	20,171				
222	13/03/11	Valdivia	20,321				
223	14/03/11	Huilo Huilo	20,408				

Geoffrey & Hilary Herdman

DAY	DATE	LOCATION Overnight	MILES	PETROL US Gallons or Litres *	Cumulative Imperial	MPG Average	Spot
224	15/03/11	Pucon	20,456 20,508	55.70 Ltrs	851.22	24.03	23.23
225	16/03/11	Vina Chillan	20,756 20,876	53.30 Ltrs	862.96	24.05	25.55
226	17/03/11	Villa El Descanso	21,083	1.5 Litres oil			
227	18/03/11	Near Santa Cruz	21,089 21,150	58.60 Ltrs	875.87	24.08	25.80
228	19/03/11	Near Santa Cruz	21,185				
229	20/03/11	Santiago	21,325				
230	21/03/11	Santiago	21,325				
231	22/03/11	Santiago	21,325				
232	23/03/11	Santiago	21,325				
233	24/03/11	Santiago	21,325				
234	25/03/11	Valparaiso	21,402				
235	26/03/11	Valparaiso	21,402				
236	27/03/11	Valparaiso	21,402				
237	28/03/11	Valparaiso	21,402				
238	29/03/11	Valparaiso	21,402	65.00 Ltrs	890.19	24.04	21.86
239	30/03/11	La Serena	21,673	52.30 Ltrs	901.71	24.04	23.52
240	31/03/11	La Serena	21,797	Changed oil			
241	01/04/11	La Serena	21,848	37.00 Ltrs	909.86	24.01	21.47
242	02/04/11	El Molle	21,868				
243	03/04/11	El Molle	21,868				
244	04/04/11	El Molle	22,018				
245	05/04/11	El Molle	22,144				

* As marked : US or Ltrs

Continues overleaf >

DAY	DATE	LOCATION Overnight	MILES	PETROL US Gallons or Litres *	Cumulative Imperial	MPG Average	Spot
246	06/04/11		22,161	52.00 Ltrs	921.31	24.05	27.33
			22,389	20.00 Ltrs Not full	925.72		
		Santiago	22,471				
247	07/04/11	Santiago	22,481				

Car shipped to Adelaide

DAY	DATE	LOCATION	MILES	PETROL	Cumulative	Average	Spot
315	14/06/11	The chrysalis arrives in Adelaide					
316	15/06/11	The butterfly emerges					
317	16/06/11	The Sanitary Inspector					
318	17/06/11	Another 405DH					
321	20/06/11	Back on the road	22,496				
322	21/06/11	405 Toboggan					
326	25/06/11	Change of Identity	22,516				
327	26/06/11	BOCA S. Australia	22,606				
328	27/06/11		22,663	45.00 Ltrs	935.63	24.22	
		Port Fairy	22,976	56.00 Ltrs	947.96	24.24	25.38
329	28/06/11	Melbourne	23,233				
330	29/06/11	Robert McDermott	23,240				
331	30/06/11		23,262	56.00 Ltrs	960.30	24.22	23.19
			23,525	44.00 Ltrs	969.99	24.25	27.14
		Canberra	23,652				
332	01/07/11	Bowral	23,755				
333	02/07/11	Kiama	23,849	56.00 Ltrs	982.32	24.28	26.27
334	03/07/11	Whale Beach	24,006				
335	04/07/11	Vaucluse	24,037				
336	05/07/11	Sydney	24,090	Brake problems			
337	06/07/11	406 Zagato	24,116	56.00 Ltrs	994.66	24.25	21.65

Geoffrey & Hilary Herdman

DAY	DATE	LOCATION Overnight	MILES	PETROL US Gallons or Litres *	PETROL Cumulative Imperial	MPG Average	MPG Spot
338	07/07/11	More brake problems	24,173				
339	08/07/11	Brakes fixed	24,196				
340	09/07/11	Armidale	24,268 24,508	33.00 Ltrs	1,001.93	24.22	20.91
341	10/07/11	Brisbane	24,524 24,808	40.00 Ltrs Not full	1,010.74		
342	11/07/11	Queensland BOCA	24,832 24,948	54.00 Ltrs	1,022.63	24.28	27.24
343	12/07/11	Chinchilla	25,072 25,186	45.00 Ltrs 20.40 Ltrs 1 litre oil	1,032.54 1,037.04	24.28 24.29	24.21 25.37
344	13/07/11	Carnarvon Gorge	25,361 25,454	30.50 Ltrs	1,043.76	24.30	26.05
345	14/07/11	Carnarvon Gorge	25,460				
346	15/07/11	Carnarvon Gorge	25,464				
347	16/07/11	Chinchilla (Beasleys)	25,557 25,727	40.30 Ltrs	1,052.63	24.28	22.08
348	17/07/11	Chinchilla (Beasleys)	25,751	Changed oil			
349	18/07/11	Brisbane	25,827 25,969	50.50 Ltrs	1,063.76	24.28	24.27
350	19/07/11	Brisbane	25,969				
351	20/07/11	Hervey Bay	26,129 26,182	52.50 Ltrs	1,075.32	24.30	26.12
352	21/07/11	Fraser Island	26,182				
356	25/07/11	Bundaberg	26,262				
357	26/07/11	Rockhampton	26,346 26,489	45.00 Ltrs	1,085.23	24.28	21.89

* As marked : US or Ltrs

FACTS & FIGURES

DAY	DATE	LOCATION Overnight	MILES	PETROL US Gallons or Litres *	Cumulative Imperial	MPG Average	Spot
358	27/07/11	Mackay	26,544 26,694	45.00 Ltrs	1,095.14	24.24	19.98
359	28/07/11	Townsville	26,703 26,945	32.00 Ltrs	1,102.19	24.23	22.56
360	29/07/11	Townsville	26,945				
366	04/08/11	Literary stuff	26,945				
367	05/08/11	Townsville Garage	26,950				
368	06/08/11	Townsville	26,955				
369	07/08/11	Townsville	26,955	55.50 Ltrs	1,114.42	24.19	20.61
370	08/08/11	Cairns	27,170				
371	09/08/11	Cairns	27,170				
372	10/08/11	Barrier Reef	27,170	41.00 Ltrs	1,123.45	24.18	23.81
373	11/08/11	Townsville	27,393				
374	12/08/11	Eungella	27,452 27,651	45.50 Ltrs 1.25 Ltrs oil	1,133.47	24.22	28.14
375	13/08/11	Eungella	27,651				
376	14/08/11	Gladstone	27,744 27,985	49.40 Ltrs	1,144.35	24.24	26.84
377	15/08/11	Heron Island	27,985				
378	16/08/11	Heron Island	27,985				
379	17/08/11	Bundaberg	28,002 28,108	46.40 Ltrs	1,154.57	24.25	25.24
380	18/08/11	Brisbane	28,278 28,342	12.75 Ltrs Not full Changed oil	1,157.38		
381	19/08/11	Back in the box	28,350				

Car shipped to Mersin

Geoffrey & Hilary Herdman

DAY	DATE	LOCATION Overnight	MILES	PETROL US Gallons or Litres *	Cumulative Imperial	MPG Average	Spot
429	06/10/11	Into Asia	28,350				
436	13/10/11	Adana	28,369 28,421	58.00 Ltrs	1,170.15	24.24	23.55
437	14/10/11	Side	28,521 28,727	29.00 Ltrs	1,176.54	24.24	23.80
438	15/10/11	Near Gocek	28,756 28,980	46.00 Ltrs	1,186.67	24.23	23.19
439	16/10/11	Chios	28,996 29,231	46.00 Ltrs	1,196.81	24.23	23.69
440	17/10/11	Chios					
441	18/10/11	One's Birthday					
442	19/10/11	Mastic					
443	20/10/11	Chios					
444	21/10/11	Kusadasi	29,235 29,334	40.00 Ltrs	1,205.62	24.25	27.13
445	22/10/11	Behramkale	29,478 29,553	47.00 Ltrs 1 Ltr oil	1,215.97	24.24	23.47
446	23/10/11	Behramkale	29,553				
447	24/10/11	Gallipoli	29,678				
448	25/10/11	Edirne	29,724 29,832	50.40 Ltr 21.00 Ltr Not full	1,227.07 1,231.70	24.22	22.16
449	26/10/11	Ruse	30,060				
450	27/10/11	Sibiu	30,068 30,310	41.00 Ltrs	1,240.73	24.23	25.19
451	28/10/11	Malancrav	30,348 30,373	47.00 Ltrs	1,251.08	24.26	27.05
452	29/10/11	Malancrav	30,373				
453	30/10/11	Sibiu	30,442				

* As marked : US or Ltrs

FACTS & FIGURES

DAY	DATE	LOCATION Overnight	MILES	PETROL US Gallons or Litres *	PETROL Cumulative Imperial	MPG Average	MPG Spot
454	31/10/11	Sibiu	30,442				
455	01/11/11	Cluj Napoca	30,555				
456	02/11/11	Brasov	30,637 30,764	54.00 Ltrs	1,262.97	24.26	24.30
457	03/11/11	Sibiu	30,901	50.00 Ltrs	1,273.99	24.26	23.97
458	04/11/11	Caransebes	31,029				
459	05/11/11	Caransebes	31,219	57.50 Ltrs	1,286.65	24.26	25.11
460	06/11/11	Lipova	31,372				
461	07/11/11	Budapest	31,431 31,580	33.00 Ltrs Not Full	1,293.92		
462	08/11/11	Budapest	31,580				
463	09/11/11	Vienna	31,630 31,786	35.60 Ltrs	1,301.76	24.30	27.20
464	10/11/11	Vienna	31,786				
465	11/11/11	Greiskirchen	31,929 31,961	49.00 Ltrs Changed oil	1,312.56	24.33	27.70
466	12/11/11	Salzburg	32,061				
467	13/11/11	Munich	32,151				
468	14/11/11	Ulm	32,191 32,310	53.60 Ltrs	1,324.36	24.31	22.19
469	15/11/11	Heidelberg	32,440				
470	16/11/11	Koblenz	32,474 32,563	55.70 Ltrs	1,336.63	24.30	23.07
471	17/11/11	Dordrecht	32,774				
472	18/11/11	Maastricht	32,794 32,916	54.00 Ltrs	1,348.52	24.32	26.90
473	19/11/11	Home	33,014 33,196	53.00 Ltrs	1,360.20	24.27	18.85

* As marked : US or Ltrs

Geoffrey & Hilary Herdman